How Language Comes to Children

How Language Comes to Children

From Birth to Two Years

Bénédicte de Boysson-Bardies

Translated by M. B. DeBevoise

A Bradford Book
The MIT Press
Cambridge, Massachusetts
London, England

First MIT Press paperback edition, 2001
© 1999 The Massachusetts Institute of Technology

This book was originally published as *Comment la parole vient aux enfants* (Éditions Odile Jacob, 1996).

Set in Bembo by Asco Typesetters, Hong Kong. Printed and bound in the United States of America.

Library of Congress Cataloging-in-Publication Data

Boysson-Bardies, Bénédicte de.
  [Comment la parole vient aux enfants. English]
  How language comes to children; from birth to two years/Bénédicte
  de Boysson-Bardies; translated by M. B. DeBevoise.
    p. cm.
  "A Bradford book."
  Includes bibliographical references and index.
  ISBN 0-262-02453-5 (hc : alk. paper), 0-262-54125-4 (pb)
  1. Language acquisition. I. Title.
P118. B65413 1999
401'.93—dc21   98-17956
                                                    CIP

For Hadrien, Charlotte, Geoffroy,
Antoine, Benoit, Martin, Clémence, and Guillaume
and for all the children who have shared their language with me.

Contents

3

The Communicative Universe of the Baby   71

4

Discovering the Meaning of Words: Nine to Seventeen Months   95

5

The First Lexical Steps: Eleven to Eighteen Months   127

6

To Each Baby His Own Style   149

Translator's Note

The original French text of *How Language Comes to Children* has been modified in a number of minor ways to make it accessible to general readers in English. Samples of infant speech in French and other languages have usually been translated, and examples of phonotactic and other rules in French have occasionally been supplemented by English examples. Some experiments that resist brief summary have been described more fully. The reader is referred to the glossary for explanations of technical terms. Certain additions have been made to this list for the sake of clarity; the list does not aim at comprehensiveness, however, since anyone requiring further detail can conveniently consult one of several existing dictionaries of phonetics and phonology. Finally, the bibliography has been slightly rearranged for ease of reference, and a number of errors found in the original edition have been corrected. In all these matters I am grateful to the author for her kind cooperation. I owe special thanks to Laura Conway Palumbo for her guidance on technical points of detail.

M. B. DeBevoise

Acknowledgments

This book has its origin in a project begun thirty years ago at the Center for the Study of Cognitive Processes and Language in Paris. I cannot mention all those who, through their learning, ideas, and friendship, have accompanied me along the way. I owe a particular debt to François Bresson and Jacques Mehler, who introduced me to the cognitive sciences. Much of the research that is cited in this book has benefited from the expertise and collaboration of Marilyn Vihman, Pierre Hallé, Nicole Bacri, Catherine Durand, and Laurent Sagart, and of other French, Swedish, and American colleagues who share my fascination with the development of the child. I have learned a great deal as well from my discussions with Peter Mac-Neilage, Peter Jusczyk, Virginia Valian, Scania de Schonen, and Josiane Bertoncini, whose thinking and work have helped organize this domain of research.

Pierre Hallé, Emmanuel Dupoux, Celia Jakubovicz, Sophie Fisher, and Kevin O'Regan were kind enough to read various chapters of this book in draft. I am grateful to them for their suggestions and comments and to Juliette Blamont for her careful copyediting of the final manuscript.

Catherine Durand has assisted me throughout these past years with both the research and the writing of this book. She deserves special thanks. Let me also express here my gratitude to the many parents and educators in daycare centers and hospitals, without whom we would not have been able to conduct our studies. The hospitality of the École des Hautes Études en Sciences Sociales permitted me to complete this book in an atmosphere that was both pleasant and conducive to hard work.

How Language Comes to Children

Introduction

It therefore matters that we inquire into the place that language still holds in the definition of man.

—Claude Hagège

It is language that informs the definition of man.

—Roland Barthes

All children learn to talk. This natural tendency to acquire language is a gift inscribed in the genetic inheritance that is ours by virtue of being human. Only extremely serious physical or psychological handicaps can prevent the development of this marvelous capacity, the hallmark of the grandeur and the uniqueness of the human race.

But what is this gift? In what does it consist? What role does the environment play in its development? What do children know before they talk, and what do they absorb from the speech of others? These are just a few of the questions that arise when we investigate how children come to speak. Only very young children who are getting ready to talk, or who are uttering their first words, can help us understand. This book grows out of our dialogue with them.

The Gift of Language

"In the beginning was the Word...."

—John 1:1

"Is he saying his first words yet?" All parents of children nearing their first birthday have been asked this question. In many traditions, the word is recognized as the supreme creative act. In the eastern Mediterranean, men founded their representation of the world on the power of the word: "I created all forms with what came out of my mouth when there was neither sky nor earth," said the Egyptian god Ptah. The world thus stands illuminated by this principle of creation: word and object are dual aspects of a single creative thought.

In the book of Genesis, at the beginning of each day, God, by the strength of His words, brought forth something out of nothing; "... God said, 'Let there be light,' and there was light," and on the sixth day, God said: "Let Us make man in Our image, according to Our likeness" (Genesis 1:26). Man, in his turn, was enabled to "say" and so to ensure his preeminence over all the animals.

The creative and revelatory power of the word is encountered in the tales of childhood as well. It is necessary to know the magic word in order to cast a spell or to gain possession of the object of one's desire. Knowledge of the phrase "Open sesame!" opens the door to a mysterious world that contains precious treasures. Without the word, the world of learning and of power cannot be entered into. And so, human beings, mythologically created by the word, have forever relied on the creative value of the word. One has only to observe the influence of writing today, and the respectful aura that surrounds writers, to see that the magical essence of words has endured. It will continue to endure, for the gift of speech permits us to create a mental world that enriches communication with others, nourishes private thought, and, by enabling us to recapture the past and imagine the future, radically alters our ordinary sense of time.

A Complex Gift

Speech is the realization of language, from which it is inseparable. The definitions given by two leading French dictionaries do not make a distinction between speech from language. According to the *Petit Robert*, language is "the function of expression of thought and of communication among men, implemented by the organs of phonation (speech) or by a notation using material signs (writing)"; speech, according to *Larousse*, is likewise "the verbal expression of thought." These definitions capture the dual function of language. At the same time, they are deliberately vague about its precise nature and the fact that it is a system. To understand the development of language and speech, it is necessary first to recall Saussure's (1972/1916) remark that "every observation about the essence of language begins by stressing the arbitrary character of the sign." The words *chien* and *dog* denote the same animal in two different languages. Neither of these words bears a physical relation to the appearance or any attribute of the animal, unlike, for example, the onomatopoeic *woof woof*. This is why a word is said to be an arbitrary sign connected with meaning. It also needs to be noted that languages are combinatory systems whose rules organize the combination of elements (phonemes[1] and words) into linguistic expressions.

Every language that is spoken in the world—and there are thousands—thus rests on a system of signs arranged according to rules that are peculiar to it. All languages have in common certain fundamental principles: all are based on sounds that combine into syllables, for example; all have the equivalents of nouns and verbs that combine into syntagms, or phrases, not by simple alignment but in more complicated ways that exhibit a hierarchical structure. Our mind is designed in accordance with these and other such principles, which manifest our genetic aptitude for language. Each language then selects and organizes these basic elements. Thus, the sequence of sounds (phonemes) /z/ and /d/ that yields /zd/ is found in certain languages but is excluded, for instance, in French. One ordering of sentence components, subject-object-verb—*the child the soup eats*, for instance—is correct in Burmese but incorrect in English. Grammatical relationships are indicated by inflections in Russian and by prepositions in French and English, and so on. Languages employ extremely varied procedures for implementing such fundamental principles, which Noam Chomsky (1957) has called *universal grammar*.

Thoughts are expressed through an organized system for transmitting information. Language is first a system of representation that makes it possible to manipulate our thoughts and our knowledge of the world. It is realized through speech. If we were purely mental beings, we would transmit our thoughts directly, but, being made of body as well as of mind, we must have some means of physical support in order to communicate. The art of communicating our ideas depends less on the organs that serve this purpose than on the specifically human faculty of having a language based on a procedure for combining arbitrary signs—as the sign language used by the deaf attests. Speech remains, however, the primary vehicle of language.

Can language therefore be identified with thought? Not necessarily. It is possible to think without language, for images can be manipulated in the mind without recourse to words. Sometimes we mentally envisage geometrical figures, routes from one place to another, artistic creations, and so on. Babies, too, form concepts before becoming acquainted with words.

The Gift of Evolution

Language is a gift—a uniquely human gift of evolution. Phylogenetically, humans did not exist before language. It is a subtle, abstract, and cultural phenomenon that no doubt came to be anchored in the human biological system at a relatively late date. Our primate cousins possess visual and auditory systems similar to ours, form organized societies, and exploit complex systems of communication. Thus, vervet monkeys warn their community of danger by cries that indicate whether the aggressor is an eagle, a snake, or a cheetah. In the case of the great apes, their capacity for acquiring language fragments is disputed, but they do not, in any case, possess articulate language. The aptitude for speech is thought to have been inscribed in the genetic code of the human species at some point between *Homo habilis* and *Homo sapiens*, our surest ancestor thus supplying the foundation for the subsequent development of mankind's mental universe.

The physical apparatus that permits articulate speech evolved with upright posture. This posture allowed the respiratory and phonatory systems to assume a vertical orientation. At the same time, the rear part of the articulatory system became vertical, but the front part did not—leading to the bent vocal tract that distinguishes humans from other primates, whose vocal tract is diagonal. The effect of this evolution was to considerably enlarge the possibilities for producing new sounds and for increasing their rhythm and control. But knowing how these phonatory possibilities were actually organized is an altogether different matter. Such changes were accompanied by an increase in brain size and a remodeling of cerebral structure. It is mainly on the basis of these modifications that the sequences of genetic changes that ultimately inscribed the aptitude for spoken language in our genetic code are thought to have developed.

The Gift of Speech and the Child

About two years after conception, or a year after birth, children will say their first words. The skill and the swiftness with which children learn to speak have always fascinated adults, who sometimes forget to marvel at the mystery of it all. Even so, what a prodigy the child is. Producing words, combining them into original sentences, understanding other people's words: these are much more remarkable feats than those that children accomplish much later and with greater difficulty. The fact that the sum of two and two is four seems a simple notion. Nonetheless, it becomes consciously accessible to children only well after they have uttered hundreds of distinct sentences. Before knowing how to coordinate their hands to catch a ball, children will have understood almost all the sentences that adults address to them, and they will have virtually mastered their language before knowing how to tie their shoelaces.

People have long suspected that the ability to acquire language so quickly could come only from a gift. Already in Egyptian gnostic texts language was referred to as a gift from God preexisting its own acquisition. Much later it was to be spoken of as a gift of reason. In his fascinating *Discours physique de la parole* (A Philosophical Discourse Concerning Speech) Géraud de Cordemoy (1970/1668) wrote, "I desire only that one observe a very important truth, which this example of children discloses to us, which is that from birth they have full reason, for finally this way of learning to speak is the effect of so great a discernment and of so perfect a reason that it is not possible to conceive of anything more wonderful. . . . It is obvious that reason is fully [theirs] from the beginning since they learn perfectly the language of the country where they are born and even in less time than it takes men [who are] already grown."

By the middle of the twentieth century, after a brief interval in which Anglo-American psychologists held the acquisition of language to be the exclusive result of learning and imitation, it came to be recognized that language development could not be reduced to a mechanism of elementary linkages between images or sensations and sounds. In 1959, Noam Chomsky demonstrated the impossibility of acquiring language with approaches of this type. The rapidity of language acquisition, the uniformity of language development despite conditions of reception that are far from ideal, the relative independence of language from differences in intelligence and experience among children, and the creativity of children's sentences: all these converged to refute theoretical approaches founded exclusively on imitation and the memorization of forms. Only a powerful innate system could allow the child to extract a model of language from adult speech. On the basis of this insight, Chomsky gave scientific shape to the age-old intuition of a gift present at birth. He affirmed that newborns possess a powerful genetic endowment that includes an implicit knowledge of the universal principles that structure languages. This endowment consists of a universal system that belongs to the human brain, which he called a *universal grammar*. This grammar is the basic schema that grounds the grammars of all human languages. A mental circuitry, inscribed in the biological constraints governing the development of the brain, underlies this schema and permits it to select the sounds, signs, and sign combinations of the mature language.

Why should the notion that the child is born with linguistic knowledge seem surprising? Every animal species possesses knowledge that is built into its specific cognitive system—the implicit knowledge that permits the swallow to build a nest and find its migratory route again, the spider to spin its remarkable webs, and the bee to build its complex hives. How could the human brain have been supposed to be a blank slate?

Must we, then, speak of a language instinct? Charles Darwin (1871) wrote in *The Descent of Man and Selection in Relation to Sex* that "language ... certainly is not a true instinct, for every language has to be learnt. It differs widely from all ordinary arts, however, for man has an instinctive tendency to speak, as we see in the babble of our young children; whilst no child has an instinctive tendency to brew, bake, or write." This "instinctive tendency" consists in a program of acquisition that develops on the basis of potentials inscribed in the genetic code of the child.

The Question of Modularity

Can this mental circuitry, which is wired into the genetic inheritance of the child, be identified with the set of general cognitive capacities peculiar to human beings? At first glance, language seems inseparable from the other higher faculties. It is remarkable to note, however, that neither mental retardation nor certain substantial deprivations—qualitative and quantitative alike—in the child's linguistic environment are sufficient to prevent the acquisition of language. Certain cases of children displaying serious intellectual deficiencies, genetic in origin, show that linguistic capacities can be preserved. By contrast, these capacities may be selectively affected in children whose intellectual faculties are sound. The system, or subsystem, of language may thus be seen as a module, independent of general cognitive abilities. The philosopher Jerry Fodor (1983) has proposed that our mental apparatus as a whole is a modular system—a system composed of specific functional subsystems, each having a distinct neural basis. These modules are characterized by, among other things, a certain autonomy with respect to function and development. Language is one of these specialized modules. Its object is linguistic information, both acoustic and visual, which it processes until such time as responsibility for this information is passed on to a central processing mechanism that can interact with various specialized modules. Learning and processing language thus depend on precise mechanisms that are specific and, up to a certain point, independent of general knowledge.

Of course, the claim that language is modular has resolute adversaries. For them, the development of language is closely related to general cognitive development, of which it is an aspect. While the discrepancies between the acquisition of language and the course of cognitive development reveal a relative independence between the two, children are capable of using language only because they have begun to understand what goes on around and inside them, what people do, what objects are, and what they feel. A minimum amount of such knowledge is required. In this sense, the use of language is not independent of the rest of cognition.

An Interactive Learning System

The child is therefore born with an implicit knowledge of the universal principles that structure language and with a genetic program for its acquisition. But for this program to operate, the child needs to hear speech. Human newborns must acquire their language; without linguistic information, their initial biological abilities remain unexploited.

What are the major initial conditions for the development of language? First, children must be able to organize sensory information. They have to distinguish, and then extract, the linguistically pertinent sounds that adults produce while speaking. The barking of the family dog is not a linguistically pertinent sound, whereas a father saying "Hello" to a friend is. Only a predisposition to process the acoustic characteristics of the sounds that constitute speech can allow its perception to be rapidly organized. Second, speech occurs as a continuous sound wave: children therefore must subsequently segment it, categorize it, and organize its variations according to their semantic value. These segmentations and categorizations are attributes of the language that children must be able to organize if they are to succeed in speaking. The third condition for the development of language concerns meaning. Children must recognize that the adult speech they hear is motivated by an intention to produce meaningful sounds.

Each of these capacities is activated according to a series of stages that are regulated by a biological clock beginning before birth. The first stage is constant in all children. As the processing of speech becomes more complete and, by virtue of this, more complex, the variety of available responses increases. The individuality of children is thus shown in their relation to language, but it will not prevent them from readily achieving full knowledge of their native language.

A critical question that psycholinguists have investigated, which we will discuss later, has to do with the reality of innate mechanisms. The next question involves the nature of these mechanisms, the way in which they operate, and the necessary and sufficient conditions of their interaction with the child's environment, taking into consideration the various forms that this environment may assume. These latter considerations highlight the role played by experience in acquiring language.

For children, then, speech is the physical host of the information that they receive about the structure of their language. But it has another essential purpose—communication.

Speech and Communication

The forms of communication between living beings are diverse— gestures, looks, cries, touches. All the senses may serve to provide information. Communication is therefore not to be confused with the faculty of language. We have seen that language, as the expression of thought through a structured system, is much more than a privileged means of communication. But spoken language is also the system of communication specific to the human species, a system whose power and efficiency have dramatically altered the possibilities for communication among members of the human community. Humans have, however, preserved other means of communication— facial gestures and expressions, gestures of the hands and body, pantomime, and so on. By means of these nonverbal pathways, children receive information from the people around them and convey information (needs, wants) to people well before they have learned to speak. Looks, smells, sounds, and caresses form a universe full of meanings to which the infant is particularly sensitive from birth. Children thus are part of a web of communication necessary to their survival. To develop normally, they must not only receive information but also desire to communicate it. They do this initially through use of the body, eyes, and smile.

Though they hear speech, children do not speak. Listening to adult speech gives them two models. The first is simply a model of behavior: the child sees that speaking is a way of communicating. The second is a model of a language: the surrounding language furnishes the child with the elements that characterize the structure of the language to be learned as well as its vocabulary. These two models must be furnished by the persons close to the child. Of course, no experiments exist in this domain to affirm that communication between actual persons is indispensable for the acquisition of language—that, for example, listening to the radio is not enough—but all indications are that this is so. Vocal communication between human beings arouses and maintains in the baby a desire to speak. The same is true for gestural communication in the language of deaf-mutes. In both cases one finds the desire to exchange feelings, needs, and demands, the desire to be included in one's family or peer group through language.

Deprived of the chance to hear language spoken, feral children actually lose the capacity to learn to speak. Similarly, young children who have been locked away from the world by their parents, and hence deprived of a certain minimum of social and linguistic support, are liable to exhibit deficiencies that sometimes prevent normal language acquisition. However, as we will see later, the mechanisms for the development of speech are robust and often withstand extreme situations. The desire to communicate is not, in and of itself, primary in establishing the mechanisms of speech. This is suggested by the experience of certain autistic children who speak but who do not use their language to communicate. They articulate expressions in stereotyped sentences that are formally correct but that seem devoid of any communicative intention. This behavior shows that an inability to employ forms of communication does not automatically hinder the development of mechanisms of speech, although it does inhibit their function.

From *Infans* to Child

The baby's entry into the world of speech is an essential step. According to the etymological sense of the Latin word *infans* (composed of the privative *in-* and a participial form of the verb *fari*, meaning "to speak"), the child—*l'enfant* in French—is one who does not speak, though this sense has been lost in French. In Latin, *infans* was contrasted with another term, *puer*, which was used to designate the older, speaking child. In English, the distinction persists in the words *infant*, used for the baby at birth and through the first year, and *child*, used for later years. English has two terms, then, to denote two ages—nonspeaker and speaker.

Our purpose, in following children from birth until their production of sentences, is to try to show how the initial capacities for language possessed by all human beings are organized in successive and definite stages by which the *infans* becomes a speaking subject. We therefore propose a cognitive approach to the acquisition of speech. This approach grows out of research into the procedures that guide the learning of speech on the basis of innate knowledge—knowledge that can, in part, be illuminated experimentally. First, we look at the predispositions that render children capable of noticing those signs that enable them to distinguish, and categorize, the linguistically pertinent aspects of sounds. Then we show how processes of selection are manifested in babbling as the baby extracts the structure and meaning of speech sounds. With the first words that link meaning with the forms produced, we see that a diversity of individual choices appears and that language and culture influence the ways in which access to language is achieved. Finally, we accompany the child as he begins to fix the parameters characterizing the particular grammar of his language. We examine the social environment in which the development of speech takes place and the exchanges of information of every type and kind that are prevalent in the environment.

Our task is complex because speech and language are complex, and phenomena can be accounted for by sometimes contradictory theories. The child also is complex, and changes occur quickly: the mental processes of the newborn who discriminates between sounds, and categorizes them, are not those of the child who attributes meaning to words and produces them. Finally, the child's environment is complex as well, differing according to the native culture, the structure of the language, the way in which information is transmitted, the habits of parents, and the process of socialization.

Understanding how children acquire speech—by witnessing the birth of the first sounds, seeing sounds organized in modulated sequences and structured in syllables, and finally seeing forms emerge that the adult can hear as words or as expressions—does not come about without misapprehensions, surprises, errors, and a sense of wonder. But this fine capacity for processing information and these subtle and efficient procedures for segmenting and categorizing sounds help guide the young child along the paths leading to entry into the world of speech.

The Infant Does Not Talk, But ...

1

Our opinion is that it is proper for man to suppose there is something unknowable, but that he must not set a limit to his research.
—Johann Wolfgang von Goethe

The Newborn Child: A Stranger

Newborns recognize the voice and smell of their mothers. They look at the faces that peer into their cradles. They distinguish smells and listen to words with endless pleasure. Only mothers, with their keen attentiveness and powers of observation, can recognize the extraordinary capacities of the newborn. According to the clichés, happily now outmoded, that for centuries surrounded newborn infants—lacking all knowledge and wrapped in their swaddling clothes—they have to learn everything from scratch, as though they need to have acoustic and spatial structures of the world transferred into their bodies. Until that happens, the newborn remains empty. In Aristotle's expression, the newborn is a blank slate.

We now know that not only is the brain of the baby not empty, but in a certain sense it is fuller than that of the most brilliant scientist. The latter's brain contains about 10 billion (10^{10}) neurons; the number in the baby's brain is reckoned to be still greater. In the developing brain, during the course of embryogenesis, neurons are generated at a rate of roughly 250,000 per minute. The creation of all cortical neurons takes place between the sixth and the seventeenth weeks of gestation. Afterward, and for the rest of one's life, not a single new neuron will be created. The loss of neurons and axons begins with the end of gestation (Rakic et al., 1986). After birth, brain development consists in pruning and arrangement, the loss of neurons being offset by an exuberant creation of synaptic junctions among neurons. These come to be linked together in associative networks whose efficiency would be the envy of all the world's media put together. Indeed, a neuron forms about 1,000 connections and receives still more. It can receive 10,000 messages at the same time. Since the human brain contains 10^{10} neurons, the number of junctions may be reckoned at 10^{15}—more than the number of stars in the universe.

If synaptic density begins to grow in the last months of gestation, it literally explodes at birth. Thanks to anatomical studies done on the brains of nonhuman primates, we have a reasonably good idea of how synaptic development occurs in human beings (allowing for the need to extrapolate rhythms of development associated with longer periods of growth and life in humans than in the nonhuman primate). In the primate, the peak of synaptic density occurs between two and four months of life, which corresponds to between eight and ten months in human babies. The creation of synapses tends then to become stabilized, reaching the adult level at sexual maturity. In young humans between nine and twenty-four months, the density of short cortical synaptic connections is still some 150 percent greater than that observed in adults. It begins to decrease in the course of the third year.

Although the significance of such exuberant growth and elimination of neurons and synapses is not yet well understood, these events are thought to be related to processes of competition and selective stabilization, so that neuronal and synaptic redundancy supply the baby with the potential for development. After birth, this maximal connectivity of still labile synaptic contacts presents an unequaled opportunity for choice, as selections and reinforcements are made in response to the outside world. The brain thus sculpts itself under the joint influence of both internal and external experiences, which determine its final architecture and its modes of functioning (Changeux and Danchin, 1976).

Thus constituted, the immature brain provides the child with a capacity for evolution and plasticity that makes possible, as Jean-Pierre Changeux has put it, a "fringe of adaptability that introduces a margin for adaptation."[1]

Speech Is Not the Infant's Language

The adaptation that permitted the production of articulate speech is altogether peculiar to the human species. With the exception of some birds—parrots and mynah birds—that are capable of unharmoniously reproducing certain aspects of the sounds that constitute speech, only human beings can articulate the range of sounds employed in spoken languages.

To speak, it is necessary to master a vocal apparatus having quite particular characteristics. It is necessary to control and coordinate the movement of the larynx, glottis, soft palate, jaw, lips, and tongue. Beyond this, the respiratory cycle must be combined and synchronized with the activity of the vocal cords. The coordination of the muscles involved by articulation is extremely complex. When you enter a room and say something as simple as "Hello, nice weather today," your normal rhythm of speech is fifteen sounds a second, and you have brought into play motor capacities involving the coordinated use of more than 100 muscles.

But evolution has not favored rapid motor development in the human species. While studies of infant perception reveal the existence of surprising and rather mysterious gifts, the picture presented by the newborn lying in a cradle is that of a fragile, helpless, and dependent creature whose head is unstable and too heavy for its body and who is incapable of controlling posture and motivity.

Thus, though their native capacity for listening is great, human beings at birth control none of the organs that will permit them to speak. So long as these organs are not functional, the vocal tract of the newborn remains physically unfit for speech.

Spoken language is a more subtle, more abstract, more cultural phenomenon than other motor behaviors, but it displays certain patterns that are found in the biology of the development of motor control. The learning of speech depends on a process of maturation

(a) Adult

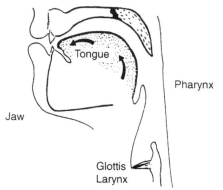

Nasal cavity

Tongue

Pharynx

Jaw

Glottis
Larynx

(b) Infant

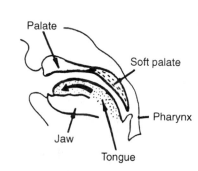

Palate

Soft palate

Pharynx

Jaw

Tongue

Figure 1.1   Vocal tract in the adult *(a)* and in the infant *(b)*.

and reorganization of the relevant organs. In the first months, physical changes accompany changes in the production of sounds. Even if these physical changes do not suffice by themselves to explain the evolution of vocal productions during the first year—hearing language spoken is also necessary—the reconfiguration of the vocal tract during the first years needs to be examined (see figure 1.1).

The vocal tract of the newborn does not exhibit the famous right-angle curve associated with upright posture that furnished the basis for the development of articulate language during the course of phylogenesis. In the newborn, the shape of the vocal tract resembles that of nonhuman primates. In fact, the infant's vocal tract is not simply a fragile miniature of the adult's. Its shape differs radically from

---

Chapter 1   *16*

that of the adult. As in primates, the curve of the oropharyngeal canal is gradual. Steven Pinker (1994, p. 265) describes the vocal tract of the newborn thus: "The larynx comes up like a periscope and engages the nasal passage, forcing the infant to breathe through the nose and making it anatomically possible to drink and breathe at the same time." The pharynx is proportionally shorter in the infant than in the adult, while the oral cavity is relatively larger. The mass of the tongue, significantly, is situated more to the front. It fills up the mouth, and so its possibility of movement is limited. The soft palate and epiglottis are relatively near each other. Thus constituted, the vocal tract does not allow the infant to produce articulate sounds (Kent and Murray, 1982). Furthermore, the infant does not control its own breathing, which feeds the production of sounds.

At three months, the palate becomes lowered and moves forward, so that it now can close off the passage of air into the nose. The tongue becomes lengthened, its musculature becomes more developed, and the opening of the pharynx permits it to move from front to back. The first clear effect of these changes is manifested in the control of the respiratory cycle. The control of phonation is thus rather rapidly acquired: at five months, babies are capable of breathing and using their larynxes roughly as adults do (Koopmans van Beinum and Van der Stelt, 1979).

The development of articulatory control takes longer. In this case it is a matter of governing the machine as a whole (tongue, lips, pharynx, larynx). While the vocal tract has been profoundly remodeled between two and six months, its transformation is still not complete at the end of the first year (Kent, 1976). In the course of the second half of the first year, the child's vocal tract begins to resemble that of the adult and allows for the production of more varied sound patterns, increasingly like those produced by the adult. But not until the age of five or six does control of all the articulators become possible. Their maturation begins with the most central organs, extending next to the peripheral organs. Gross movements are mastered before specific movements, and control of the tip of the tongue and of the lips is the last to be acquired, shortly before the age of five or six.

This general remodeling continues to affect the infant's ability to produce certain groups of sounds during the first three or four years.

This slow evolution explains why, for example, French children go on until a rather late age saying "Alisk" for "Alix" or "Obélisk" for "Obélix."

A Competent Newborn

When everything is already known,
but when nothing is begun.

—Madame de Staël

If the human brain possesses an innate disposition or even, as some would say, an instinct for the acquisition of language, behavioral correlations with this genetic specification must exist from the earliest age, no doubt from birth. But what are they? And how can babies be questioned about them? They cannot be expected to give, with their heads or hands, any signs of either agreement or disagreement or, of course, any vocal responses.

Recent research provides a plausible picture of how infants, making use of a sophisticated biological and cognitive apparatus, perceive the sounds that constitute speech—not only how they hear them but also how they extract, dissect, recognize, and analyze them. A huge problem immediately arises, however, from the fact that no strict correspondence exists between the acoustic signal and phonetic segments. Despite years of research, and despite the study of all the acoustic parameters involved in the realization of a phoneme, phoneticians have always been disappointed in their quest: the occurrences of a single segment are never acoustically identical. They depend on the contexts in which the segment is found. Thus the [p] in the word *purchase* is acoustically different than the [p] in the word *stop*. How, then, can we recognize the sounds that permit words to be identified? How can we attribute to segments whose physical manifestation is highly variable a stable value that enables them to be recognized as identical in all contexts? Researchers at Haskins Laboratories in New Haven, Connecticut, devoted themselves to this problem in the 1940s. They found the answer to the enigma not in the characteristics of the acoustic signal but in the human being's biological abilities.

Let us look first at what happens in the adult. The human psychoacoustic system automatically imposes boundaries within which sounds that are heard form stable categories. Thus, despite the physical continuity of the signal, listeners cut up the acoustic space into successive categories. This capacity of the psychoacoustic system to perceive sounds discontinuously and in the form of discrete units is known as *categorical perception* (Liberman, Harris, Kinney, and Lane, 1961): phonemes are perceived in a discontinuous manner throughout a sound series that physically is continuous. It seems reasonable to suppose that a property of the auditory system in primates was exploited over the course of evolution for the purpose of organizing the sounds that constitute speech. In humans, in any case, categorical perception became one of the fundamental mechanisms serving to distinguish these speech sounds.

If things are thus in the case of the adult, what happens with newborns? Are they born with a fundamental capacity for organizing the speech they hear? And if so, how is this known? How can we confirm the hypothesis that language learning is due to innate biological mechanisms?

In 1969, Einar Siqueland and Clement DeLucia had the remarkable idea of making use of the only behavior mastered by the newborn—sucking. To survive, newborns must know how to suck. For the most part, they do so enthusiastically. Thanks to this enthusiasm, Siqueland and DeLucia were able to employ a method that made it possible for the first time to carry out experimental research on newborns and language learning.

This method is known as *high-amplitude sucking* (HAS) or, to use Siqueland's and DeLucia's (1969) term, *nonnutritive sucking*. One begins by putting the infant in a baby carrier. A rubber nipple, supported by a rigid rod, is connected to a computer. The amplitude of the infant's sucking activity is measured for two minutes in the case of each child to define a personal baseline measure in the absence of any sound presentation. Once the baseline has been established, the period of familiarization begins. During this period, each sucking action whose amplitude exceeds the baseline activates the sound circuit and gives rise to the presentation of a sound. Thus, the number of sounds presented depends on the baby's attentiveness in sucking on the nipple. After a certain time has lapsed, the rate of sucking decreases.

The procedure passes then to the next phase, which makes up the test proper and begins with a change in the type of stimulus. The sound that the baby receives on the occasion of the next strong sucking action is different from the one heard during the familiarization period. The idea is that, on the one hand, babies like to be stimulated and, on the other, they have a great capacity for relating events to each other. They therefore establish a relation between the appearance of sounds and their sucking. At first, interested by what they hear, they suck vigorously. Then, monotony being mother to boredom (as the French proverb has it), lassitude sets in, and their ardor for sucking diminishes. The opposite is true as well: novelty arouses renewed interest and, once perceived, leads the child to resume sucking to take advantage of the new stimulation. Thus, the resumption of sucking as a result of a change in stimulus indicates that the baby has indeed perceived a difference between the two stimuli. Conversely, the absence of revived vigorous sucking indicates that the difference between the stimuli has gone unnoticed.

This ingenious way of measuring nonnutritive sucking made it possible to investigate the ability of infants to distinguish the sounds that form the framework of the languages spoken around them. The first question was whether babies discriminate among speech sounds categorically, as adults do.

Peter Eimas, E. Siqueland, P. Jusczyk, and J. Vigorito (1971) gave a preliminary answer. They found that four-month-old babies distinguish the syllable [ba] from the syllable [pa], not by identifying their acoustic difference alone but by identifying when this acoustic difference locates the syllables on either side of a boundary that is close to the one used by adults to distinguish [ba] and [pa]. Infants do indeed discriminate categorically (see figure 1.2).

Since 1971, dozens of experiments, some of them conducted with babies as young as three and four days old, have shown that infants are capable of distinguishing almost all the phonetic contrasts found across natural languages (Jusczyk, 1985). They discriminate between the contrasts of voicing, place, and manner of articulation

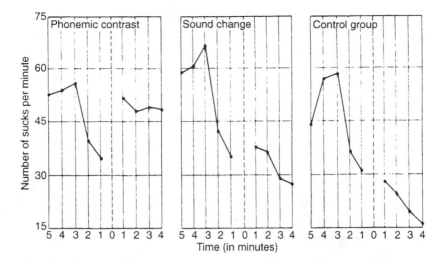

Figure 1.2   Rates of sucking among infants signalling their reactions to a change of stimulus. The graph shows variations in the rate of sucking among infants when they are presented with a phonological contrast (the phoneme /p/ versus /b/), a sound change (/p/ versus /p'/), and the same stimulus (/p/ versus /p/) (the control group). The dotted vertical line indicates the moment of the stimulus change. Only the first group of babies clearly increased the rate of sucking following the change of stimulus, thus showing that these babies perceived a difference between the two sounds. This reaction cannot be explained by a discrepancy in voicing lag between the two sounds, since the voicing lag between /p/ and /b/ is of the same order as that between /p/ and /p'/ (from Eimas, Siqueland, Jusczyk, and Vigorito, 1971).

that constitute phonetic categories. Babies who are only a few days old show themselves to be small geniuses in this domain.

Questions then began to multiply. Is the predisposition to process language sounds limited to a talent for distinguishing language segments? Or are babies also precociously sensitive to other particularly important aspects of language, such as the prosodic contours of sentences, with their melody and rhythm? Experiments quickly confirmed the importance of prosody. Newborns only a few days old prefer to listen to the voice of their mother when this is presented in competition with that of another mother talking to her baby. But the mother's intonation must be natural; if a tape recording of her voice is played backward, the child's preference no longer holds. This preference is related to the dynamic aspects of maternal speech, such as intonation, rather than to the static aspects of sounds, which are preserved when the tape is played backward. The child's attention therefore is not related to the static characteristics of the voice but on those characteristics of the voice present under normal conversational circumstances (Mehler, Bertoncini, Barriere, and Jassik-Gershenfeld, 1978).

In addition to a preference for the mother's voice, the child shows a preference for the mother's language (Mehler et al., 1988). When sequences of French speech are presented following sequences of Russian speech, four-day-old French infants show stronger renewed sucking than when these sequences are presented in the reverse order. Since the two samples are recorded by a single bilingual speaker, it is not a matter of different speakers. Furthermore, this preference is maintained when the sequences have been filtered to remove most of the phonetic information while leaving the prosody intact. The prosodic differences between the child's native language and the foreign language are therefore sufficient to arouse a livelier reaction during the presentation of the native language. Is this familiarity with the native language uniquely the product of the baby's contact with the mother during the first few days following birth? Is so short a time really sufficient to orient the infant's attention to certain general properties that characterize the prosody of the language spoken in its environment? Or might this process of familiarization have begun earlier, during the course of prenatal life?

The Infant Is Prepared Before Birth

The embryo of the first months does not seem to have much to tell us about language, but the fetus of the final months does. Traditionally, it was supposed that the future child, comfortably insulated inside its mother, bathed in amniotic fluid, enjoys an agreeable silence that enables it to develop peacefully before having to brave the noisy, air-filled atmosphere in which it will later live. Physicians long dismissed as maternal imagination the observations of mothers who felt the fetus react to sharp noises and jump at the sound of a loud telephone ring. It is now known that the child's senses gradually begin to function before birth. The auditory system of the fetus is functional from the twenty-fifth week of gestation, and its level of hearing toward the thirty-fifth week approaches that of an adult. Auditory sensory data reach the fetus both from the intrauterine area—from the mother's living body—and from the outside world. The first recordings of sounds reaching the fetus gave the impression of a very loud atmosphere within the womb. Internal sounds (respiratory, cardiovascular, and gastrointestinal noises) were therefore thought to partly mask external sounds, already muffled by the uterine membrane and the beating of the mother's heart. More recent recordings have somewhat changed this picture of the fetus's acoustic environment. These recordings, made by slipping a hydrophone inside the uterus of pregnant women at rest, show that intrauterine background noise is located in the low frequencies, which limits its masking effect (Querleu, Renard, and Versyp, 1981). The mother's voice and the voices of others in the environment thus manage to pass through this background noise. The intensity of the mother's voice *in utero* is not far removed from its intensity *ex utero*. The high frequencies are attenuated, but the spectral properties of the mother's speech remain the same, and the chief acoustic properties of the signal are preserved. Words spoken by the mother are transmitted through the air and also through her own body. They are therefore more perceptible than sounds coming from the outside alone, though these too are perfectly audible by the fetus. The prosody is particularly well preserved: the intonation of the speech recorded *in utero* was faultlessly recognized by adult listeners; the same was true for 30 percent of the phonemes.

But how can we explore prenatal capacities for speech? The technique of nonnutritive sucking involves an interruption, and then a revival, of attention during a change of stimulus. This same type of approach can be used to test perception in the fetus. We possess physiological measures of its behavior in more or less profound states of waking and sleeping. Cardiac and motor responses can give us some idea of what surprises and alerts the fetus when it is in a state of rest. When presented with a repetitive sound, by means of a speaker positioned twenty centimeters (or about eight inches) above the mother's abdomen, the fetus gradually becomes used to it. The beginning of the presentation of the sound provokes an initial reaction of arousal, which is manifested by a reduced heart rate. Cardiac deceleration then subsides and finally disappears, and the heart resumes its normal rhythm with repeated presentations of the sound. This is the period of habituation. If, after habituation, the sound is changed, a new round of cardiac deceleration indicates that the novelty of the sound has been perceived. This habituation-dishabituation paradigm is the basis of methods used to test the capacities of the fetus (Lecanuet et al., 1987).

A number of studies reveal how the fetus reacts to variations of the physical characteristics of the stimulation by examining its behavioral state (see, for example, Lecanuet and Granier-Deferre, 1993; see also Lecanuet, Granier-Deferre, and Schaal, 1993). Differences in both the intensity and frequency of sound stimuli elicit discriminatory reactions in the form of cardiac deceleration. The same is true for variation in the order of speech sounds. Jean-Pierre Lecanuet and C. Granier-Deferre (1993) presented fetuses between thirty-six and forty weeks old with sixteen repetitions of the disyllable [babi]; when the fetus was habituated, this disyllable was changed to [biba]. The change in the order of the syllables provoked a deceleration in the rate of the heartbeat of the fetus, tested in a state of calm sleep. This deceleration indicates that the two sequences were distinguished. Nothing allows us to say that the fetus recognized them. Nonetheless, the fetus did react to a simple change in the order of the two phonetically similar syllables that made up the disyllables. The second disyllable was new to it by comparison with the first.

The question arises, then, whether exposing fetuses to their mother's language before birth favors perceptual adjustment to the phonetic and prosodic parameters that characterize this language and differentiate it from others. We have seen that categorical discrimination is universal in newborns. At the same time, however, they recognize the voice of their mother only when prosody is preserved. Does there exist a prenatal framework that helps regulate certain sophisticated infant perceptual capacities? Does external stimulation leave an imprint on the brain of the fetus? Or are the observed reactions simply signs of intermittent arousal in response to changes in stimulation?

To better determine the source of the discriminations observed in the fetus and their impact on the capacities of newborns, attempts were made to discover whether memories of prenatal experiences persist. Using the well-tested method of nonnutritive sucking, it was first asked simply whether newborns between one and three days old were able, by virtue of the prenatal experience of their mother's voice, to distinguish this voice from that of other speakers (DeCasper and Fifer, 1980). When they had no more than twelve hours of effective contact (*ex utero*) with her, newborns preferred the voice of their mother to that of another woman. The questions that followed were more specific. Are the effects of exposing the fetus to important acoustic characteristics for speech carried forward with the newborn? To find out, Anthony DeCasper and Melanie Spence (1986) used a more sensitive variant of the procedure of nonnutritive sucking. In their procedure, one of the stimuli is presented while the newborn makes long pauses between suckings; the other is presented during brief pauses. Newborns regulate the rhythm of their sucking according to their preference for the stimulus: slow sucking generates one of the stimuli, and rapid sucking the other.

Using this method, the authors showed that newborns would give one rhythm to their sucking to hear a passage of prose that had been recited by the mother in a loud voice during the last six weeks of pregnancy and another rhythm to hear a new prose passage read by the mother but not previously heard during pregnancy. One might suppose that the mother's voice simply enjoys an altogether special status and serves as the model for recognizing the intonation and the regularities of the passage that had been heard *in utero*. But the newborns preferred the passage read by the mother before their birth even if it was read by another woman during the test. The fetus therefore appeared to be responsive to the general acoustic properties of the speech signal and not simply to the voice and specific intonations of the mother.

This conclusion called for verification: the authors carried out another experiment, now testing recognition not in newborns but in the fetus (DeCasper and Spence, 1986). They asked future mothers to read a poem in a loud voice every day for four weeks. At the end of these four weeks, when the mother was in the thirty-seventh week of gestation, the fetus listened to the poem that the mother had recited in alternation with another poem never heard before. These alternating sequences were recorded by a third person and retransmitted through a speaker positioned at the level of the head of the fetus. Variations in the heart rate served as an index of discrimination. This technique confirmed the role of prenatal exposure. In fact, the heart rate systematically decreased only in response to the poem read by the mother during the preceding four weeks and did not vary during the reading of the other poem. What cues enabled the fetus to react to the familiar poem? These were not characteristics of the mother's voice, since the test poems were recorded by another woman. It was not a matter of some distinctive rhythm peculiar to a quite particular poem, chosen for just this reason, for precautions had been taken not to habituate all the fetuses to the same poem. It must be concluded, then, that every language event with normal intonation and rhythm alerts the fetus and leads it to regulate its listening to this linguistic model, whose imprint persists at least for a certain time.

Familiarization with the mother's language therefore takes place in the last months of prenatal life. Sound stimulations received during the last months of intrauterine development are likely to contribute to the priming of sensory pathways and to attune the perceptual calibration to certain characteristics of speech sounds.

The Talents of Infants

But let us return to infants, who are not so naive as had been thought, since they are prepared for listening during the prenatal period. At birth, they are capable of distinguishing a broad range of consonant and vowel contrasts, whether or not these contrasts belong to the repertoire of the language spoken in their immediate environment. What is more, babies very quickly show evidence of perceptual constancy: they recognize the similarity of sounds belonging to a single phonetic category, despite physical variations. A single sound can be phonetically realized in many different ways, yet each variant must be recognized as the same sound. Let us take an example: the sound [a] spoken by a man with a deep bass voice, by a child with a high-pitched voice, by a person with a southern accent, by a person with a northern accent, with a rising intonation or with a falling tone, in different contexts, must be categorized as the same vowel /a/.

Studies have shown that at five months, infants are able to neglect the variations of a vowel due to changes in speaker and intonation (Kuhl, 1983). They arrange the different samples of a single sound into a single category.

Another talent of two-month-old newborns is the particular status that they accord the syllable. The syllable is perceived by them as a whole rather than as a combination of distinct elements. This has been demonstrated experimentally. Two-month-old babies were familiarized with a series of syllables—for example, [bi], [si], [li], [mi] (that is, a common vowel with different consonants). It was then observed that the infants were capable of detecting the addition of a new syllable—for example, [di] or [bu]—following a series of syllables that they were familiar with. The babies noticed that [bu] is different from [bo] [ba] [be] and also from [du]. The fact that they noticed the novelty of [bu] shows that the babies did not extract the phoneme /b/ as the property common to the habituation stimuli— that is, they did not decompose the syllables into smaller elements (Juscyzk and Derrah, 1987; see also Bertoncini et al., 1988). This study showed that babies distinguish between sequences of disyllables and sequences of trisyllables, even when the total duration of the sequences remains the same (Bijeljac-Babic, Bertoncini, and Mehler, 1993). This again indicates that the perception of a sound series is organized by syllables.

These aptitudes of the infant are highlighted by experiments in which the acoustic cues are presented in isolation. However, we may ask whether the same discriminatory performance will be found when other auditory promptings, such as prosody, compete for the baby's attention. Recent experiments by Denise Mandel, P. Jusczyk, and D. Kemler-Nelson (1994) sought to establish that performance is similar. They formed the hypothesis that the prosodic cues detected by infants in the first weeks after birth are likely to play an important role in helping the infant organize speech information. They there-fore tested the discrimination of phonetic contrasts presented in sen-tences and compared it against phonetic contrasts presented in word lists. The results of these experiments confirmed their hypothesis: babies of two months detect changes of phonemes better when they occur as part of short sentences than in lists of words. The babies' rate of sucking strongly increased when a series of sentences of the type *The (r)at chases the white mouse* follows the sentence *The (c)at chases the white mouse*. The babies reacted less strongly to the change of the phoneme /r/ to /k/ when it appeared in a list of words read in succession than when it appeared in sentences uttered with a natural intonation.

In everyday life, the natural prosody of the language of infants' mothers commands their listening attention. As the authors suggest, prosody serves as a sort of perceptual glue that holds together sequences of speech. Certainly mothers, who amplify the variations of intonation and play with their voices when they talk to their children, feel this to be so. Thanks to such variations, babies not only retain their capacity for discrimination but find their capacity reinforced by the exaggeration of rhythm and prosodic contours. One observes furthermore that babies better distinguish phonetic contrasts when sentences are read by a woman speaking directly to a child than when they are read by an adult addressing another adult.

What's in a Name?

Are newborns sensitive only to the superficial characteristics of speech? Do some patterns in particular come to acquire a meaning?

The infant's name is often spoken when her parents cuddle or play with her. Does this sound form, which is often associated with feelings of personal well-being, take on particular significance? Can the child recognize when her name is pronounced? Denise Mandel, P. Jusczyk, and D. Pisoni (1995) studied infants of four and a half months to determine whether their names had special status for them.

The method of nonnutritive sucking no longer works for infants at this age. Fortunately, it becomes possible to inquire into their preferences more directly. Two speakers are placed on either side of the infant. Above each speaker there is a small light. So long as the child gazes toward one of the lights, a sound stimulus (the child's own name, on the one hand, and, on the other, three other names spoken with the same tone) is broadcast through the corresponding speaker. The cumulative listening time—or, more exactly, the amount of time spent looking at the light sources—indicates the child's preference for one or the other stimulus.

It turns out that babies listen more attentively to their own name than to the names of their friends. One's name is therefore a recognized signal. However, to say that it is a signal does not imply that the baby of four months connects sound patterns with meanings. Dogs recognize their name, which is as much of a signal for them as the sight of their leash or that of their masters putting on their coats. For the dog as for the baby, names are sound signals arousing attention in one or more particular situations. Babies of four months react to their name, without necessarily realizing that the sound forms have a referential function.

The brain of the newborn is therefore far from being empty. But is the newborn's language capacity organized like that of an adult?

The Organization of Language in the Brain

The principal characteristic of the cerebral cortex is its subdivision into zones that support particular modules—motor or sensory modules, for instance—and cognitive functions. For a century it has been known that discrete areas of the cortex are involved in processes specific to the comprehension and production of speech and language (see figure 1.3). In the adult, the cognitive aspects of language are represented in the left hemisphere of the cerebral cortex, along the Sylvian sulcus (or fissure). The two areas chiefly involved in the comprehension and production of speech are Broca's area (Broca, 1969/1861) and Wernicke's area (Wernicke, 1874), whose functions, until the recent advent of cerebral imaging in clinical research, were determined on the basis of studies of pathology. Lesions involving Broca's area, located in the lower part of the third convolution of the frontal lobe, beneath the Sylvian sulcus, entail the near impossibility of producing speech, due to the loss of articulatory control, while leaving intact the understanding of words and sentences. Adjacent to Broca's area is the system of representations responsible for the precise control of the muscles of the mouth and larynx.

Lesions involving Wernicke's area, in the rear and upper part of the temporal lobe at its junction with the parietal and occipital

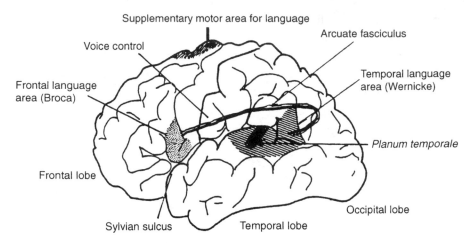

Figure 1.3 Location of Broca's and Wernicke's areas in the human brain and the motor areas involved in articulation and phonation (supplementary motor area and voice control area).

lobes, entail a loss of comprehension while leaving intact the ability to speak, though the speech of such patients is for the most part incomprehensible. The arcuate fasciculus (identified by Burdach) connects Wernicke's area with Broca's.

The left hemisphere has a fundamental role in the processing of rapid acoustical changes and consequently in the processing of speech sounds. The right hemisphere, by contrast, has responsibility for the perception of acoustical events distributed over a long period of time. This hemisphere controls prosody. Lesions of the right hemisphere do not produce aphasias or apraxias, but they do cause problems in the processing and production of prosody and music. The elements of prosody as well as variations in intonation due to affectivity are processed on the right side, and their anatomical organization is located in mirror image to that of the cognitive and analytical language processed on the left side.

Prosodic elements are particularly important for the acquisition of speech. As we have seen, babies are attentive first to intonation; they vocalize prosodic contours before they articulate. They produce isolated syllables before producing sequences of syllables; the phonological and syntactical organization of speech comes later. We now know that the right hemisphere, *in utero* and at birth, matures more rapidly than the left hemisphere. The discrepancy between the maturational rhythms of the two hemispheres in the first year is the source of differences in the emergence of functional capacities (De Schonen, Van Hout, Mancini, and Livet, 1994). It may explain certain characteristics of language development, such as the form in which words are first coded. This is a point to which we return later.

Cerebral imaging provides additional information: the localization of fundamental processes is more variable than had previously been thought, exhibiting patterns that are liable to differ from individual to individual. More elaborate functions are derived from interconnections among several regions of the brain.

Corresponding to the left lateralization of language-processing areas are anatomical and histological asymmetries. The *planum temporale,* including Wernicke's area, which plays a primary role in language comprehension, is larger on the left side of the brain than on the right in 65 percent of individuals (Geschwind and Galaburda, 1987).

Since infants are born without fully functional language abilities—they cannot talk at birth—why should they display such cerebral lateralization? Does it exist from birth, or does it develop at the same time as language? Broca (1969/1865) hypothesized that it accompanies the development of language. The model of acquisition developed by Eric Lenneberg in 1967 rests on the same idea. For Lenneberg, lateralization and the acquisition of language arise in complementary fashion, beginning at two years and concluding with the onset of puberty between the ages of ten and twelve. Rather surprising observations show, in fact, that brain-damaged young children learn to speak and to speak well. These children, whether victims of a perinatal injury to the left side of the brain or of a disease requiring surgical removal of the left hemisphere (lobotomy), more completely recover the capacity to speak the earlier the accident or operation. When the lesion occurs before the age of one year, recuperation is total. In the case of later lesions, deficits are observed over the long term in certain aspects of syntactic processing. It is possible, therefore, in infants and small children for the architecture of the cortex and that of its connections to be restructured, and the propensity of the left hemisphere to process and produce language reversed, cerebral plasticity enabling the damaged brain to furnish substrates for language in the right hemisphere instead. Lenneberg concluded from this that a functional equipotentiality of the two hemispheres exists during the first two years and that cerebral lateralization is the result of learning processes.

The possibility of early functional and structural reorganization, however, does not necessarily indicate that responsibility for language is not one of the purposes of the left hemisphere. In a normal brain, linguistic functions depend on the operation of certain cerebral structures in the left hemisphere. Only a dramatic change that profoundly alters cerebral activity leads other structures to support these processes. The plasticity of the brain, while it is significant in the very young child, does not inevitably amount to a congenital hemispheric equipotentiality.

Among the anatomical asymmetries in the newborn and the infant is that of the *planum temporale*, which is larger on the left side than on the right from the thirty-first week of gestation (Geschwind and Galaburda, 1987). Why do functional asymmetries matter? To be able to refute the idea of initial equipotentiality and progressive lateralization, it is necessary to demonstrate the early specialization of the left hemisphere for speech processing. Is such a demonstration possible?

Indications—but nothing more—of early functional lateralization have been reported thanks to a variety of ingenious techniques. Researchers have racked their brains thinking up ways to lead newborns to indicate whether they prefer using one hemisphere or the other in processing language sounds. Psychological approaches, such as nonnutritive sucking, along with certain physiological approaches have made it possible to investigate whether one hemisphere rather than another seems specially involved in tasks of discriminating syllables or musical notes. The method researchers developed draws on a phenomenon known as *dichotic listening*.

Dichotic listening rests on the fact that the principal transmission pathways for auditory signals are crossed: sounds reaching the right ear are transmitted first to the left hemisphere, while sounds reaching the left ear are sent first to the right hemisphere (see figure 1.4). In dichotic listening, when two different sounds are simultaneously presented in a synchronized way, one to the right ear and the other to

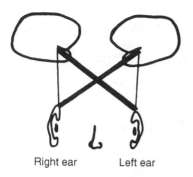

Right hemisphere   Left hemisphere

Right ear   Left ear

Figure 1.4   Diagram showing the crossing of auditory pathways. The presentation of a sound to the right ear goes first to the left hemisphere.

the left ear, the hearer reports a single sound—the dominant sound. In adults, the sound presented to the right ear—which travels, then, to the left hemisphere—is dominant when a speech sound is involved. The sound presented to the left ear—traveling to the right hemisphere—is dominant when a musical sound is involved.

In 1977, Anne Entus made use of this phenomenon by combining it with nonnutritive sucking to examine hemisphere preference in newborns. Infants of two months were presented with a musical sound in one ear and a speech sound in the other. These sounds were repeated until the point of habituation and the babies resumed their normal sucking rhythm. At this moment, one of the sounds was replaced by another of the same kind. The increase in the rate of sucking indicated that the child had perceived the change. This increase was clearer following a change of the speech sound in the right ear (as opposed to the left) and following a change of musical notes in the left ear (as opposed to the right). Though sometimes questioned, these results have more often than not been reproduced, either using the same experimental approach (Bertoncini et al., 1989), or event-related potentials (Molfese and Molfese, 1979), or measures of cardiac deceleration (Glanville, Best, and Levenson, 1977; see also Best, Hoffman, and Glanville, 1982). They seem to indicate, in any case, that at the age of two to three months the left hemisphere does a better job discriminating between speech sounds and the right hemisphere a better job discriminating between musical sounds.

Auditory event-related potentials produced in response to phonetic and musical presentations provide measures of the electrical activity of the brain generated by acoustic stimuli. These responses are difficult to interpret, particularly in babies, but the data they supply are important. The first studies in this domain favored the thesis of a preferential activation of the left hemisphere during the presentation of syllables. Using the same method, Ghyslaine Dehaene-Lambertz and Stanislas Dehaene (1994) recently showed that three-month-old infants can very rapidly detect, in less than 400 milliseconds, a change in the first consonant of a syllable. The electrophysiological correlates of this phonetic discrimination indicate a moderate temporal functional asymmetry favoring the left hemisphere. This hemisphere seems to possess an advantage in acoustically and phonetically processing short syllables. However, the ERP responses obtained in this experiment were subject to considerable individual variations that obliged the authors to qualify their assessment. They concluded that "lateralization in favor of the potentiality of rapid syllable discrimination in the left hemisphere appears to be a modest advantage for this hemisphere rather than a radical division of functions between the two hemispheres" (Dehaene-Lambertz, 1994, pp. 43–49).

It follows that there is something the brain encodes asymmetrically in the case of speech stimuli and that such encoding occurs early in life. But one can only speculate about the nature of the mechanism that produces this asymmetry. It is possible that acoustic stimuli have neuronal substrates similar to those that are useful for processing speech. Thus, the left hemisphere might serve the purpose of perceiving sequences of auditory stimuli characterized by constantly changing acoustic spectra. This kind of analysis may account for early auditory discrimination and a tendency to lateralization, without requiring the inference that speech is processed by the left hemisphere in three-month-old babies. But it might also be supposed that a functional asymmetry corresponding to the anatomical asymmetry observed in newborns underlies a tendency for the left hemisphere to process syllables rather than melodic sounds or sounds that cannot be articulated in languages (Bertoncini et al., 1989).

The process of language acquisition may, in fact, be essential to cortical maturation and hemispheric lateralization. If, for external reasons, language cannot be acquired within the normal time period, lateralization seems to be greatly affected. In the case of Genie (Curtiss, 1977) a child who was isolated shortly after birth and not exposed to a normal linguistic atmosphere until the age of twelve, the right hemisphere was dominant for the incomplete form of language that she was able to acquire. Generalization from the small number of similar cases is not possible, but Genie's case may suggest that the architecture of language centers and the experience of linguistic events are related.

In sum, newborns are far from being the blank slate described by Aristotle. They manifest innate gifts for processing the linguistic environment: they distinguish and categorize the phonemes of languages, and they are sensitive to the voices and prosodic characteristics of their maternal language. Their perceptual system is prepared in advance for processing language sounds. But infants are not only brilliant listeners. Although speech is not yet at their disposal, they are nonetheless preparing themselves for this moment by sharpening their vocal capabilities, organizing their perceptual capacities, and conversing with adults through looks, sounds, and gestures.

The Emergence of Speech

2

In the beginner's mind there are many possibilities, but in the expert's there are few.

—Shunzya Suzuki

Vocal Expressions of the First Months

The newborn comes into the world crying. Unless interrupted by sickness, the production of sounds is constant in human beings, from the first cry to the last breath. From the first syllable to the last word, humans are machines for generating speech.

During the two months that follow birth, the infant's vocal production is completely constrained by the physiology of the vocal tract and by physiological states. Apart from tears, infants emit only reactional sounds that signal their well-being or discomfort.

Infants are, however, as we have seen, extraordinarily attentive to speech: they look and listen. They carefully follow the movements of another's mouth and try to imitate them. They distinguish voices, showing a particular preference for that of their mother. They are sensitive to the rhythms and intonations of adult talk and, being accustomed to the prosody of their native language, are apt to express astonishment when a foreign friend of the family begins to speak. Antoine Grégoire, a psychologist from the French-speaking region of Wallonia in Belgium, published in 1937 a remarkable book about the first two years of language, based on observation of his two sons. He noted that the speech produced by others interests and excites infants as much as events with which they are more directly acquainted. The experimental approach of recent years has made it possible to confirm his observations. However, newborns' interest in speech barely manifests itself at all in the first sounds that they produce.

Between two and five months, babies vocalize only while lying down. For this reason their productions, the celebrated "arrheu" and "ageu", are almost uniquely made up of sounds issuing from the larynx and the soft palate (Koopmans van Beinum and Van der Stelt, 1979). Infants have not yet mastered the art of phonation: it is only toward the fourth or fifth month that they become capable of modulating their voices in various ways. Their vocalizations then become progressively more voluntary. Vocalizing is, in fact, one of the first voluntary behaviors in the infant. From this moment on, infants seek to extend their sound repertoire. They develop an entire series of vocal games, in the course of which they manipulate both prosodic cues such as the pitch of the voice (sharp cries and grunts) and the sound level (howls and murmurs) as well as consonantal features: friction noises, nasal murmuring ("m:::"), rolled labials ("prrr", "brrr"), uvular trills (a kind of cooing). Babies also play with their articulators, clicking the tongue, opening and closing the mouth, and so on. The first vowels appear during this period.

Toward the sixteenth week, one hears the first laughter and cries of joy emitted with the mouth wide open. Babies' laughter is as wonderful to look at as it is to hear. Their whole being is suffused by a succession of chuckles that all but suffocates them. On acquiring control of phonation, toward the fifth month, the child can more specifically modulate the duration, pitch, and intensity of their vocal productions. The fundamental frequency of these vocalizations is about 450 Hz for most babies. However, surprising variations in pitch may occur within a single vocalization, up to three octaves. Infants seem already to take infinite delight in playing with their voices—a foretaste of the pleasure that words, spoken and heard alike, will bring them later. Often they are amazed by what they can do; sometimes their own voices make them laugh. But most of all they seem to have become aware of the impact their cooing, or prebabbling vocal play, has on others and to have begun to make use of it socially to communicate their emotions and demands.

Toward the end of the sixth month, babies are capable of globally coordinating phonatory and supraglottal adjustments: they begin to be able to interrupt their vocalizations at will, which is an essential condition of vocal control. They can also model the pitch of their vocalizations on those of their interlocutor: their voice is higher when they are with their mother than when they are with their father. They can also imitate simple patterns of intonation on the basis of adult examples (Masataka, 1992; see also Kuhl and Meltzoff, 1984). This capacity for imitating the vocal behavior of others will be regularly enriched in the following months.

Between four and seven months, the infant also extends its repertoire of articulatory movements to include gestures that bring the forward part of the articulatory apparatus into play. Coming after the initial "arrheu" and "ageu" are sounds that, while somewhat tentative, contain the quasi-consonants [aw:a], [abwa], and [am:am], as well as isolated vowels that are lengthened and modulated. At four or five months, certain productions are shorter and include sounds of a consonantal sort that resemble syllables. But these pseudosyllables do not have the characteristics required of the syllables of spoken languages (Oller, 1980). Infants are practicing scales, in effect, by manipulating the vocalic sounds [aï], [eï], and [a:e] during the period preparatory to babbling. They play at varying the intonation, succession, and duration of these sounds. By repeating certain familiar types, babies familiarize themselves with a number of routines and become increasingly capable of producing varied sound effects.

It is probable that these games enable infants to discover, on the one hand, the relationship between the intensity and the duration of the sounds they produce and, on the other, how to coordinate the articulatory movements that such productions require. Gradually, babies practice small movements involved in closing the front part of the vocal tract, which permits them to specify the appropriate activity of the jaw, lips, and tongue. The cooing of the baby's first months— "the combined result of attention, sensations, feelings, and unconscious imitation" (Grégoire, 1937, p. 46)—has come to an end. The infant is getting ready to babble and is now in the antechamber of speech.

Quick Studies of Their Native Language

All languages are accessible to children at birth, but they will not speak all of them. Acquiring a language requires associating sounds and meanings according to the phonological and syntactic rules of the language. First, children must select the sounds (phonetic segments or syllables) that constitute the repertoire of the sounds used in their language and acquaint themselves with the combinations of these sounds. They must also assimilate the prosodic cues (accent, rhyme, and intonation) that link linguistic units in organized forms (words, phrases, sentences). The various languages spoken in the world differ from each other in a great many of these respects. But children will learn only their native language or, in the case of bilingual families, their native languages.

From the first days, as we have seen, they begin to pick out and memorize the prosodic characteristics of the native language. Discrimination among phonetic contrasts, on the other hand, is universal, rather than specific, in infants. However, it will not remain so. As adults, we are unable—or are able only with the greatest difficulty— to distinguish sound contrasts belonging to foreign languages when they do not exist in our own language. When does this loss of ability occur—early on, or relatively late? As Shunzya Suzuki wisely observed in connection with problem solving, there are many possibilities in the mind of the beginner but only a few in the mind of the expert. To become expert in the native language, the child has to select the right movements to make and the right sound signals to listen to.

Patricia Kuhl (1993) has tried to determine when infants recognize the vowel categories specific to the language spoken around them. Each language possesses a typical way of pronouncing vowels. The prototypes of each vowel are not the same in every language. Thus, both English and French have a vowel /i/, which is pronounced differently in the two languages. To organize vowel categories in terms of the vowel space peculiar to their own language, children acquire a vowel model typical of the phonological system of that language. To test the organization of babies' vowel space, Kuhl and her team (Kuhl et al., 1992) studied the discrimination of /i/ vowels in six-month-old American and Swedish babies to determine whether the effect of this vowel prototype is manifested in each of the two languages at this age. Her idea was that if children already have a mental representation of the vowels of their language organized around the prototypes of this language, the difference between English and Swedish prototypes will be exhibited, in American and Swedish infants, by differences in their assimilation of vowels distinct from their respective prototypes. This would imply that children no longer have a universal representation of the vowel space but one that is adapted to their specific language.

To determine the existence of vowel categories organized around prototypes, the infant was presented with a reference sound that was repeated once a second. Then this sound changed. If the child turned his head at the moment it changed, he was rewarded: a small wind-up toy was lit up. If the child did not turn his head, the toy, enclosed in a clear plastic box, remained invisible. Thus, the child learned to turn his head when the reference sound changed, making it possible to observe the differences between sounds that were perceived.

American and Swedish babies did not react to this experiment in the same way. The former had greater difficulty distinguishing samples of /i/ the nearer these were to the English prototype of the vowel /i/. By contrast, the proximity of samples of /i/ to the English prototype did not matter to the Swedish babies; but they had trouble distinguishing instances of /i/ the nearer these were to the Swedish /i/ prototype. This is because a prototype attracts adjacent vowels in such a way that native speakers have a hard time telling them apart from the prototype. Nonprototypical vowels do not attract adjacent vowels. As a result, a speaker's discrimination in the neighborhood of a vowel prototype is less good in his or her own language than in another language. At six months, babies therefore have a representation of vowel space adapted to their own tongue, just as adults do.

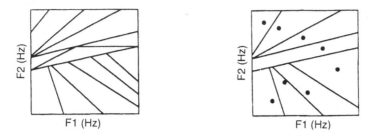

Figure 2.1 Hypothetical partition of acoustic space underlying phonetic distinctions in a universal way (left) and boundaries of vowel space in spoken English (right) (from Kuhl, 1993).

According to Kuhl, the initial sound space is divided by universal psychoacoustic boundaries. By six months, as a result of contact with the language spoken around them, babies have reorganized and simplified this space: they have made it pertinent to their particular language. Thus, nonpertinent categories in the native language disappear, and those remaining pick out pronunciations sufficiently close to the prototypes of this language (see figure 2.1).

In a matter of weeks, then, infants have selected the elements compatible with their linguistic environments. They begin to fail to hear those elements that are generally absent from the phonetic structures that they perceive in their usual experience of language.

This selection mechanism compares the internal representations constantly generated by the brain with forms that present themselves in the linguistic environment (Changeux, 1992). Those that are compatible with the contrasts, syllabic structures, and prosodic cues that exist in children's language are retained. The engrams constituted in this way will stay in their brain. Thus, children's perceptual capacities are reorganized, through what they hear, to select and process the elements of their native language. Babies of bilingual families, no less ingenious than others, will have to manage to successfully carry out these selections and reorganizations in parallel for the two languages that they hear.

Toward five to six months, the baby's encyclopedic hearing begins to fade away, and a phonetic genius begins to emerge. A few months later, infants will have managed to organize a particular object—the language of their environment.

If, at this point, a sensitivity to the vowel categories of their native language appears in infants, it is not until around ten months that a decline in their capacity to distinguish universal consonantal contrasts begins. Vowels and consonants have, in fact, very different roles in speech. The former, which carry prosodic information, are better suited to "magnetizing" the child's attention.

In a lovely set of experiments, Janet Werker and Richard Tees (1984) compared the capacity of English-speaking children in Canada for distinguishing the consonants of Hindi, a language spoken in India, and of Salish (or Thompson), an Indian language spoken in Canada. English-speaking adults are unable to discern the difference between the /ḱi/ and /q́i/ of Salish and are similarly unable to discern the retroflex/dental contrast in Hindi. For them, these phonemes— quite distinct for the speakers of these languages—are heard as a single sound. All English-speaking babies of six to eight months are perfectly capable of distinguishing the foreign phonemes. But between ten and twelve months, they become incapable of distinguishing the phonemes of Salish or of Hindi. The performance of infants of eight to ten months lies between these two extremes: about half still discriminate between the contrasts, while the other half are no longer able to do so (see figure 2.2).

The incapacity to discriminate between /r/ and /l/, which surprises us in Japanese adults (and which, at the airport in Tokyo, almost resulted in my departure for Bali rather than Paris), has its origin in this early loss of attention in Japanese children to a contrast that does not exist in their language.

The reorganization of consonantal discriminations occurs later than in the case of vowels and seems tied to the beginnings of word– recognition. This accelerates the processes of selection: what is not pertinent must not be allowed to obstruct the brain at the moment when children start to memorize the verbal forms that will constitute their lexicon. At this point, sound discrimination ceases to be free and is used instead to register differences in meaning.

The process by which the perception of consonant categories is reorganized is not so straightforward. When children begin to select the consonant categories peculiar to their language and to detect their

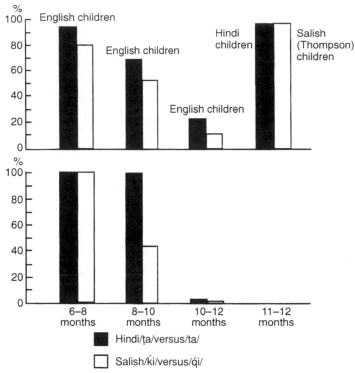

Figure 2.2 Percentage of children of English-speaking parentage who distinguish the Hindi and Salish (Thompson) contrasts tested. In the upper panel, the age groups correspond to different groups of children. In the lower panel, the study is longitudinal. The English-speaking children gradually lose their ability to distinguish contrasts foreign to their language (from Werker and Tees, 1984).

specific properties, their perception of nonpertinent contrasts in the language is modified. But not all nonpertinent contrasts are eliminated by the age of ten to twelve months: some will remain assimilated to categories of the language for some time. Eventually, all contrasts are assigned a linguistic value within the framework of the phonological system of the child's language. This occurs at about the age of two. Subtle experiments by Catherine Best (1993) show the evolution of this reorganization, some elements of which leave traces in adult speech.

Babbling

One might, in following the same example, show how a child learns finally to speak, but it suffices to have observed the beginnings, and one may easily understand what comes after.

—Géraud de Cordemoy (1970/1668)

At last, the long-anticipated day arrives: the child begins to babble. The onset of babbling, perceived at once by adults, is generally very sudden. Following the uncertain sounds of the preceding days is the first "*pa pa pa*" or "*ba ba ba*", clear and well articulated and immediately noticed by parents. Parents sometimes tend to interpret them as rough drafts of the child's first words. Some fathers conclude, a bit hastily, that they have actually heard their child's first word and that this word, naturally, is *papa* (or *dada*).

Babbling marks an important stage in the development of speech. Mumblings give way to productions that constitute the beginning of this development. Babbling is not the same as language, of course, but it is a form of language that provides a framework for the development of speech. To quote Grégoire's poetic phrase (1937, p. 73), "It is a language whose phonetic fabric frequently flutters but that nonetheless obeys the principles of phonetic possibility." Less poetically, we may say that the babbling child begins to produce syllables that respect the syllabic constraints of natural languages (Oller and Lynch, 1992).

Without entering too far into the details that occupy linguists, one may regard the syllable as the basic rhythmic unit of natural languages. All languages are syllabic. In all languages, syllabic structure is built out of consonants and vowels—that is, it is formed through the opposition of features of a contracted vocal tract (consonants) and an open vocal tract (vowels), by aperiodic sounds (consonants) and periodic sounds (vowels). The syllable is composed of a nucleus (the vowel), one or more margins (consonants), and a transition between the formants of the vowel nucleus and the consonantal margins.

Corresponding to each vowel is a syllable. The duration of a syllable in natural languages is between 100 and 500 milliseconds. Its nucleus is a vowel—a sound emitted by a source of periodic energy whose resonance pattern corresponds to that of an open vocal tract. Transitions between one or more consonantal margins and the vowel nucleus must be continuous.

These notions allow us to identify the changes in articulation that mark the passage from the quasi-syllables produced between four and seven months—prior to babbling—to the syllables of babbling, whose characteristics, similar to the ones we have just defined, correspond to the material form of adult syllables.

What Do Children Say Between Seven and Ten Months?

Between six and ten months, often toward seven months but with substantial variation from child to child, children's first babblings are heard. These first forms—which make up what is called *canonical babbling*—are most frequently characterized by the production of simple syllables in a consonant-vowel sequence, such as [pa], [ba], [ma]. The consonant sounds introducing the syllable are typically occlusives and nasals. The sounds [p], [b], [t], [d], and [m] are generally combined with low central vowels: the vowel [a] as in the adult word *hot*, low front vowels ([æ] as in *bat*), and central vowels (e.g., Λ, as in *mud*) form the basis of babbling. Until ten months, other vowels are relatively rare in productions. Some children prefer to produce velar consonants—[g] or [k]—rather than labials. (Grégoire's son, for example, was fond of these.) Individual variation among children appears early. Syllables are very often grouped in repetitive sequences: [bababa], [dædædæ], [bebebe]. However, this is not the only type of production. From the moment they begin to babble, children can indulge certain whims with regard to phonetic transformations—but not too quickly. They proceed bit by bit, sometimes with a more original variation. Grégoire (1937), who noted the productions of his eight-month-old son in the early hours of the morning, found other series amid the frequent instances of [papa] and [tatata]: [dədədə], [emawma], [aba/abwu], [goaguga], [goage/eka]. Open syllables, with their vowel-consonant-vowel series (such as [aba], [ædæ], and [eka]) are fairly frequent, whereas closed syllables—that is, syllables having a final consonant, such as [dat] or [bam]—are rare.

The rhythmic sequences formed by repeated consonant-vowel combinations, such as [bababa], which characterize canonical babbling, may help relate the sensory and motor aspects of vocalizations. By repeating the same patterns of articulation, the child learns to associate the sound patterns corresponding to them. In addition, the child's learning of phonetic possibilities is facilitated by the acoustic and articulatory variations of these rhythmic repetitions.

What is the role of articulator motivity in the productions of babbling? Series of repeated syllables are produced by the rhythmic alternation of opening and closing the mouth, accompanied by phonation. A relatively open vocal tract during phonation leads to the production of a vowel, while the production of consonant sounds implies a relatively closed vocal tract. For Peter MacNeilage and Barbara Davis (1991), this oral oscillation cycle supplies the basis for babbling and accounts for the form of its productions. The categories of consonants that require the greatest closing off (or constriction) of the vocal tract are the occlusive consonants (/p/, /b/, /t/, /d/, /k/, /g/) and the nasal consonants (/m/, /n/, /ng/). They represent more than 80 percent of the consonants at the beginning of babbling, with consonants that bring the upper articulators into play—labials and dentals—enjoying an advantage. Corresponding to the early tendency to maximal closure of the vocal tract in consonants is a preference for a large opening of the mouth in the case of vowels. The most frequent vowels are therefore [a] and [æ]. Thus, productions of the type /bababa/, /dadada/, and /mam mam mam/ at the beginning of babbling are explained by the relatively simple movement of a succession of openings and closings of the jaw. This mandibular oscillation furnishes the articulatory frame whose content is given next by the movements of the tongue. Babbling, with its characteristic repeated syllables, reflects the formation of frames within which the different phonetic segments will be inserted as they become accessible to the child.

This model predicts the observed high frequency of [bababa] (labial and low central vowel) productions, of [dedede] (dental and front vowel), and of [gogogo] (velar and back vowel) in early babbling. But if these first productions may be interpreted in terms of such a description, we shall see that babies quickly prove to be too clever to allow themselves to be confined within a rigid frame.

In the first months, children practice varying their voices and their intonations. They have thus acquired a certain control over the duration, intensity, and pitch of their vocalizations. But what role does intonation play in babbling? From one point of view, now considered to be outmoded, intonation is a simple addition, super-imposed on phonetic productions. But the diversity of the prosodies displayed by natural languages implies a mastery of the temporal relations and variations of intonation as well as of the modalities of approach and release in the articulation of sounds.

Acoustic analyses by Ray Kent and Ann Murray (1982) on the vocalization of babies in the United States offer a uniform picture of falling contours, which were thought to be a general tendency rep-resenting the physiological correlate of the "breath group ending." However, careful listening to babies from different countries aged seven to eight months holds surprises for the investigator: their bab-blings resemble each other, to be sure, but they are never identical. Listening to them, my colleagues Laurent Sagart and Catherine Durand and I had the impression that there existed characteristics that define a quality of voice and a manner of articulating and modulating syllables that were wholly independent of what was said and that were peculiar to each baby. But quality of voice and manner of speaking were not only individual; they depended also on a particular language and culture. We found French babies already to have a way of vocalizing—of approaching and releasing sounds—that differed from that of Arab babies. Was this impression, so contrary to the standard academic views of the 1970s, a figment of our imagination? It needed to be checked.

A simple experiment, in which we presented adults with sample pairs of babbling by eight-month-old French babies (recorded in Paris), Arab babies (recorded in Algiers), and Cantonese babies (recorded in Hong Kong) assured us we were not mistaken (Boysson-Bardies, Sagart, and Durand, 1984). The adults were asked to indi-cate—by guessing, if necessary—which one of two successively heard samples they thought was the babbling of the French baby. Their answers were correct more than 70 percent of the time and suggested that, in the case of eight-month-old babies, characteristics of intonation and vocal quality specific to each language had already influenced their manner of producing sounds and of grouping them in intonation contours. The Algerian babies were found to exhibit abrupt onsets, friction noises in the release of sounds, and stressed syllables. The French babies displayed lengthenings and softer modulations, whereas the abrupt endings of productions with an "entering tone" found in the Cantonese babies, along with numerous small variations in pitch, prefigured the variation in tones characteristic of their language. Thus one may conclude that the type of phonation, the rhythmic organization, and the intonation contours of babbling reflect the characteristics of the language of the baby's environment by the eighth month.

What Do Babies Say Between Ten and Twelve Months?

Toward the age of ten or eleven months, articulation becomes clearer and more assured, and series of varied syllables become more numerous. After the so-called canonical period of babbling, during which series of repeated syllables form the majority of the productions, the moment comes when children considerably augment their production of polysyllabic utterances in which vowels and consonants are systematically varied. Although the field of combinations is still restricted and phonetically circumscribed, certain children are particularly fond of difficulty: "Apabouyé oyé oyé pabouyé," said one French baby we observed, named Jeanne, while Léa made a brief speech: "Baepach:ebape'hae chlxo." The majority of productions remain mono- or disyllabic, however, with occlusives and nasals continuing to be predominant.

Or take Pierre, a baby of ten months. Putting a microphone not too far away from him, we withdrew to an adjacent room and watched him through the open door. Pierre played and babbled. When he banged on a block, he produced brief sounds that were isolated syllables. Then he stopped and, staring into space, produced a long series [bababa], followed by a series [dadada], then [gagaga]. What was the baby doing in running through this range of sounds? It is not by chance that these three series came one after another, for they involve successive places of articulation—labial, dental, velar. Pierre modulated his productions from front to back by retracting his tongue and changing the place of articulation in the vocal tract. The following day, Pierre produced [apff] and [pepff] series. This time, he kept the place of articulation the same but varied the manner of articulation ([p] is an occlusive labial and [f] a labial fricative). Other regularities were noted: isolated syllables preceded series of syllables but rarely followed them; sequences of repeated sounds preceded series of varied sounds. Observing babies of this age on a daily basis, one notices, in addition to regularities in the order of their productions, an evolution in the way in which they contrast the effects of the place and manner of articulation of sounds. Between canonical babbling and the varied babbling that one finds during this period, babies will have rather systematically explored the range of articulatory play and come to find amusement in producing series of variations according to the position of the articulators. They have thus somehow constructed a springboard for speech.

Despite these regularities, great variability is already seen among children. Carole's babbling contained many series with the velars /g/ and /k/: these represented half of the occlusives she produced; Charles, by contrast, produced hardly any velars. Noël produced no /l/ in his babbling, while Laurent included them in more than a third of his productions. No labial occlusives (/p/, /b/) were found in Laurent's babbling at ten months, which is rare: for Charles, Carole, Marie, and Noël, series introduced by [b] and [p] were very frequent; for Marie, they represented more than a third of her productions. Anne, less skillful at varying her syllables, toyed a great deal with their prosodic envelope instead. She grouped series of [mememe] along rising and falling intonation contours, which give the impression of short sentences in animated conversations. Her springboard for speech was more prosodic.

Preferences for certain configurations are thus clearly signaled in the productions of children of ten to twelve months, although no children systematically explore the range of articulatory possibilities at their disposal. They choose and privilege certain production routines that they will make use of when the time comes to program words. Even so, what is important is that the training of their articulatory capacities has given them the faculty to choose the rhythmic and syllabic frame that will furnish the bases for the articulatory programming of their first words.

Wherein the Babbling of Babes Is Subjected to the Seriousness of Scientists

Why do children babble? What are children doing when they babble? Is babbling a game? Is it a prelanguage? Are they interested only in playing with their voices? Why should we be interested in the sounds of babbling at all when, historically, its study has long left psychologists and phoneticians—with some remarkable exceptions—relatively indifferent?

Antoine Grégoire is one of these exceptions. In his 1937 book, *L'Apprentissage du langage* (The Learning of Language), he argues for the hypothesis that language sounds exert great early influence on the vocalizations of babies. But means of verifying his intuitions were lacking. Without recourse to recordings that allow transcriptions made by different observers to be checked against one another, it is difficult to compare observations and notes about the vocalizations of babies belonging to different linguistic environments, no matter how meticulous and conscientious these observations may be.

The first 120 pages of Grégoire's book, devoted to the phonetic analysis of cooing and babbling sounds, reveal the importance he assigned to babies' vocalizations. Relying on systematic observations of the first months, Grégoire tried to chart the course of what he called *phonetic normalization*. He reckoned that this occurs quite early. He thought that cooing is subject to environmental influence and that the articulatory modalities of adult language serve as models for the productions of babbling: "If one were to follow infants from various countries from day to day, one would surely observe, among a mass of apparently disorganized facts, [the same process of] relative phonetic normalization" (Grégoire, 1937, p. 73).

Meticulous analysis of the babbling produced by his two sons led him to this prediction in 1937: "To insist yet again on the material aspect of speech, during what period does the regularization of the phonetic system—in other words, its gradual development in accordance with local usage—begin? The opinion generally adopted assigns a rather late date to this new phase, the end of the first year or so. Until this moment, babbling is presumed to escape the influence of the child's environment. In this regard, we are already justified in expressing some doubt. We believe in the likelihood of earlier effects" (Grégoire, 1937, p. 74).

Antoine Grégoire would have liked to have been able to compare the cooing of the babies of the Swiss Alps around Berne with that of small children in Paris. This area of the Swiss Alps was not chosen at random: the region's variations in vocal register make it possible, in principle, to test whether a difference between the gutteral articulation of Swiss babies and the front articulation of Parisian babies correspond to the adult pronunciation peculiar to each of the two places. Unfortunately, the means of doing this were not available to him. That did not prevent Grégoire from identifying cooing and babbling as stages of early phonetic normalization, a sort of laboratory where preparations are carried out for the production of language sounds in their full articulatory specificity.

Structuralist and generative approaches, on the other hand, emphasized the universal factors of development in language. In this framework, at least at first, the genesis of the development of language appeared to be of little interest. The great structuralist linguist Roman Jakobson (1972/1941), in his famous book *Child Language Aphasia and Phonological Universals*, posited a radical discontinuity between the productions of babbling and those that belong to language. These productions, on his view, bore no relation to the repertoire of first words. Straight off, then, he rejected all studies of babbling sounds as irrelevant to the acquisition of speech. Babbling was only an exercise giving rise to random and extremely varied series of sounds. Furthermore, a period of silence separated these productions, which were not linguistic, from the production of the first genuine linguistic sounds that appeared with the child's first words.

Despite its radical character, this opinion, coming as it did from so respected a scholar as Jakobson, eventually came to determine how researchers regarded prelinguistic productions—all the more as his analysis coincided with that of Lenneberg (1964) and Chomsky (1959), as well as of most of their disciples during the 1960s. For them, the productions of babbling corresponded to a given stage of maturation and evolved in accordance with maturational processes. Their forms being universal, they must be found in all children of the same age, even in deaf children—and before phonological regularities manifest themselves.

The advantage of Jakobson's propositions lay in the fact that they could be tested. They stimulated research, and studies of phonological development multiplied, soon followed by studies bearing on pre-linguistic forms. But the empirical data that were expected to support Jakobson's claims turned out to be quite unconvincing. Neither the claim that babbling has no relation to later productions nor the universal pattern proposed for phonological development has been borne out by the analysis of children's productions (Oller, Wieman, Doyle, and Ross, 1975).

In the 1970s, another approach to understanding the nature of babbling emerged. A group of linguists focused on the biomechanical constraints on the articulatory apparatus and on its relation to perception (MacNeilage, 1980; see also Lindblom, MacNeilage, and Studdert-Kennedy, 1983; and Studdert-Kennedy, 1991). This approach seemed to converge with Lenneberg's position in insisting on biological factors in linguistic development but it departed from Lenneberg in its rejection of privileged, specialized mechanisms for language and in its interpretation of the nature and function of babbling.

On this view, all the movements due to the biological equipment of human beings possess fundamental structural characteristics displaying comparable forms of organization based on an assembly of coordinated movements (Thelen, 1991). A fundamental gesture underlies all the articulatory productions of babbling. It involves a cyclical movement, alternately opening and closing the vocal tract, first produced by the opening and closing of the mouth (MacNeilage and Davis, 1991). This motor configuration, which accounts for the canonical syllables of babbling, does not require a specific motor control. A simple mechanism furnishes the regularities that account for the syllables that are found in all the babbling of all children, no matter what their linguistic group may be. The causal explanation of prelinguistic patterns, as well as the patterns of first words, rests therefore on biomechanics. Anatomical changes are a necessary, if not sufficient, factor of development. Proponents of the biomechanical model sought to show that phonetic systems emerge as adaptations to constraints on the production and reception of language (Lindblom, 1992).

The biomechanical approach linked up with the work of phoneticians on the nature of the phonetic inventories of languages spoken in the world. According to these researchers, the general aspects of babbling could be explained by the presence in every language of a common core of sounds—a subset of articulations that forms the basis of the systems of sounds that children have to learn. This core develops sooner and more systematically than rarer and more elaborate combinations of segments.

On this view, the chance that a child will escape the universality of babbling patterns is small. The variability that is observed among children's vocalizations is to be explained by individual preferences for certain of these patterns, within the limits imposed by the biomechanical tendencies that control consonant-vowel co-occurrences.

Biomechanical models of articulation have the merit of putting babbling back in the context of general phonetic development. With this type of model, the forms of canonical babbling are related to the gestures that ground the basic structures of articulation in languages. Their value for the development of speech is thus recognized. But the influence of the linguistic environment on babbling has continued to be underestimated in these approaches. Curiously, it was just at the moment when the perceptual capacities of infants had come to be appreciated that theories that minimized the effect of perceptual capacities on speech production came along.

The propositions generated by an essentially biomechanical interpretation do contain an element of truth. They account for the frequency of certain types of productions in babbling. However, they underestimate the role of the selection processes that permit the rearrangement of early perceptual capacities. Of course, these propositions do not reject the role of auditory, visual, and proprioceptive sources of information, which establish a self-regulating relationship between listening and production, but they see this role as operating only at a late stage and then without great force.

And yet the fact that children hear words by itself modifies their vocal behavior. Proof of this is given by the differences that are found between the speech of deaf children and the speech of hearing children (Oller, Eilers, Steffens, Lynch, and Urbano, 1994). The former do not begin to babble until several months after hearing children.

Does perceptual processing therefore have no influence on speech productions? This would be quite a surprise, considering what a remarkable machine the baby is when it comes to establishing correspondences. Babies are attentive to speech, from the earliest days prefer their native language, from birth readily distinguish /ba/ from /be/, /da/, /bi/, /ga/, and /gu/, from the first months imitate the gestures adults make with their mouths, at four to five months connect sounds with movements of the mouth, and at the same age reproduce intonation contours. Are they really passive in the face of what they hear, see, and feel, when the time comes to manage their own productions?

In the 1980s, the hypothesis of early interaction appeared (or, rather, reappeared, having been first proposed by psycholinguists such as Grégoire) (Boysson-Bardies, Hallé, Sagart, and Durand, 1989). This hypothesis posits a process of mutual adjustment between the genetic and physiological equipment of children, on the one hand, and the effects of experience with the language spoken by their parents, on the other. Before birth, this interaction modulates the perceptual capacities for prosody. In the second quarter of the first year, as we have seen, it performs the same role with regard to phonetics. In production, this interaction is marked by the evolution of the phonetic and intonational organization of babbling. The mechanism that governs it is biologically determined and therefore universal: this is what allows children to make selections on the basis of the data presented by their environment. Children's brains constantly produce internal variations, which can be regarded as hypotheses by means of which they test the external world (Changeux and Dehaene, 1989; see also Edelman, 1987). The process of development thus rests on the selection of empirical data that allow certain hypotheses to be established. Little by little, levels of organization are built up that are increasingly adapted to the external world.

The vocal productions of children are thus modeled by selection processes. The phonetic forms and intonation patterns specific to the language of the child's environment are progressively retained at the expense of forms that are not pertinent to the phonological system of this language. The process begins at birth, if not before. However, the first effects on vocal performances are delayed, particularly by the slow course of motor development.

The answers to the propositions generated by these different models—maturational, biomechanical, and interactive—are found in the empirical data. But interpretable answers are not easily obtained from babies, and their whims sometimes muddy the waters. Fortunately, the facts are stubborn, and the urgings of the children themselves grow more and more insistent, with the result that we find ourselves sharing the sympathetic appreciation Antoine Grégoire showed for their vocal productions.

Do French Babies Babble in French and Yoruba Babies in Yoruba?

To hear the babbling of a little English girl of ten months named Mary, one would think one were listening to Mrs. Thatcher. The series of "djodj" sounds that she makes with a somewhat clipped tone are unlikely in a French baby or a Chinese baby. But do such exaggerated examples suffice to show the influence of one's native language on vocalizations? Perhaps Mary is simply a good imitator of some woman in her family circle, deploring the silliness of a certain George.

Only systematic cross-linguistic analysis can provide the answer, for it allows us, in principle, to separate what is universal from the systematic modifications that are made based on one's experience of a particular language.

The influence of the native language on children's babbling has been brought out by parallel experiments and observations of children belonging to different linguistic communities. General features, common to all children, characterize the first productions of babbling, but the variability that appears during the last trimester of the first year shows that by this point they are no longer simply a function of biomechanics. Does such variability merely indicate the random possibilities that exist for more numerous productions, or does it point to the operation of selection processes that reveal a certain level of phonetic organization?

To answer this question, it was necessary to combine comparative and predictive approaches. But do the phonological systems of different languages allow predictions to be made about the epigenetic processes that underlie the development of prelinguistic forms? We mentioned earlier that, at eight months, the prosodic and rhythmic organization of babbling allows adults to pick out, from different samples, those produced by children of their own linguistic community. When the first experiments in this domain were carried out, it remained an open question whether the phonological organization of the native language exercises an influence on the phonetic structure of babbling.

The systematic, comparative, and cross-linguistic study of babbling must begin by studying vowels. Vowels are perceptually salient in the speech chain and demand less precision than consonants with respect to articulatory control. In 1980, Philip Lieberman called attention to the emergence in the babbling of English babies of a coherent vowel space during the last quarter of the first year. Researchers were interested to see whether, in the course of this development, evidence of early influence by the linguistic environment could be found. A study of the vowels produced by children of ten months belonging to very different linguistic groups was to decide the matter.

Each language, in fact, has its own vowel space. The number of vowels in languages may differ very considerably: some may have as few as three, and others as many as sixteen or more. The vowel system of a language can be studied by means of spectral analysis of the vowels produced by speakers of this language: a vowel is in some sense a musical sound, produced by the vibration of the vocal cords and modulated by the configuration of the vocal tract, which amplifies certain frequencies and weakens others. Every vowel has a timbre, or color, that is specific to it. This timbre is tied to the pattern of formants. For example, a [u] has a dark timbre: its first two formants are located at low frequencies; an [i] has a clear timbre: its second and third formants are located at high frequencies. In short, the color or timbre of a vowel is defined by the position of the different articulators—the lips, tongue, larynx, and so on.

If environment has an early influence on phonetic selection in babbling, it must be possible to find systematic differences in the distribution of vowel sounds between linguistic groups. Furthermore, these differences ought to reflect those that are found in the vowel repertory of adult languages.

The answer had to be sought in the four corners of the globe. It was necessary, first, to find languages having quite different vowel spaces. Thus, we paid visits to French, English, Chinese (again Cantonese), and Algerian babies (Boysson-Bardies et al., 1989). Adult English speakers have more front vowels (/i/, /I/, /æ/), French speakers more rounded vowels (/œ/, /ø/), Cantonese speakers more back vowels (/ɔ/, /ɑ/), and Algerians, who speak Arabic, have only three vowels in their phonological system, the realizations of which are more central than front or back. Babies are so sensitive to language sounds that it was necessary to interview them in their native countries, where it might be assumed they had not heard other languages. We therefore made recordings of the English babies in Sussex, the Cantonese babies in Hong Kong, and the Algerian babies in Algiers. The French babies—like all the others, ten months old—were recorded in Paris.

Each of the five children from each of the four linguistic communities was recorded for sixty minutes. Their productions supplied between fifty and sixty analyzable vowels per child. We measured the acoustic characteristics of these vowels (that is, the frequencies of the first and second formants, F1 and F2). This allowed the vowels to be represented according to the classic F1 × F2 plan, illustrated, for example, by the famous vowel triangle /a/, /i/, and /u/.

Figure 2.3 presents the data for all the children of each group (the ellipses include 75 percent of the vowels for each group).

The distribution of vowels can be seen to be quite different for the four groups. The English children have a tendency to produce more high front vowels (/i/ and /I/), while the Cantonese, at the opposite extreme, favor the low back vowels /ɔ/, and /o/. The Algerians have a more centralized vowel space than the French,

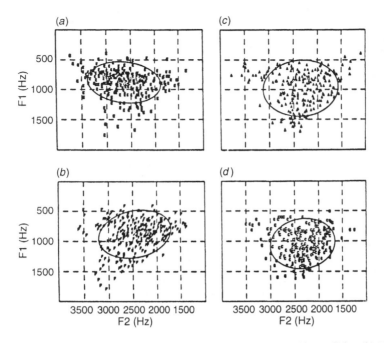

Figure 2.3   Vowel space of ten-month-old babies: *(a)* English, *(b)* French, *(c)* Algerian, *(d)* Cantonese. The vowels found in their babbling have been reported with reference to the value of the first and second formants. Different tendencies among the linguistic groups can be seen (from Boysson-Bardies, Hallé, Sagart, and Durand, 1989).

whose /a/ is already distinguished from the English /æ/ and sounds very French.

Do these variations reflect vowel characteristics in the languages of each child? To find out, we chose to analyze the relative compactness of vowels in each group and to compare the degree of compactness of the vowel space in adults with that in children for the different groups: the relationship between the first two formants of the vowels determines the vowels' relative compactness or diffuseness. For compact vowels, the F2/F1 relation is weaker than for diffuse vowels, which in general are high and front (/i/ and /é/). Comparing vowels along this compact/diffuse axis is convenient because it captures a dimension unaffected by the length of the vocal tract. Figure 2.4 gives the F2/F1 relation for the children tested and for speakers of the adult language.

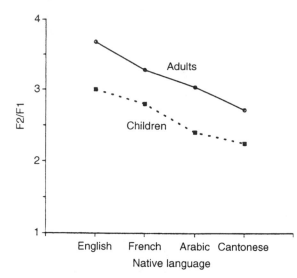

Figure 2.4   The relationship between the second and first vowel formants in the babbling of children of ten months from different linguistic groups corresponds to the relationship found in their native language.

A parallelism was observed in the compactness relation between the vowels of the children of the different groups and the vowels of the adult languages: the F2/F1 relation was highest among the English and weakest among the Cantonese. This parallelism shows that children already have a representation of the vowel space of the language that allows them to realize vowels as a function of the perceived characteristics of vowels they have heard.

Kuhl's research (Kuhl et al., 1992) on perceptual categorizations, conducted in the United States and in Sweden, later showed that babies exhibit greater sensitivity, already at six months, to the prototypical vowels of their language. This early encoding of the vowel categories of the language spoken around them agrees with the data showing early differences in productions. Moreover, these differences testify to a use of the perceptual encoding of vowels for production in babbling. This convergence establishes that an interaction between the perceptual processing and encoding of elements of the phonetic repertoire takes place over the course of the first year.

It remained to be seen whether the repertoire of the language has an influence on consonants and syllables. There was strong resistance to this view at the time. Conventional approaches to the problem of articulation were based on the marked predominance of occlusives—particularly of labials and dentals—in the babbling of babies and in their first words: consonants are more complex to produce than vowels, which are more stable, and therefore require more motor skill. The dominant view was that consonants are uniquely determined by articulatory mechanisms.

Japanese and Swedish babies, along with French and American babies, were kind enough to provide us with information (Boysson-Bardies et al., 1992; see also Boysson-Bardies and Vihman, 1991). Like our American and Swedish colleagues with whom we carried out this research, we began by recording the children in their native countries when they were ten months old and had not yet produced any words. Our study continued until the children produced about twenty-five words in the course of a session: they were then between sixteen and nineteen months. Babbling and words were analyzed independently and grouped according to the different age brackets. The distribution of consonants was studied according to the place of articulation for three principal categories (labials, dentals, and velars) and according to the manner of articulation (occlusives, fricatives, nasals, and liquids).

In the data on babbling, as in that on first words, the sizable percentage of labial and dental consonants, the preponderance of occlusives, and the rarity of fricatives and of laterals (/l/ and /r/) matched the universal general tendencies predicted by physiological considerations (see figure 2.5). Clear differences were found, however, in the distribution of places of articulation and modes of consonant production among the four groups of children. Thus, at the age of ten months, French children produced more labials than Japanese or Swedish children did.

Cross-linguistic analysis also confirmed that the repertoire of consonants, in babbling as well as in the production of first words, resembled the distribution that was later to be found in children's commonest words: the process of constructing phonetic representations specific to their language had begun. At ten months, the children we studied had already selected a repertoire of consonants that reflected the statistical tendencies of their native language (see figure 2.6).

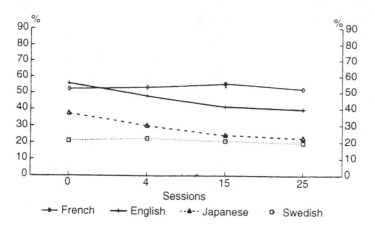

Figure 2.5   The percentage of labial consonants per session in the productions of French, English, Japanese, and Swedish children. These percentages are indicated at four stages—when the children had not yet spoken words, when four different words were spoken in a recording session, when fifteen different words were spoken, and when twenty-five different words were spoken. The differences in the production of labials among the linguistic groups remained stable through the period studied, beginning with children of ten months and ending at about the age of seventeen months for the majority of the children (from Boysson-Bardies and Vihman, 1991).

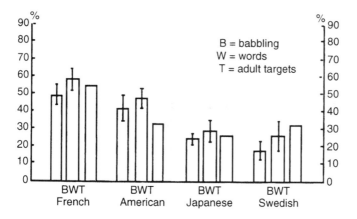

Figure 2.6   Percentage of labials in babbling, first words, and the forms predicted by the native tongues of French, American, Swedish, and Japanese children. This bar graph shows the early influence of the native language on the production of labials (from Boysson-Bardies and Vihman, 1991).

The distribution of consonants does not change significantly between babbling and first words. One finds some differences, however. The repertoire of first words is simpler and includes a still higher percentage of occlusives and labials. In fact, the production of a word demands the elaboration of a specific motor program, which imposes constraints on the forms and order of articulatory sequences. If these constraints are too strong, children return to simpler forms and try to adapt them to the word they wish to produce. This leads to different strategies in different children.

The syllable, as a unit of production, grounds the organization of speech. But in young children, motor limitations impose constraints on the structure of syllables. The predominant structures in babbling are simple: consonant-vowel for the most part, sometimes consonant-vowel-consonant. Vowel-consonant-vowel and consonant-vowel-consonant-vowel series are frequently found.

Biomechanical approaches make strong predictions about the consonant-vowel co-occurrences that ought to be found in babbling as well as in the basic syllable of languages. A maximal synergy among the articulators and minimal changes in articulation are assumed in order to predict privileged forms of consonant-vowel association. According to these same approaches, the consonant-vowel structure is strongly privileged, and three associations—labial consonant + central vowel, dental consonant | front vowel, and velar consonant + back vowel—are universally favored (MacNeilage and Davis, 1991).

If one believes that the influence of the local language matters, predictions are a function of particular languages. Thus, Nigerian babies speaking Yoruba, a language in which most of the words begin with a vowel, ought very early to produce more vowel-consonant-vowel forms than French children.[1] And, indeed, Yoruba children do merrily mock mechanical constraints and produce many more vowel-consonant-vowel forms than consonant-vowel forms. After all, they have to learn to speak Yoruba. Between 65 and 75 percent of the disyllables produced by the French, English, and Swedish children we studied were of the form consonant-vowel-consonant-vowel, as against 38 percent for Yoruba children, the balance of whose disyllabic productions (62 percent) were of the form vowel-consonant-vowel (Boysson-Bardies, 1993).

Common tendencies are found, of course, but the consonant-vowel associations at ten to twelve months show that the associations predicted by the biomechanical approach and its principle of minimal articulation are found in babbling only when they are also predicted by the structure of the native language. Good learners that babies are, they tend to prefer the most frequent associations in the common words of their native language. Thus, the Yoruba-speaking children whom we called on to help check the data showed a predilection for the forms /ki/ and /ké/, forms that ought to be relatively rare according to motor-based predictions.

This last study further emphasizes how early the selections by the child are made. Between nine and ten months, the interaction between perception and motor performances permits children to organize their babbling. This reveals an agreement between the re-organization of perception and the first productions. The experiments on sound-discrimination capacities suggest that, toward ten to twelve months, babies lose interest in sounds that do not belong to the phonological system of their language. At the same moment, children's performances become oriented toward the production of the vowels, consonants, and syllables privileged in their own language.

Of course, the differences between modes of acquisition and the variability in forms that one finds among children of a given linguistic group indicate the need for caution in generalizing about all the children belonging to it. However, the fact that individual variations do not manage to mask the specific tendencies of different linguistic groups reinforces the view that selective processes organize a phonetic level in production at nine to ten months.

They Begin Speaking Their Language Without an Accent

As we have seen, French adults are able to distinguish the vocalizations of French children of eight months from vocalizations produced by foreign babies. When asked to explain the reasons for their decisions, they point to signs such as intonation and rhythm. But are these kinds of coloring, which are given very early to vocalizations, related to characteristics of prosodic organization specific to French? Prosodic cues make it easier to break utterances into segments, and at two months children are already sensitive to them. But do they use them before their productions come to be organized into words and sentences?

Andrea Levitt and Qi Wang (1991) have analyzed forms of babbling consisting of repeated syllables in French and American children aged seven to eleven months. They were able to identify patterns of pitch and temporal organization of the terminal syllable for these ages that tend to draw it closer to the characteristic form of the terminal syllable of the ambiant language. Thus, lengthened duration of the terminal syllable and a rise in its fundamental frequency (F0) contours were observed much more often in French children than in English-speaking children (54 percent versus 24 percent). Pierre Hallé, B. de Boysson-Bardies, and M. Vihman (1991) have compared temporal organization and F0 contours in the disyllables of French and Japanese children of eighteen months. Rising voice and terminal lengthening are usual in French children, whereas in the Japanese a falling contour and the absence of terminal lengthening characterize the final syllables of disyllabic productions. These data agree with the characteristics of prosody in French and in Japanese. In Japanese, unlike in French, terminal syllables are not lengthened (see figures 2.7 and 2.8).

One of the most interesting aspects of how children acquire language that remains to be studied is surely the organization of intonation and rhythm at five to six months—before the first productions of babbling occur but after the infant has mastered phonation. If prosody has the role attributed to it in the segmentation of continuous speech, the possibility of checking its contribution to the perceptual processing of organized forms through the productions of children seems extremely important. Factors such as oral posture, overall laryngeal position in relation to the modes of production characteristic of certain languages, and organization of intonation contours resembling those of the native language may manifest themselves before six months. This would confirm a parallel evolution, albeit moved forward, of perceptual processing and organization of productions with respect to prosody.

As we have seen, children do not begin by speaking with the rhythm and intonation of a universal Esperanto. The voices of

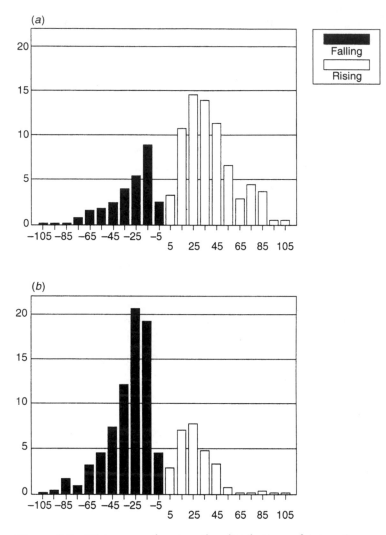

Figure 2.7 Histograms showing the distribution of intonation contours in disyllables: (a) French children, (b) Japanese children. The French children produce more rising contours, Japanese children produce more falling contours (from Hallé, Boysson-Bardies, and Vihman, 1991).

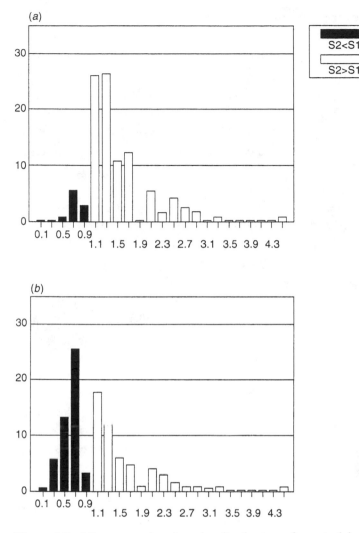

Figure 2.8   Histograms showing the distribution of terminal lengthenings in disyllables: *(a)* French children, *(b)* Japanese children. The French children conform to the tendency of French adults to lengthen the terminal syllable, whereas Japanese children, like Japanese adults, shorten it (from Hallé, Boysson–Bardies, and Vihman, 1991).

children all over the world do, of course, have much in common; but listening to their babbling and first words, we see that young language learners have already captured the characteristic color and tone of their native languages.

Babbling in Sign Language

The importance of babbling in the attainment of language is seen in the universality of this stage, which transcends the physical ways in which language is realized. Until five or six months, the congenitally deaf baby vocalizes as a hearing baby does. A rupture appears only at the moment of babbling: deaf babies do not babble. They do not begin to vocalize syllables or series of syllables at the age when hearing babies begin to do so, at about seven months. To the contrary, after this age, the vocalizations of deaf babies tend to diminish. It is only after a year that one finds vocal babbling, composed principally of labial syllables ([ba]) that the baby can "see" how to pronounce. Deaf babies who grow up in an environment with a sign language are immersed from birth, like hearing babies, in a linguistic world. The form of language that the child receives and the sensory modalities involved are radically different: linguistic information is transmitted through manual gestures, and they are received visually. The motor control of oral and manual gestures puts distinct circuits into play. Although the task that awaits the child differs in its physical realization, the attainment of language occurs according to stages of development very similar to those that one finds in hearing children who learn to speak. Thus, one observes that deaf babies babble manually toward eight months. Laura Ann Petitto and P. F. Marentette (1991), who have studied these forms of babbling, think that the gestures are comparable to the syllables of the babbling of the hearing child. Like the latter, the deaf baby produces gratuitous gestures that evoke sublexical elements of the structure of the signs serving to represent words. These gestures are distinguished both from the gestures usual in other manual activities and from gestures of communication that can be found in the hearing child, such as finger pointing. They consist in rhythmic movements of opening and closing the hand and in particular manual configurations. These gestures, made within a circumscribed space and under particular circumstances, are clearly related to the gestures used in sign language. Systematic comparisons with the body language of hearing children clearly confirm its specificity.

Thus, very early, both deaf and hearing infants are subject to the influence of the language spoken within their family circle. Within the limits imposed by their lack of articulatory skill, they select a phonetic and accentual repertoire appropriate to their language. As Antoine Grégoire (1937, p. 254) remarked in his study of his two sons, "at a moment that is difficult to fix precisely, but fairly close to birth, the two children gave the impression of practicing, in its general features, the pronunciation of French." Since then, experimental studies have confirmed the reality of these impressions and shown that at least in the second half of the first year—if not before—the intonation and phonetics of the productions of children tend in the direction of those found in their language environment. The notion that prelinguistic productions are completely independent of first words is today no longer sustainable.

There exists no smooth, continuous transition between the phonetics and intonation of the productions of babbling, on the one hand, and those of the first forms recognized as words, on the other. The occurrence of words, or of expressions possessing a meaning, nonetheless marks an essential stage in the child's development. From now on phonetic and intonational selections will no longer be randomly drawn from his repertoire but rather directed toward an end. There then begins a process of adaptation in the course of which the researcher's interest shifts to new questions: How does the acquisition of the lexicon come about? How, using this lexicon, is the phonological system of the language acquired? How do words come to have meaning? What relationship exists between cognition and the learning of words? Help in answering these questions comes from children in their second year.

The Communicative Universe of the Baby

3

Speech, being the first social institution, owes its form to natural causes alone.
—Jean-Jacques Rousseau

Communication and Expression

Since Darwin (1872), it has been known that certain human behaviors may be understood in terms of phylogenetic evolution. This is particularly true for the faculty of communication. In animal species, this faculty exists in various forms, with quite varied means of transmission (smells, songs, attitudes, gestures, expressions, colors, vocalizations). In most species, the very early—if not instantaneous—reaction of the young to signals of the species allows them to survive. It grounds their social reactions (that is, their reactions of attachment and avoidance) and later organizes their sexual life and the defense of their territory.

While still in the egg, the chick reacts to the clucking of the mother hen: this sound encourages it to break through its shell and later serves as the rallying signal that enables it and the other members of the brood to follow the mother.

In the human newborn, genetically programmed responses exist for receiving the communication signals of the species. The newborn's faculty of communication rests on modes of transmission and reception of information whose extreme precocity, if not innateness, can be demonstrated. In fact, most—if not all—of the behaviors associated with so-called innate communication are affected by the first interactions with the environment. Very early—sometimes even before birth—cognitive mechanisms are triggered and calibrated by factors and aspects of the environment specific to the species. The mechanisms that make communication possible also result from these first interactions.

Quite particular interactions establish themselves in the mother-child pair, requiring only a minimum of experience. Newborns know the voice of their mother from having heard it in the uterus. They prefer listening to their mother's voice than to the voice of another woman (Mehler, Bertoncini, Barrière, Jassik-Gershenfeld, 1978). They react to their mother's smell, likewise detected before birth, by turning in the direction of clothes having this smell (MacFarlane, 1975; see also Schaal et al., 1980). They also are sensitive from birth to human faces and turn toward them (Johnson and Morton, 1991). Very early on they recognize their mother's face and certain of its expressions (De Schonen, De Diaz, and Mathivet, 1986; see also Trevarthen, 1977). They interact with their mother's behavior from birth as well, influencing it by their particular way of feeding at her breast via micromovements to which she unconsciously responds (Zack, 1987). Newborns receive information, then, but they also deliver it, thus permitting a reciprocal adaptation between the behaviors of mother and infant.

Individuals must recognize and accept their fellow species members. The human species has developed mechanisms and strategies appropriate for dealing with this problem. Recognition of the human face and responses to vocal promptings, as well as the expression of emotions through gestures, are among the genetic programs that allow the infant to take its place within a system of relations.

The signals used in communication rest on an innate, universal repertoire of facial expressions and gestures. A system for recognizing expressions, as innate and universal as the system for producing sounds, encodes their meaning. The experimental study of the facial expression of emotions shows that emotional gestures are stereotyped. The fundamental gestures and expressions (pleasure, fear, distress, calm) are similar in all human beings, regardless of race or social and educational environment (Eibl-Eibesfeldt, 1970). They are found in blind as well as sighted babies and therefore owe nothing to imitation. They ground social relations by permitting social partners to interpret each other's emotions. Not only do these expressive gestures occur at an early stage, but they are precise. When infants only a few weeks old are given either a spoonful of sweet liquid or a spoonful of bitter liquid, they react with gestures that are already quite typical: they part their lips and perform little rhythmic lickings in the case of the sweet liquid, and they close their mouths, pull down the corners, and blink their eyes in the case of the bitter liquid.

Venturing into the vast field of means and modes of communication available to the human child is beyond the scope of this book. What interests us here is the development of a particular and special mode of communication—speech. This grows in large part out of its own roots. But the reciprocal behaviors and the interpretations of the emotions and behaviors of others whose evolution structures the child's system of communication during the course of the first year constitute the natural environment in which language anchors itself. Functional equivalences between nonlinguistic forms of communication and certain of the first linguistic expressions will provide evidence of the bond that exists between these modes of communication. We therefore present certain nonlinguistic relationships and modes of expression whose impact is particularly important in establishing the child as interlocutor.

Looking

Newborns often stare at the mouth of an adult, particularly when the adult is talking, but it is above all the eyes that retain their attention. Looking is an essential component of nonverbal communication. In everyday life, it is often by means of the gaze, or look, of others that we interpret their emotional states—vivacity, languor, anxiety, gaiety, sadness. All these emotions can be read in the eyes. "One speaks much better to the eyes than to the ears," as Rousseau said (1817, p. 503). The search for eye contact activates and maintains a strong bond of communication that not only arouses affective relations but organizes the temporality of the contacts.

Faced with a "dreamy" infant, what does a mother do to communicate with her? She tries to establish contact by her eyes. Establishing eye contact permits a first modification of the baby's behavior. The mother knows this. By calling her, talking to her, and touching her, she arouses the child's attention. The bond between the two is fragile and intermittent at first, but when it is established, the mother is able to capture and retain the baby's attention. This behavior of seeking to make contact, using the eyes, is itself very fundamentally a part of human nature. One finds an analogous process in the baby who is born blind: she turns her face toward the voice of her mother and keeps it fixed there.

Mothers have a profound reaction when the child begins, around the fourth week, to systematically seek eye contact with them. Between two and three months, this contact—sustained by gestures and expressions—allows emotional states to be linked to temporally organized relationships. Thus, together with affective bonds, exchanges of looks (mutual gaze) prepare the way for other kinds of relationships—namely, those that rest on reciprocal behaviors.

Reciprocal Behaviors

Imitation is one of the interactions in which infants participate from the first days of life. Many experimental studies, including one by Andrew Meltzoff and Keith Moore (1977) have shown that they stick out their tongues, open their mouths, and close their eyes when an adult makes these gestures in front of them, slowly and in a repetitive fashion. These gestures are chosen because they belong to the roster of the newborn's spontaneous productions.

Do these early imitations have the same status as those found later, toward eight to nine months? This question has been the object of long and contradictory debates. For Henri Wallon (1942) they manifest a mimetic mechanism that leads to the sharing of emotions. For Meltzoff and Moore, they are founded on the capacity of children to mentally note equivalences between transformations of their own bodies and those that they see in another. These first imitations may also help the child to pick out and identify the members of the family circle who are recognized not only by their faces but also by their gestures and behaviors. These gestures and behaviors thus promote social identification.

The evolution of what psychologists call *intermodal processing* is particularly important for cognitive organization. At two months, children detect equivalences between touch and sight (Streri, 1987). They can visually recognize an object that they held in their hand, without seeing it, a moment before. At five months, the baby notices the correspondence between words and the movements of the mouth. This can be proved by a simple experiment: the child is placed in front of two television screens, between which there is an audio speaker. On one of the screens, a woman silently articulates a sound such as [mi]. On the other screen, the same woman articulates, again silently, the sound [ta]. The speaker transmits one of the two sounds. The child will systematically choose to look at the picture that corresponds to the sound transmitted (Kuhl and Meltzoff, 1984; see also MacKain, Studdert-Kennedy, Spieker, and Stern, 1983). This aptitude for relating vision and hearing is of extreme importance for the development of speech. In looking at the face and mouth of their mother while she speaks, children deepen their knowledge of the relation between the perception of sounds and their articulation. We have seen that the most visible sounds—labials—are among the earliest and most frequent in babbling. They are also the first ones to be uttered by hearing-impaired children.

Elaborate forms of imitation develop from the fifth month (Uzgiris, 1993). Frequently, it is the mother who elicits them by imitating a gesture or a vocalization. Through these reciprocal exchanges—in the course of which the infant adopts at first a passive, then an active, role—the child learns to recognize and share emotions and knowledge of the world. Games such as hide-and-go-seek, exchanges of looks, and greetings will take over a bit later from the first interactive behaviors and, in scarcely more elaborate forms, maintain themselves throughout the whole of adult social life.

Turn-Taking

Among the behaviors connected with early imitation, a special place must be assigned to the vocal exchanges of the third month. Toward three months (between ten and sixteen weeks, generally), and only for a short period, the strange and, until now, rather little-studied behavior called *turn-taking* appears. It is marked by a spectacular exchange of vocalizations, in the course of which mother and child respond to each other by taking turns vocalizing. The child's response to the vocal prompting of the adult takes the form of echoes. The infant begins to vocalize when the adult stops talking to him—a situation that occurs again several times, giving the impression of a conversation. This stereotyped behavior is fleeting; it lasts for only two to three weeks and corresponds to a very limited period of maturational development. Turn-taking is also observed in the deaf child, a sign that it is triggered by the whole set of physical components that signals a vocal production—the vocal sound, the sight of the movements of the mouth, breathing, and exchanges of looks. Moreover, the maintenance of attention that underlies the rhythms of turn-taking in infants is essentially visual: intermittent eye contact regulates the mutual expectation of the ending of a vocalization.

As a programmed part of development, the function of turn-taking is still poorly understood, but it is believed to determine certain functions programmed for communication. Its adaptive value appears to be particularly rich. It brings into play intermodal stimulations for the recognition and production of speech-related behaviors. The attention brought to bear on the visual factors involved in turn-taking no doubt prefigures the aptitude of five-month-old babies for putting sounds into correspondence with the movements of the mouth. It is one of the sources of intermodal processing of acoustic and visual information. Cognitive organization is therefore structured through turn-taking, but this behavior also allows the child to construct a more personal system of exchange within the context of communication. Finally, turn-taking maximizes the child's opportunity to hear and respond to her mother and the mother's opportunity to hear and respond to her child. It makes them partners in speech.

Expression of Emotion

Newborns express their physiological states and their emotions through crying (signaling hunger, distress, or simply uneasiness), making facial expressions, arm waving, foot stamping, staring, and, very soon, smiling. Smiling occurs quite early, in fact. The baby already smiles at birth, even when delivered prematurely. According to a medieval legend, the starry sky, passing overhead, produces an enchanted music that is perceived by infants, who imagine that they are hearing angels sing in heaven and smile in their sleep. But this "smiling at the angels"—an expression of the bliss and feeling of well-being of the satisfied infant, half-asleep—is not children's only reason for smiling. They also display spontaneous smiles—a true smile in the waking state, a responsive, social smile. This too belongs to those basic behaviors inscribed in the genome of the human species: beyond the pleasure it expresses, it has a social function. It serves to calm others and to establish affective bonds with them. The baby's smile delights the mother and, if the legend of Cypsclus is to be believed, softens even the most hardened adults. According to this legend, Cypselus, the future king of Corinth, was to have been killed at birth, but he smiled at his assassins; moved and disarmed by this, they spared him.

Rather quickly the range of gestures and expressions grows. In the child of seven or eight months, various gestures express joy, fear, disgust, pleasure, tenderness—all expressions that the adult easily interprets (Izard et al., 1980).

But does the baby manage to interpret the fundamental expressions of adults? From the first days of life, newborns are sensitive to the expressivity of faces. Their uneasiness in the presence of a fixed and unexpressive face can actually lead to tears, signaling distress at the absence of signs of movement, of life. At the age of ten weeks, infants react in an appropriate fashion to the expressions of their mothers: smiles and vocal encouragements provoke positive reactions; sad faces trouble them (Termine and Izard, 1988). At four months, if one familiarizes infants with portraits of smiling women, they react to a change of expression on the portraits that are next presented to them. In a 1927 study of babies in a home for abandoned children, Charlotte Bühler noticed that, at five months, children responded to emotions when they were expressed both by the face and the voice; at six months, the voice alone sufficed; and at seven months, a slight facial expression was enough to inform children of a happy or angry attitude on the part of the adult. But Bühler added that at eight or nine months children sometimes misinterpret an angry facial expression as a joke or a bit of kidding—perhaps because they are unable to imagine any ground for blame on their side. The capacity for interpretation that comes through in this behavior suggests a considerable degree of cognitive evolution. The child's responses are no longer systematically—or, one might add, physically—tied to the gestures and expressions of the adult, which are now perceived as being able to be treated in a different way. Another type of communication is born with the child's first propensities to understand small jokes and, soon, to make them.

Does the attribution of meaning to the various emotions betrayed by the expressions of a face allow the child to share such emotions? In *The Expression of Emotions in Man and Animals* (1872), Darwin remarked that his son at six months assumed a melancholy expression, with the corners of the mouth turned down, when he saw his nurse pretend to cry. But such copying did not imply that the child shared the same emotion; he only imitated its effects, without the same sensation being aroused in him. The true sharing of emotions seems to occur later: it accompanies this capacity for interpretation that we have seen emerge at the end of the first year.

The baby's expressions exercise a regulating effect on the behavior of the adult, and the expressions of the adult exercise a regulating effect in turn on the behavior of the baby. Thus, at one year, children interpret and take into account the adult's reactions to guide their exploration of the world. When they are about to touch a new object or venture into an unknown space or react to the presence of an unknown person, babies turn back toward their mother's faces in the expectation of being able to read there some sign of approval or disapproval of what they propose to do. They treat their mother's expressions as a commentary that is directed at them and that they need to take into account. Positive expressions encourage babies to act or to smile at the unknown, whereas negative expressions cause them to withdraw and curl up next to their parents.

Sharing Information About the Outside World

Communicating is also a matter of transmitting information about the outside world. Infants for the most part communicate their inner sensations. Later, when they begin to take an interest in the objects and events of the world, their looks and gestures are interpreted by adults as a function of the environment. Mothers have a tendency to give a meaning to these gestures, to comment on them, and thus to share a semantic context with their children.

This sharing of information about the external world may be analyzed experimentally by observing the evolution of the mutual regard of mother and child (Butterworth and Grover, 1988). Toward six months, children are able to follow the direction of their mother's gaze, on the condition, however, that the object she is looking at is in plain view. At twelve months, they interpret the adult's look more precisely: in the presence of two identical targets, they can isolate the one that the adult is staring at. But they are still incapable, on the evidence of the gaze alone, of determining the location of an object placed behind them or outside their visual field. They will be able to do this only at eighteen months.

At eighteen months, however, vocal communication has taken over and permitted many other exchanges of information about the world of objects. Nonetheless, the interpretation of vocal modulations, facial expressions, and the direction of the eyes provide—and will continue to provide—the child, and the adult as well, with indispensable additional information and support.

Joint attention also underlies the gesture of pointing, whose importance has been much—sometimes too much—stressed. This gesture rests on the ability to look in the direction indicated by another person's finger and, secondarily, on the attribution to the other person of a corresponding ability to look toward what one indicates oneself in making this gesture (Scaife and Bruner, 1975; see also Butterworth and Cochran, 1980).

At twelve months, almost all children are capable of looking in the direction indicated by an adult's gesture. However, it is only between eleven and fifteen months that most children begin to point toward a distant object. At first, they point solely at nearby objects that can be seen by a third party. This gesture, intended to signal a demand or to call attention to interesting objects, will later be used to ask the name of an object. The gesture of pointing is fundamentally a gesture of communication, but there is no relation between the development of language and the early habit of children to point at objects. Many children who point to find out the name of an object store up their knowledge and only later reveal the vocabulary thus accumulated.

Babies have at their disposal a natural "language" that is common to all cultures and consists in the interplay of facial appearances, expressions, gestures, tones of voice, and looks. This interplay, which manifests the "passions of the soul," often accompanies the oral expression of adults. It helps children when they come to interpret words. Family members and friends, by understanding and responding to babies' signals in a practical or affective way, establish a stream of communication with them that quickly becomes enriched during the following months. Without this coordinated exchange of affective and cognitive messages, the development and flowering of the baby's personality are liable to be compromised. Many examples exist of the harm caused by a lack of affectionate care and by the absence of a family circle ready to listen to, and understand, the baby's bodily messages. Deprived of a minimum of love and interaction with adults, infants suffer and become sickly (Cyrulnik, 1993). At bottom, however, the development of speech proceeds by listening. To be fully realized, the child's capacities have an essential need for a model of the native language. In English as in French, after all, the language of the society in which the child grows up is called the *mother tongue*. The mother occupies a special place—though she is not the only person involved—in the emergence of language by furnishing this model in a format to which the child is quite particularly sensitive. How does she do this? And why?

Motherese

Who has not seen a mother, father, or grandparent peer into the cradle, with a slightly mocking, yet tender look, and tell the baby strange "stories" that mix together affectionate words, onomatopoeia, vocalizations, and gestures of encouragement—all in a falsetto voice with broad glissandi? Who has not noticed the mother's concentration, her clear articulation and emphasis on the word or message that she wishes to convey when she explains a detail of everyday life to a young child?

Victor Hugo (1985/1881) knew not only the art of being a grandfather but also that of recreating in words the flash of images and emotions. In a delightful poem, he showed the effect of an excess of maternal love on the mother's vocabulary:

She coos. . . . And then in her tenderest voice,
Looking lovingly at the child whom God made glow,
Searching for the sweetest name that she can give,
To her joy, to her flowering angel, to her chimera:
"Oh, horror! There I've gone and woken you."

The tender voice of a mother, the clear and modulated intonation of airport terminal announcers, the dynamic baritone of advertising pitchmen, the sugary speech of soap opera heroines, the doctrinal tone of professors: all these uses of vocal register, intonation, and tempo are so many indications that serve to locate and complete the semantic content of spoken words. Most hortatory, erotic, and didactic speech depends on modifying the way one speaks, whether the speaker does this consciously or unconsciously.

Imagine that you are in a bus and that you are asked to guess to whom the man or woman behind you is speaking. If the unknown person behind you is speaking to a small child, you will not mistake this. Indeed, no adult will be mistaken: almost all adults, no matter their sex or age, modify their way of speaking when talking to infants and very young children. Adults show a concern and a willingness to adapt to the capacities of the child by adjusting the register of their voices, adopting an affectionate tone, and articulating words clearly and more slowly.

The linguistic environment of young children is made up, at least in large part, by particular forms of language called *motherese* and *baby talk* in the literature in English. Though the term *baby talk* is used in French (*parler bébé*), there is no corresponding word for *motherese*. This term refers to the modulations of the prosody and voice of mothers (or other adults) speaking to babies, whereas *baby talk* indicates the simplification of vocabulary, syntax, and the form of the words of the language addressed to a slightly older child, without, however, neglecting the modes of intonation that are associated with it. Whether peering into the infant's cradle or taking care of the baby, adults, when they speak, first attempt to establish affective contact and to elicit vocalizations.

The poet Zanzotto (1986) has coined the word *petel* (from the Italian word for "breast") to refer to this maternal language. "*Petel* . . . is the cuddling language mothers use to address very small children, which tries to mimic the language these children use to express themselves." What are the characteristics of this maternal language? One notes, in particular, modifications of voice and prosody—a higher vocal register than usual; and a restricted range of intonation contours (but with very exaggerated modulations and variations of pitch), and long, soft melodic forms with sudden glissandi and large F0 excursions. The effect of prosodic rhythmicity in these productions is amplified by the frequency of repetition. The raised pitch of the voice, the exaggerated modulations of the intonation contours, and the frequency of syllabic repetition and prosodic pattern are perfectly adapted to the capacities of young infants for perception and attention—all the more so as the mother often accompanies these vocal modifications with exaggerated facial expressions (eye contact, raising of the eyebrows, big smiles) as well as with rhythmic movements of the body and adjustments in posture (holding the baby in her arms, bringing her face near the baby, and so on) that focus the baby's attention, heightening interest and helping establish a preference for this form of communication (Fernald and Simon, 1984; see also Fernald and Kuhl, 1987; and Papousek, Papousek, and Haekel, 1987).

The special interest shown by the child in speech having the melodic characteristics of motherese is confirmed by all experiments.

Infants at two to four weeks prefer the voice of their mothers to that of other women, but only if the mother speaks with a normal intonation. At seven weeks, babies prefer to listen to a woman speaking to a baby—that is, speech having the melodic and rhythmic characteristics of motherese—rather than to words extracted from conversations between adults in which these characteristics are absent or at least much attenuated (Fernald, 1985; Pegg, Werker, and McLeod, 1992). This preference, which is very strong, is found until children reach preschool age. It is independent of the language used by the adult. Janet Werker, J. Pegg, and P. McLeod (1994) have studied the reactions of five-month-old American and Cantonese babies when presented with two audio-video recordings—one of a Cantonese woman speaking to her baby of four months and another of this same woman talking with an adult friend. The English-speaking babies, like their Cantonese counterparts, listened longer to the recording of the Cantonese mother speaking to her baby. A second tally, taking into account the affective preferences of the babies, yielded the same results. Babies prefer to listen to speech directed at babies, whether it is in their own language or whether their own mother or a foreign woman speaks. Motherese has a quite particular appeal for them.

What is the point of motherese? These first vocal messages—which are intended, on the one hand, to capture the child's attention and, on the other, to encourage exchanges—convey affective values through melodic contours. The voice, more than any other stimulus, provokes smiles in infants, attracts their gaze, allows face-to-face contact to be maintained with them, and, finally, motivates exchanges of verbal communication. These early vocal exchanges with the mother orient the baby toward a mode of oral communication. Thus, the behavior of turn-taking emerges toward the end of the second month, when infants react to the vocal promptings of the mother by cooing when she stops talking.

Parents' use of a higher pitch of voice, nearer that of children, lets their child know that they are talking to her. Babies are so sensitive to this identification by vocal pitch that, at five months, as we have seen, they respond to their father with a lower voice than the one they use in the presence of their mother. The way in which parents modify melodic patterns as a function of the context of their exchange with their child is "so regular and so consistent that melodic contours are the first aspect of vocal messages that the baby can process and imitate before being able to produce the first syllables" (Papousek and Papousek, 1993). Thus, at four months, the baby responds with more positive affective signs to gratifying vocalizations than to neutral ones or vocalizations whose tone is more reproving.

Baby Talk

Parental attitudes, and the style and content of maternal language, become modified over the course of the infant's development, but the principal prosodic characteristics of motherese are found to be preserved until the third year.

In Western societies, from six to seven months, the nature and form of the comments made by parents clearly change. Mothers' subjects of conversation with their babies consist in commentaries on the sensations they are apt to feel and on their inner states. From six months, mothers talk more of the external world and show a greater interest in the child's activity. When their babies reach seven or eight months, parents realize that they are beginning to recognize words and then to understand them: the remarks that are directed to them must therefore prepare them for this (Cohen and Beckwith, 1976). These remarks become clearer and better articulated, utterances shorter and spoken more slowly, with longer pauses in between. Adults seek to make themselves understood. Prosodic characteristics remain important. The voice continues to be higher, and intonation, like the emphasis placed on ends of sentences, is quite pronounced. Prosodic organization thus tends to assign value to the phonetic and rhythmic structure of words and sentences. Sentences are simple, short, and repeated. The frequency of words containing reduplicated syllables is important. Already in the Middle Ages, Bartholomaeus Anglicus (Riché and Alexandre-Bidon, 1994) advised the nurse to "say her words as if she had a stutter"—thinking the repetition of syllables ought to be a help to the child in learning.[1] During the same period, in the thirteenth century, Aldobrandino da Siena (Landouzy and Pépin, 1911) gave advice to mothers so that their children could comfortably say their first words: "Rub the mouth with rock salt or with honey, wash the mouth with barley milk, above all if he is slow to speak. That he may be made to say words that do not have too many letters and that make the tongue move, such as *mama, papa, baboir*."[2] This advice is connected with the idea that the teeth are necessary for talking, but already exhibits subtle observation of the articulatory tendencies of babies. It accords with present-day research that finds labials and syllables not involving too many movements of the upper articulators appear with the greatest frequency in the first productions of babies and in the vocabulary of mothers, who spontaneously employ more words beginning with labials ([m], [b], [f], [v]) when they speak to children. In all the linguistic groups that we have studied, the maternal phonetic repertoire includes more labials than the repertoire of their language would predict. Parents stand a greater chance, in fact, of obtaining "good" results by providing models containing words that are easy to pronounce and whose pronunciation is readily visible. Such words are particularly represented in the lexicon used with children. Thus, in French, among the most frequent words in infantile vocabulary one encounters *maman, papa, poupée, bébé, bravo, pain, bain, poum, boum, balle, biberon, miam*, and so on; in English, one finds a series of words of the same sort, including *mommy, baby, ball, bunny, bottle*; in Swedish, *pappa, mamma, blomma, bil, bulle*, and so on. But in structuring the child's speech, each mother's particular way of speaking is less important than the forms of the language employed within the child's linguistic and cultural environment. An analysis of the influence of the phonetic structure of the words used by the mothers of one-year-old children belonging to four cultural groups shows that there is no direct relation between the phonetic repertoire of the mother and that of the child in each of the mother-child dyads (Vihman, Kay, Boysson-Bardies, Durand, and Sundberg, 1994). The child's repertoire reflects that of the language spoken in the family circle more than any particular aspect of the mother's phonetic repertoire.

Cultures and Modes of Speaking to Babies

In studying the universality of parental speech behavior, Charles Ferguson (1964) identified some twenty characteristics common to different linguistic groups throughout the world, including repetition of words and sentences, exaggeration of intonation contours, decelerated pronunciation, lengthening or reduplication of stress placed on an important consonant or vowel, freedom in shifting stress in homonyms, strong presence of labial or palatal consonants that "soften" pronunciation, deletion of clusters and consonants that are hard to produce (such as [r] and [l]), consonant or vowel "harmonization" through simplified structures of the consonant-vowel-consonant-vowel type (in French, for example, *dodo*, meaning "sleep"), and nasal harmony (the addition of an extra nasal consonant in a word containing only one: in Japanese, for example, "meme" for *dame*, meaning "bad"). The generality of these processes has encouraged the view that they reflect a universal behavior on the part of adults and, more particularly, of parents when they address their little ones. But is this true?

The use of a distinct register in talking to children seems well attested—if not actually verified—in a good many diverse cultures, including ones in which Arabic (Ferguson, 1964), Spanish (Blount and Padgug, 1976), and Marathi (Kelkar, 1964) are spoken. The prosody of maternal speech in American English (Garnica, 1977; see also Stern, Spieker, Barnett, and MacKain, 1983), Japanese (Fernald and Morikawa, 1993), and Mandarin Chinese (Grieser and Kuhl, 1988), has been systematically studied with the help of acoustic analyses and also through cross-linguistic studies involving American English, British English, French, Italian, and Japanese (Fernald et al., 1989). In all these studies, one finds significant differences between speech directed at children and speech intended for adults. All mothers and fathers in these cultures raise the pitch of their voices and produce short utterances that include long pauses. But one finds fairly clear differences between cultural groups in the forms common characteristics assume: American parents modify their intonation more systematically and to a greater degree than do parents in other countries. The same is true of the exaggeration of facial expressions that accompanies this behavior. French fathers, by contrast, like Japanese mothers and fathers, modulate their intonation relatively little when they address their children.

One may thus ask whether this adaptation of speech behavior on the part of adults toward their children is really a universal, biologically rooted phenomenon of adult–child communication in the human species.

Some cultural studies call into question the universality of the characteristics noted by Ferguson. Elevation of vocal pitch is not usual is certain non-Western languages, particularly in tone languages, such as Mandarin Chinese (Grieser and Kuhl, 1988) and Thai (Tuaycharoen, 1979), in which falling contours are prevalent. There is no special prosodic register for babies and young children among American Indians speaking Quiche Mayan (Ratner and Pye, 1984). Raised vocal pitch in this language is a general sign of deference that is not used with children. By contrast, mothers often lower their voice to a whisper when they address babies. In other cultures the elevation of the voice depends on the sex of the child to whom one is speaking. In the American Indian populations of Guatemala, adults use a monotone with children. On the other hand, they are prepared to repeat a word or phrase as many times as is necessary to facilitate comprehension. In these cultures, the practice of repetition may replace prosodic modifications.

Among the Kwara'ae of the Solomon islands, mothers speak to infants indirectly: a frequent behavior consists in speaking about children or on behalf of children, turning them toward the person who is being addressed. Its purpose, in this and other such cultures, is to integrate children into the social community as soon as possible and in the best possible way, rather than to make them precocious speakers (Watson-Gegeo and Gegeo, 1986). Among the Kaluli of New Guinea, adults speak seldom to infants and rarely look at them directly. It is not supposed that babies understand language. At six to eight months, they receive certain instructions. They are prevented from touching an object by being made to feel ashamed: "Does this belong to you?" they are asked, or "Who do you think you are?" Of course, babies in this society are brought up as part of a community and hear a good deal of language spoken around them, but, until they are able to speak, speech is rarely transmitted to them other than in the form of orders. When they do begin to speak, in particular when they say certain words that mark their entry into the community of speakers, such as *no* (mother) and *bo* (bosom), Kaluli adults apply a very directive teaching technique. After each sentence they add *elema*, which means "Say like that." Errors of pronunciation are corrected, as well as substantive mistakes. Mothers do not try to show children objects and teach them their names; they make them repeat words and sentences. It would be interesting to know more precisely how language is acquired by Kaluli children. Unfortunately, the authors of the principal studies on the subject have not inquired into this aspect particularly, indicating only that by their second year these children repeat very well (Schieffelin, 1986).

In societies more similar to ours, when children reach one year of age, the particular features of motherese, while preserving the functions that they have had until this point, are reshaped to facilitate the teaching of new words to children and assist their comprehension of the meaning of the sentences they hear. Parents continue to exaggerate the prosody of their sentences while seeking to enlarge the child's linguistic horizon. In one study, Richard Aslin (1993) showed that to teach their children new words, mothers presented these words in sentences and not as isolated words. The children must therefore extract the word to be learned. In this they are aided by two maternal strategies. The first strategy is prosodic: in more than two-thirds of cases, American mothers placed greater emphasis on the words that they desired to teach. The second strategy is syntactic: the mothers place the new words at the end of the sentence—where they are more easily extracted—more than 89 percent of the time. One finds this strategy even in the behavior of Turkish mothers, although it is not grammatical in the Turkish language to place a noun at the end of a sentence, the canonical order requiring the verb to appear in this position.

One expects children, then, to respond to the messages that they receive from adults. They therefore have to analyze the content and form of messages. Mothers employ several tricks to make their children understand. One of them consists in the repetition of sentences. Psycholinguists who have analyzed maternal discourse have found that a third of the sentences in their productions consist in repetitions, often simplified, of the previous utterance. Other mothers reformulate their utterance, or that of the child, expressing it in a different way. Japanese mothers rather systematically reformulate children's utterances to make them culturally acceptable. Other mothers choose to clarify their remarks by commenting on them. This latter technique is much more profitable for the child.

The sentences of adults are, on the whole, short and grammatically correct, although often unfinished. In fact, relatively few adult phrases in the language addressed to children are ungrammatical (Newport, 1976; Valian, forthcoming). They concern objects or events present in the field of vision, which helps children in their efforts at understanding what is said to them.

In Western cultures, children are generally considered to be autonomous in their choice of activities. They are therefore asked many questions to which they have the choice of responding yes or no. Interrogative sentences are all the more numerous in the speech of parents to the extent that they amount to a polite version of what in other cultures appears in the form of an order—for example, *Can you do that for me?* Interrogative sentences also frequently convey the meaning of a deictic sentence: *You see that balloon?*

May we conclude from this that the form of sentence varies depending on whether adults address a child or another adult? Elissa Newport (1976) has compared the percentage of sentence structures in the two situations. She found fewer declarative sentences (30 percent) used with regard to children than with adults (87 percent), more imperative sentences (18 percent as against 2 percent), and many more interrogative sentences (44 percent as against 9 percent).

In societies like ours, imperative sentences are relatively infrequent—and this both when one speaks to little girls and to little boys. But it is not the case everywhere. In certain cultures, the forms of sentences vary depending on whether one is speaking to man or to a woman or to a little boy or to a little girl. Among the Luo, one finds that 3 percent of sentences are in the imperative in the case of a father speaking to his two-year-old son, and 43 percent when the father addresses a little girl of the same age (Blount, 1970). In Luo society, under most circumstances, the man gives orders to the woman. Adults addressing a little girl—especially men—will therefore employ a greater number of sentences in the imperative than when addressing a little boy. On the other hand, in this culture as in many others, children are considered to be inferior interlocutors, lacking initiative in their speech behavior: one asks them questions or gives them instructions. The percentage of declarative sentences addressed to them is low (10 percent).

Cultural variations must not be allowed, however, to mask specific language behaviors employed by adults in addressing children to bring them into the language community. There is a special mode of adult–child verbal communication that is very generally, if not universally, found. Its characteristics may vary. Certain social groups have ritualized the learning of speech with the aim mainly of integrating the child into a highly organized and structured social group. Before everything else, children must know their place in the group and know how to play the role assigned to them. In other cultures, mothers favor the child's affective relations and individual performances. In all cultures, however, the transmission of language accompanies the integration of children into a social community. And so they are subject to the rules and expectations of this community.

Despite cultural variations affecting the modes of presentation of the language, all babies in the world learn to speak at roughly the same age. Furthermore, most studies show that there is little correlation between the child-directed speech of the mother and the linguistic development of the child. Parents do not teach language to their children; they furnish them with models—a model of the language and a cultural model. In the linguistic model, children attempt to find signs that will permit them to grasp the structure and meaning of utterances; in the model of their culture, they find the social forms of their status as interlocutors. Later, no doubt, the quality and richness of the linguistic environment will more directly influence the language development of children. But so far as the foundations of language are concerned, the genetic mechanism is powerful enough to reduce normal disparities in reception found across cultures. In fact, it will sometimes permit certain gaps to be filled. Thus, children raised in an environment in which an impoverished language (called a *pidgin* or *creole*) is spoken tend to use forms that are more grammatical than those of their parents. Is this genetic mechanism therefore so powerful that it knows no constraints? The answer is no.

Critical Periods

The term *critical period* is used to refer to a window of time during which the influence of experience on a given behavior is significant. Experience can have several functions: it may allow certain capacities to be maintained that, in its absence, would disappear; in other cases, only the rhythm of development is affected by a lack of experience; finally, in a third class of cases, experience can be indispensable to the appearance of a behavior. In animal species, many examples illustrate the indispensable role of the environment in triggering the normal development of mechanisms specific to the species. This is the case with song in a number of species of singing birds: the young birds develop the song of their species only if they have heard it sung by other species members during their first few weeks of life (Marler, 1984). Is there also a critical period for human beings in learning to speak?

We all know from personal experience that critical periods exist for certain aptitudes. Consider, for example, the learning of a second language. Whereas children learn one or more foreign languages without any trouble, adults often have great difficulty—all the more as they grow older and the longer they remain monolingual. The ability to learn a foreign language (and, especially, to speak it without an accent) declines sharply with age. It is thought that a foreign language learned after adolescence will always be spoken with an accent.

In describing the perceptual capacities of babies, we saw that toward eleven months they begin to lose their talent for discriminating between phonetic contrasts that are not pertinent to their mother tongue. Japanese children two years of age, like Japanese adults, are incapable of distinguishing /r/ from /l/. They will have extreme difficulty distinguishing these sounds when they begin to learn a foreign language, and this difficulty will become almost insurmountable when it comes to reproducing them.

The evidence suggests, then, that there are critical periods for certain linguistic aptitudes. These critical periods are not a property of growth as such, but they do reveal the loss of plasticity that occurs when neuronal connections become specialized.

Can comparable evidence be developed with regard to first language acquisition? This is a difficult question to answer. Experimentation is impossible in such a case, and one must rely on more or less pertinent observations to fix a possible period beyond which language cannot be attained. No one today is prepared to revive the attempts attributed to the pharaoh Psantik I of Egypt and, much later, Frederick of Prussia. Psantik caused babies to be raised in an isolated place and directed that no one should speak to them. He reasoned that the language such children learned to speak on their own would be the "original" language of mankind—which shows how anciently rooted the modern notion of a gift, or an instinct, for speech actually is. The pharaoh's experimental subjects turned out to speak Phrygian: the shepherd in whose care they were placed is said to have been Phrygian; taking pity on the infants, he disobeyed the pharaoh's orders. The babies isolated from all linguistic contact on the orders of Frederick III, however, wasted away and died.

Generally, the question of whether there exists a critical period after which language can no longer be learned has been answered affirmatively. Lenneberg (1967) thought that the critical period extended until puberty. Currently, it is believed to end at about the age of seven. Children past this age, who have heard no human language during childhood until then, should be incapable of acquiring language. What evidence was found to justify pushing back the threshold age to seven?

Cases of feral children (or wolf children) are relatively rare, thankfully, although more than a dozen have been reported since the seventeenth century. These children were discovered in isolated places and were supposed to have grown up without human contact. They produced no human vocalization, walked on four legs, and ate like animals. The stories of such children, though dramatic, are not easy to investigate scientifically. Jean Itard (1981/1801) recounted the case of Victor, the wolf child discovered in the eighteenth century at the age of ten to twelve years in the Aveyron in France. Despite the prolonged and intelligent efforts of his teacher, Victor never managed to acquire language. But in this case, as in the few others of which we are aware, it is not known whether his abandonment may have been due to the prior presence of handicaps, such as profound debility or autism. In any case, the conditions of life—or, rather, survival—faced by these children were so abnormal that it is hard to draw valid conclusions about their inability to learn to speak.

The case of children who have been locked away and raised in circumstances of extreme deprivation is a bit different. They have heard speech, although for the most part only minimally (Skuse, 1993). All of them, except Genie, were restored to a normal environment before the age of seven, and almost all, with the exception of those in whom serious sensory or cognitive problems were found, recovered normal (or nearly normal) language. The case of Genie is special (Curtiss, 1977). Genie was discovered when she was thirteen years old. She had been deprived of normal exposure to language from the age of about eighteen months. Despite considerable efforts on the part of the therapists who subsequently took charge of her rehabilitation, she never learned to speak normally. She acquired a certain vocabulary but remained incapable of putting together syntactically correct sentences. The case of Genie may indeed confirm that there exists a temporal limit for the acquisition of language. But the horribly painful conditions of life that she knew for thirteen years produced major psychological and cognitive disorders, and it is impossible to say whether she was really normal before her confinement. Her case, like that of Victor of Aveyron, nonetheless may suggest there is a critical period beyond which language capacities are diminished, or actually disappear, in the absence of a linguistic model.

The congenitally deaf, if exposed from birth to sign language—just as blind children are exposed, altogether naturally, to spoken language—acquire language at the same (or nearly the same) rate as children without sensory handicaps. While it is known that profound deafness has severe consequences for the acquisition of spoken language, it is less often realized that more modest levels of hearing loss or repeated middle-ear infections during the first two years sometimes entail a lasting deficit in language reception. They affect the ability to process speech and thus show that impoverished or skewed hearing in the first two years, even if only intermittently defective, distorts phonological development.

To speak, children need to grow up in a linguistic environment. The linguistic input need not be very rich, and there is no need that it be based on direct instruction; but the received model must be sufficient for the child to be able to categorize speech sounds and to specify the principal parameters of his language. It is also necessary that this linguistic environment be provided by physically present human beings. We think we know—or at least we like to believe—that hearing speech over the radio or television is not enough to guarantee access to language. The linguistic model must be presented within a framework of interactive communication involving the child and those around him.

We have deliberately avoided insisting here on the importance of affectivity. This is not to downplay its fundamental role. We know how essential the tender and loving care of adults is for the survival and mental integrity of the young child: the babies raised in isolation by Frederick of Prussia died. We know also how important normal social integration is. Even if lasting problems in acquiring language are not an inevitable consequence of deprivation, they arise from deficient psychological and social conditions. We have also avoided examining the psychological suffering that leads to temporary episodes of mutism. Instead, we wish to emphasize the robustness of the genetic mechanism for the acquisition of language. An intact mechanism generally allows a child to acquire language in spite of deficits (sometimes quite serious) in sensory, affective, or cognitive abilities. But acquisition is possible only on the (necessary and sufficient) condition that the child has the company of one or more human beings who communicate using one of the languages spoken by human beings. This fact is as remarkable as it is reassuring.

Discovering the Meaning of Words: Nine to Seventeen Months

4

What is important, what is acquired during development, is not an abstract representation of the product but the possibility of recreating procedures.
—Gerald Edelman

Dividing Up and Assembling

Children face several tasks in putting together their lexicon. In the first place, they have to extract units of meaning from the talk that they hear. This is not a simple matter. Speech occurs as a relatively continuous sound wave, and the boundaries between words provide children with few distinct acoustic cues.

The study of infant processes of speech segmentation has long been the Loch Ness monster of developmental psycholinguistics. Of all the enigmas that have arisen in trying to understand how the child acquires the words of a language, the segmentation of speech during the first year has remained the most disconcerting; even today, the way in which the child manages to distinguish and extract words from a continuous sound wave retains a certain mystery. Natural speech rushes forth like a flood: there are no systematic pauses between words. Unlike the blank spaces of a written text that allow words to be distinguished, the silences in a spoken sentence do not constitute an adequate basis for extracting units of meaning.

Adults, of course, in attempting to make themselves intelligible to children, do speak more slowly, but they do not stop between each word. The question arises, then, how children succeed in extracting from the speech signal—this continuous flood of sound—sentences, phrases, and words. How, that is, do they extract the units that make up meaning?

As adult speakers who are able to divide speech into meaningful units on the basis of our prior knowledge of the terms that make it up, we intuitively tend to suppose that the process of segmentation depends on the recognition of words. As we shall see, such a view is only partially correct. It does not hold for young children: babies do not know the words that make up the remarks addressed to them or to others around them. Children are confronted with a thorny problem: unlike adults, who dispose of an established lexicon in which each word is coded with its semantic and grammatical characteristics, they do not have the help of such a lexicon in trying to partition speech into words. Certain words, of course, are sometimes isolated and repeated by the mother and in this way can be more easily spotted by the baby. But we have seen that this type of maternal behavior is rare. And the possibility of localizing a word in a series is, in any case, not sufficient to permit other units of discourse to be isolated.

The key to the problem has been sought in the linguistic gifts of infants and particularly in their remarkable capacity for detecting variations in the physical characteristics of speech sounds. If physical—that is, acoustic—cues for segmentation in speech exist, then it is possible infants are sensitive to them. Do they in fact exist? What are they? Are babies really capable of detecting them?

In all languages, rhythm and intonation are part of the formal structure of speech. In some, melodic features convey differences of meaning and structure. Thus, in Mandarin Chinese, the form *ma* can have four different meanings, corresponding to the four tones used in this language. In the early days of structuralism, and especially after the appearance of Chomsky and Halle's book in 1968, prosodic variables were neglected by linguists; they were not considered pertinent to the problem of characterizing linguistic universals. Since then, this position has been reconsidered. The heterogeneous use of prosodic cues in different languages, it is now realized, is evidence that they play a role in the structuring of these languages. Psycholinguists also have come to recognize the importance of prosodic cues in speech processing. Recognition of their influence in organizing babies' perceptual capacities has made it possible to formulate the problem of how infants segment continuous speech in a new way.

Because adults dispose of a fully constituted lexicon in which each word is coded with its phonological, grammatical, and semantic specifications, they are sometimes supposed to have no need for explicit segmentation procedures other than those connected with the recognition of words. This is not the case. The time spent in processing messages would be uselessly prolonged if all the possibilities for segmenting an acoustic-phonetic form had to be explored in the course of listening. Attempts to match a given form with the words in the lexicon may also prove to be misleading. Long words, for example, contain embedded acoustic-phonetic forms corresponding to words in the lexicon. In the French word *courgette* (zucchini), one finds the homophones *cour* (courtyard), *cours* (course), and *court* (a present form of the verb *courir*, to run), as well as *jette* (a present form of the verb *jeter*, to throw)—none of which needs to be activated in the lexicon to extract the meaning of a sentence such as *In a zucchini there are seeds*. Extracting the word *cour* would lead one down a false trail (*In a courtyard there are seeds*), taking up processing time. The absence of a segmentation marker between *cour* and *jette*, along with the short-long metrics of French words, make it possible to avoid a mistaken segmentation in which the words *cour* and *jette* are activated.

Of course, if an error is made, context enables listeners who have been misled to eliminate erroneous choices fairly quickly, but the efficiency and rapidity of comprehension are affected. Similarly, rapid decisions between certain homophones of the *vert/vers* type in French are enforced by the meaning of sentences in which they occur. In fact, prosodic cues allow the correct word to be extracted even before the semantic context intervenes. Thus, phonologically similar sentences—for example, *Derrière ce pré vert, lequel nous appartient ...* (Behind this green meadow, which belongs to us ...) and *Derrière ce pré vers lequel nous nous dirigeons ...* (Behind this meadow we are heading toward ...)—lose their ambiguity before the end of either one is reached, thanks to prosodic segmentation cues that mark off the relevant phonological groups in each case. In the first sentence, the boundary is located after *vert* and, in the second, after *ce pré*. In these utterances, the rest of the sentence serves to confirm the proper interpretation.

But in other sentences, ambiguity can be dispelled only by paying attention to intonational cues. Thus, to distinguish two sentences such as *J'ai admiré le chapeau élégant que ce dandy de Paul a acheté ce matin* (I admired the elegant hat that Paul, that dandy, bought this morning) and *J'ai admiré le chapeau et les gants que ce dandy de Paul a acheté ce matin* (I admired the hat and gloves that Paul, that dandy, bought this morning), the presence of intonational segmentation cues is indispensable. Rapid processing of speech in real time thus involves perceptual processing of prosodic cues.

The first of these cues is pause, which, while not usual, may occur between important boundaries, as in the case of clauses and sentences, and may be created by hesitations or resumptions of speech. Stronger boundaries, such as those between clauses and sentences, are better marked in prosody than the weaker boundaries that divide phrases and content words.

More specific and more subtle than pauses, and varying across languages, are rhythmic patterns of duration, modulations of the pitch of the voice, and differences in syllabic intensity. Variations in syllabic duration at the boundaries between units of meaning consist in the lengthening or shortening of the duration of vowels and consonants. Variations in intonation—the rise or fall of vocal pitch—also signal boundaries between words, phrases, and sentences. Finally, variations in intensity are important, particularly in pitch languages.

Prosodic rules are peculiar to each language. In French, boundaries are marked principally by a lengthening of syllables as well as by variations in fundamental frequency and intensity. More than other speakers, the French tend to clearly raise their intonation at the end of the noun phrase (Hirst and Di Cristo, 1984) (see figure 4.1). In English, stress—which generally falls on the initial syllable of a word—is an important segmentation cue. Experiments by Ann Cutler and Dennis Norris (1988) have illuminated the strategies of English adults, who segment the speech stream at the beginning of

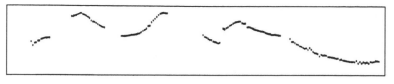

[Le chameau beige] s'en va dans le désert

Figure 4.1   Intonation contour of a French sentence (*The beige camel goes off into the desert*). A rise in intonation is observable at the end of the noun phrase (with the word *beige*).

stressed syllables. These speakers implicitly make the assumption, justified by the frequency of words beginning by a strong syllable in English, that such a syllable has a greater chance of indicating the beginning of a word than an unstressed syllable does. Prosodic cues are not the only ones that assist the segmentation of speech, however.

Word structure obeys different rules of phonemic construction in different languages. Thus, endings that are admissible in one language cannot be met with in another. Certain sequences of phonemes are possible only at the boundary between two words, and therefore function as segmentation cues. In French, a word cannot end with the sound [ls], so that the series *elle sait voir* [elsevwa:R] is segmented by French speakers after [el] and not between [els] and [evwa:R]. In German, by contrast, an [ls] sound is possible at the end of a word, and so the series [derfelsistGro:s] may be segmented after [ls]: *Der fels ist gross.*

The boundaries between words in different languages are therefore regulated by principles that govern the succession of admissible sounds in the language. These principles make it possible to identify boundary probabilities between words. One might object that prosodic cues do not always fit well with the syntactic structure of utterances and that the relative independence of intonation and the fact that it conveys important affective and pragmatic information disqualify it as a wholly reliable factor. However, the advantages of these prosodic and phonetic strategies of segmentation for adults are obvious. Such strategies exploit more information and thus permit more rapid and reliable processing. But are they possible strategies for babies as they try to break the speech code?

The Infant in Action

For the baby, the task of segmenting the units of continuous speech must be perceptual. The organized properties of speech are recognizable because they are embedded in the physical properties of the signal: prosodic cues take the form of temporal markers and variations in frequency. As we have seen, infants are experts when it comes to detecting these prosodic cues. The question now becomes one of determining when and how, through the selection of these cues, detection of organized forms such as sentences, phrases, words, and syllables is carried out.

Developmental psycholinguists are veritable Sherlock Holmeses when it comes to searching for the cues that babies exploit in their attempts to segment speech. Indeed, they have to be because infants are themselves gifted detectives when it comes to discovering what may be useful to them in preparing their entry into the community of speakers. Destined to master speech, and equipped with all the tools needed to penetrate its mysteries, babies are tough nuts to crack. They force psycholinguists to be ever more imaginative. Psycholinguists, for their part, refuse to become discouraged and go on thinking up new questions to put to their infant subjects.

Anne Christophe, E. Dupoux, J. Bertoncini, and J. Mehler (1995) have studied the reaction of three-day-old French newborns to the temporal markers of word boundaries. These markers are principally the duration of the initial consonant and the duration of the terminal vowel. The experimental stimuli consisted in disyllables of the type [mati]. In one case, the disyllable [mati] was first extracted from a word such as _mathématicien_, pronounced naturally. Then the syllable was extracted from two words, again pronounced in a normal way, one after the other, such as _schema tigré_. In the latter instance, where the disyllable [mati] emerges from the sequence of two words, one finds cues between [ma] and [ti] that mark a word boundary—namely, a lengthening of the terminal vowel of the first syllable as well as a lengthening of the initial consonant of the second syllable. These cues ought to make it possible to distinguish the interword disyllable occurring at the junction of two words from the internal intraword disyllable contained within a single word. Newborns tested with reference to the nonnutritive sucking paradigm reacted by sucking harder when interword [mati] disyllables succeeded a series of [mati] intrawords. Christophe and her colleagues concluded that something perceptible by newborns occurs around word boundaries. She was, of course, wary of concluding that babies actually segment speech at word boundaries. But she did suppose that the existence of a necessary condition, if prelexical prosodic cues are to support the infant's capacity for detecting how speech is organized, had been established.

So far, few experiments involving infants have been specifically devoted to this problem. It is known, however, that infants are sensitive to variations in rhythm and pitch (Demany, McKenzie, and Vurpillot, 1977; see also Trehub, Bull, and Thorpe, 1984). But one must not forget that infants and older babies do not work with the same object. For infants, this object consists in sounds for which they possess fine mechanisms of discrimination. With age, babies become sensitized to the characteristics of a different object: they no longer process sounds but process speech—that is, sounds bearing meaning.

Putting Together the Pieces of the Puzzle

When, and how, does the aptitude for perceiving potential boundary cues in the continuous flood of speech come to organize units of meaning in the form of clauses, phrases, and words? This is what the recent studies of teams directed by Kathy Hirsh-Pasek (Hirsh-Pasek et al., 1987) and Peter Jusczyk (Jusczyk et al., 1992; see also Myers et al., 1996) sought to analyze. Thanks to these studies, it has been possible to show that different types of units of speech—clauses, phrases, and words—are progressively noticed as *organized forms:* the first segmentations bear on large, prosodically well-defined units, which then facilitate the identification of finer structures that, in turn, will permit the identification of words.

The researchers made use once more of the method, described earlier, of preferential listening. The child is placed between two speakers emitting different stimuli. Each speaker is connected to a light that comes on when the sound stimulus that it emits is triggered. So long as the child looks at the light bulb while it is illuminated, he hears the stimulus. If he turns his head away for more than two seconds, the light goes off, and, with it, so does the presentation of the sound. The child thus learns that listening time is connected with his gaze and that he can regulate it. One may therefore determine a preference for this or that stimulus, depending on whether the child listens to it for a longer or shorter time.

To determine which prosodic boundaries are pertinent for the child, artificial pauses a second in length are inserted into the sentences broadcast through the speakers. These pauses may or may not correspond to the natural prosodic division of sentences. The experimental measure is the time the child spends listening to the different versions: a longer listening time is treated as a measure of preference. If the child finds that a pause is more appropriate at one moment in a sentence than another, he will prefer to hear the sentence that contains a "correct" interruption (see figure 4.2).

First, pauses were inserted at the boundaries of clauses, or within clauses. Thus, five-month-old babies were presented with the choice of listening to series such as the following:

Cinderella lived in a great big house // but it was sort of dark // because she had this mean mean stepmother.

Cinderella lived in a great big house but it was // sort of dark because she had // this mean mean stepmother.

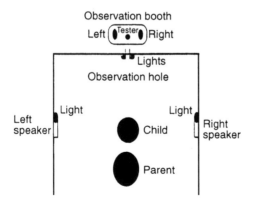

Figure 4.2 Experimental setup for testing the preference of children presented with two auditory stimuli.

At five months, children show a preference for stories with pauses inserted at the boundaries of clauses—the top example above —on the condition that the story be read with the characteristic intonation of motherese. This effect is maintained when the phonetic content is eliminated using a filter that leaves the prosody intact but erases consonants and vowels. The role of prosodic cues now appears more clearly. The capacity for dividing up clauses is initially very general, since one finds a preference for scansions at the boundaries of clauses when the infant is given sentences in foreign languages to hear. But this general sensitivity is restricted quite quickly. Very soon, at nine months, babies lose the capacity to react to the boundaries of clauses in foreign languages. At the same time there occurs a refinement in their ability to recognize the pertinent pauses of their native language.

The same methods have been used to test the sensitivity of children to the prosodic markers of segmentation for smaller units such as phrases. Babies six to nine months old were presented with sentences such as the following:

The little boy at the piano // is having a birthday party. All the friends // like to sing . . .

The little boy is having // a birthday party. All the friends like to // sing . . .

Infants of six months showed no preference for either one of these sentences. By contrast, at nine months children showed a preference for the first, in which the pauses coincide with the boundaries dividing subject from predicate.

Infants are therefore sensitive to the prosodic markers of segmentation—temporal variations (duration of segments, lengthening of terminal syllables, pauses) and variations in pitch. During the first months, children respond to very general properties found in most languages. Then the organization provided by prosodic traits becomes refined and, after six months, adjusted to the characteristics of the maternal language.

Prosody must therefore supply children with some of the clues for segmenting continuous speech into meaningful units. Of course, the correlations between syntactic units and prosodic forms are far from being perfect in the speech of adults. But the simplification of structures and the particular intonation that characterizes the verbal forms that mothers and other adults use in speaking to children facilitate their syntactic segmentation. In motherese, as we noted earlier, clauses are generally grouped under an intonation contour that is well formed—that is, plainly marked by the lengthening of the terminal segment and the modulation of vocal pitch at the end of the clause. This prosodic grouping—or envelope—is generally consistent with the organization of the principal syntactic units. The relationship between prosodic and syntactic cues thus comes out more clearly and reliably in motherese than in the language used by adults with each other.

The temporal and frequency-related values that mark the segmentation of utterances are not absolute properties of segmentation. These values have different weights in different languages. At nine months, babies' sensitivity is restricted to the rhythmic models and prosodic markers of the language spoken in their immediate environment and that language only. The rapidity with which children have been able to notice and select complex pieces of information, pertinent to their language, shows how prepared and channeled the development of language and speech is in humans.

We have come a long way since the 1960s, when certain "grammatists" concluded from what they took to be the primacy of syntax that prosody was useless in processing sentences. Prosody, they held, could guide children toward syntax only after the child first recognized syntactic structure, which was essential in picking out prosodic cues.

Certain details of our story so far may seem strange. We know that infants are capable of discriminating between brief auditory stimuli: 40 milliseconds is enough time for them, in fact, to distinguish consonants according to their place of articulation, as well as vowel quality, in syllables of the consonant-vowel type. Anne Christophe's studies (Christophe et al., 1995) reveal that newborns are sensitive to weak variations in temporal cues, on the order of 15 milliseconds for vowels and 20 milliseconds for closure of consonant sounds. However, studies of older infants show that, at six months, the spectral and temporal cues they register involve longer periods of time, such as those that mark sentence boundaries. Only at about nine to ten months do briefer prosodic cues become pertinent for marking finer and more specific forms of linguistic organization. Why this gap? The factors of attention and memory, which come into play when children process everyday speech, change between the first months and the second half of the first year. Aptitudes at this age (nine to ten months) differ from early capacities of discrimination.

Children engaged in collecting information about the pertinent properties of the linguistic units of spoken language have discovered —probably toward eight or nine months—that the organization of speech sounds has a function: it conveys meaning. Newborns operate in a sophisticated fashion in pursuit of a particular end—the ability to discriminate phonemes and syllables. At a later age they react in a much less differentiated way and in pursuit of a different end—the ability to process units of meaning and therefore to recognize words.

It was necessary, we felt, to pose some further questions to our babies: "Does the programmed acoustic system you were born with permit you to pick out the characteristics of the syllabic organization of words? Even though (depending on the language) these units may not always be coextensive with adult words, can you tell us whether salient, or stressed, syllables furnish you with a valuable basis for extracting words? Do you notice when syllables are organized more or less systematically for forming words? How do you spot this organization? We know, on the other hand, that phonotactic cues are also involved in the processing of words. Do the phonological regularities of languages help you to segment what you hear?"

We could justify these questions by explaining that a model that presumes that children have perceptual predispositions for extracting and representing words also demands that we study these predispositions in terms of their perceptual salience and validity in the language. This model also must account for children's capacities for processing frequency distributions in the local language. We felt sure our experimental subjects had answers for all of our questions—if only we could formulate them in such a way that they would reply.

In English, as in many other languages, stress falls on content words and, within these words, on the root and not on the inflections. This is why English is comprised mainly of words that carry the accent on the first syllable. In a corpus of 200,000 words, Cutler and Carter (1987) found that only 4 percent of polysyllabic words begin with a weak initial syllable. English-speaking adults can use the massive predominance of the strong-weak rhythm to segment the speech stream into words. Do babies in an English-speaking environment manifest a similar tendency, and, if so, beginning when? They should then prefer trochaic sequences (sequences consisting in a first stressed syllable and a second unstressed one) rather than iambic sequences (which exhibit an unstressed-stressed pattern).

One team of researchers had American babies of six and nine months listen to lists of disyllabic words consisting of a stressed syllable followed by an unstressed syllable and lists of disyllabic words composed of an unstressed syllable followed by a stressed syllable (Jusczyk, Cutler, and Redanz, 1993). At six months, the children showed no preference, but at nine months they were more interested in lists of words with a strong-weak stress pattern than in lists of words exhibiting a weak-strong pattern. Does this preference reveal only a general bias for a strong-weak tempo in nine-month-old children? No, since babies hearing Hebrew at the same age prefer the iambic (weak-strong) pattern that is predominant in Hebrew. One may therefore conclude that the linguistic environment has influenced the preference of babies for the distribution of accents predominant in the language spoken around them.

In French, rhythm is syllabic; it is not founded on a strong-weak alternation. One ought therefore find no preference. But this question has yet to be put to French babies.

The Problem of Small Pieces

The role of stress must not be overestimated, however. In certain languages, its distribution may hinder rather than help segmentation. Thus in Quiche Mayan, an American Indian language, morphemes and syllable boundaries do not coincide (Pye, 1983). The strategy of extracting stressed syllables often ends up with a linguistic unit that has no meaning in the adult language, for it contains only the end of one morpheme and the beginning of another (as if one were to say *tenquick* on hearing the phrase *was eaten quickly*).

We are faced with a chicken-and-egg problem. On the one hand, the tendency to extract stressed syllables cannot come from a preprogramming of the organism but must emerge instead from its actual experience in processing the local language. On the other hand, this processing derives its power from innate specialized mechanisms that human beings make use of to solve the problems posed by the perception of language.

Do babies pay attention to phonetic characteristics in segmenting and extracting words? We have seen that infants come into the world with a certain amount of experience, a sensitivity to phonetic contrasts, and the ability to represent syllables. This shows that, at a very early stage, speech sounds trigger a level of processing that organizes acoustic information to arrive at a number of pertinent constitutive varieties of these sounds (Jusczyk and Bertoncini, 1993).

Children must learn that, in their language, certain successions of phonemes are impossible at the beginning or end of words, some are frequent, and others are possible but rare. French children, for example, must be able to reject sequences such as [gd] as a beginning of a word. This sequence of sounds exists, on the other hand, in a language such as Polish. Accordingly, Polish children have to learn that this sequence is well formed. When do babies become sensitive to these aspects of the distribution of sounds in their language environment?

American children of six and nine months were given lists of English words and lists of Dutch words to listen to (Jusczyk, Friederici, Wessels, Svenkerud, and Jusczyk, 1993). Certain segmental and phonotactic properties of Dutch violate the phonetic structure and phonotactic constraints of English. Thus, the Dutch words *zwetsen* and *vlakte* would be impossible in English, where the series [zv] and [vl] are not allowed. By contrast, the prosodic structures of English and Dutch are similar. Each list contained fifteen words that had been chosen because they were abstract and therefore likely to be unfamiliar to children. In keeping with the usual procedure, the time spent listening to each of the lists served as a measure of preference. No preference was found among the six-month-old children, for whom the listening time in each case was comparable. On the other hand, the nine-month-old children listened longer to the list of English words (8.93 seconds) than to the list of Dutch words (5.03 seconds). This experiment shows that phonotactic cues may be accessible to children by the age of nine months.

When differences of prosodic organization are added to the phonotactic contrasts of word lists of two languages, which is the case in a comparison of English and Norwegian, one sees that by six months babies prefer to listen to the words of their own language. Sensitivity to differences in prosodic organization therefore occurs earlier, or at least is better established, than sensitivity to phonotactic organization.

Of course, as Peter Jusczyk et al. (1993) rightly remark, showing that children recognize when unfamiliar items conform to the phonotactic constraints of their native language is not the same as showing that they use such constraints to segment speech. However, the fact that between six and nine months children extract regularities and phonotactic properties of their language supports the hypothesis that they may, in fact, use these properties to process speech.

But once more we find ourselves faced with a contradiction, this time between children's aptitude for processing speech and their aptitude for extracting words. The perception of word boundary cues has been studied using the same technique with babies of five, nine, and eleven months (Myers et al., 1996). Pauses of one second were inserted in stories told to children. They were inserted without reference to clauses but placed between two different words or between two syllables of a single word. Are these infants, like those in Anne Christophe's experiment, sensitive to the cues that allow word boundaries to be distinguished?

It turns out that only at eleven months do children show a fairly clear preference for samples in which the pauses coincide with word boundaries. While the cues that mark prosodic grouping enable the child to prefer clauses at six months and phrases at nine months, one must wait until eleven months to obtain comparable data for words. Are prosodic and rhythmic cues alone, then, not enough to permit children to segment words before this age? Surely the child recognizes individual words well before eleven months. It must therefore be supposed that other cues have been superimposed on prosodic cues in the apprehension of word boundaries.

Recognizing and Understanding

So when do children begin to understand, to respond in a new and different way to words and phrases used by members of their families? Certain parents, who also happen to be psycholinguists, have kept notebooks with precise observations of the productions, gestures, and reactions of their children. The earliest reactions to words seem to occur toward six or seven months. Morris Lewis, to whom we owe a good study (from 1936) of the beginnings of language, noted that his son waved his hand between eight and nine months when one said "goodbye" to him. At seven months, one of the babies we studied, Henri, clapped his hands when one said "bravo" to him and refrained from touching an object when one whispered "hush." Many parents will have observed early behaviors of this type. But, before nine months, most of these gestures are related to specific situations and are learned in response to words said in well-defined contexts. It is believed that most children begin to understand words only toward nine months, even if it is not easy to determine how far this understanding extends. More often than not, the mother's tone of voice and the particular situation continue to be decisive in obtaining a response from the child. A particular intonation on the mother's part sometimes suffices to enable the child to understand an intention or a situation.

At eight months, Henri crawled very well and liked to tug at the leaves of a green plant that was located within his reach. Up to that point, this behavior was met with raised eyebrows, a deep voice, and a light tap on the hand, and with Henri being rapidly relocated away from the object of his lively curiosity. One day, however, he approached the plant and held out his hand. This time a firm "no" stopped him. But then a game began. Henri stuck out his hand once more and, smiling, looked up expecting to hear the "no" that indeed was not long in coming. He withdrew his hand, without touching the plant. Then he began his little game again. He had connected the gesture and the prohibition perfectly and, because he was capable of imagining the reaction his behavior would produce, looked to play a joke on the person watching him. The game continued for quite a while, to Henri's great pleasure. Did he, for all of that, understand the meaning of the word *no*? A "yes," uttered with the same abrupt intonation as "no," would have had the same effect. The child of nine months, who reacts to the sentence "We're going for a walk" by moving toward the door, is often assisted by cues such as the presence of the parka and knit cap that he puts on to go out. Let us not forget that children are marvelous at making connections. At this age, they have identified sound forms and, in relating them to contexts, managed to memorize a sequence of sounds together with the situation to which they correspond.

It has still not been possible to prove that the perceptual capacities displayed by infants include the representation of pieces of knowledge—that is, forms associated with meaning. But one does note an evolution in the processing of speech. The decline in the capacity to discriminate between speech sounds that are not phonological in the native language and the loss of the ability to segment foreign languages signal a shift in interest on the part of the child in processing speech. The processing of organized linguistic entities now converges with perceptual selection to permit the encoding of units of representation and therefore of words.

Words have a stable phonological form as well as meaning. Memorizing and remembering a phonetic pattern and coding a linguistic representation are two different tasks. But they are complementary aspects of installing a system that permits the child first to recognize words, then to attach a meaning to them, and a bit later to organize a mental dictionary of the adult type.

In our quest to detect the emergence of vocabulary, the first question that arises is how stable phonetic forms are recognized and memorized, independently of their meaning.

Finding the Same Object Again

To determine when children memorize stable, organized forms and recognize them in various contexts, babies of seven to eight months were "questioned"—on the assumption that they would display a preference for known forms rather than for unknown forms. Peter Jusczyk and Richard Aslin (1995) thus familiarized children with monosyllabic and disyllabic words. For sixty seconds the babies heard these words repeated every two seconds. They were then tested with the usual procedure for listening preference. Each child could choose to listen to one of two stories: in one, the familiar word was inserted several times; in the other, an unknown word appeared with the same frequency.

Let us look at Jusczyk and Aslin's experiment more closely and observe the behavior of their eight-month-old subject, Alice. Alice sat on her mother's knee in the observation cubicle. For sixty seconds, the word *cup* was presented to her. Then, through the speaker located to her left, Alice heard a story with the word *cup* in it: "The cup was bright and shiny. A clown drank from the red cup. Meg put the red cup back on the table," and so on. The word *cup* occurs fifteen times in this story, sometimes at the beginning and sometimes in the middle of a sentence. From the other side, on the right, Alice heard another story containing the word *dog,* which also occurs fifteen times: "The dog runs around the yard. The mailman called the big dog," and so forth.

Alice, having been familiarized with the word *cup,* showed a clear preference for the first story, turning her head for a longer time toward the left speaker, while Paul, familiarized with the word *dog,* preferred the second: he turned his head for a longer time toward the right speaker. Similar results were obtained with two-syllable words such as *hamlet* and *kingdom* and also when the children were trained on sentences containing the target words and then tested for their recognition of these words.

The term "word" is to be understood here as being subject to all the limitations these experiments involved. No appeal to meaning was made. The children recognized the phonetic forms with which they were familiarized without necessarily attaching any significance to them. In these experiments, words were not chosen in order to be understood by the infants. Acceptable nonwords in the language such as /kark/ and /poup/ would have led to the same results.

This memorization is nonetheless long lasting. Jusczyk and Aslin managed to show that, fifteen days after the end of the familiarization period, eight-month-old babies continue to exhibit more interest in stories containing words with which they have been familiarized or in words figuring in stories that they have heard every day for a week. However, these results are obtained only if the phonetic form of the words remains stable over the course of the experiment. The human speaker may change without this unduly bothering the child, but the modification of a consonant within the word with which the child has been familiarized prevents the recognition of this word. From this comes the idea that the recognition of words, before comprehension intervenes, rests on a strict agreement between the memorized phonetic form and the form presented in the stories. Children of seven to eight months display the ability to generalize, since they are capable of ignoring certain acoustic dimensions such as the timbre of the speaker's voice and its prosody while being sensitive to the modification of a segment, whether consonant or vowel. In other words, the memorized words are coded in memory in detailed form, and they are recognized later only if they correspond exactly to this form.

May we assume, then, that the sound repertoire that forms the basis of the lexicon is prepared in this way? In daily life, children are not trained to listen to words repeatedly, though, of course, a number of words and expressions do frequently recur in the adult speech they hear around them. But babies must extract these words from sentences and code them as examples received at various moments during the day, if not on days more or less remote in time. In fact, the assignment of too strict a description to a unit of speech can make recognition of this unit in everyday speech difficult. The agreement between a representation stored in memory and new examples of this word is often far from good. Speakers, pronunciations, intonations, and conditions of insertion in speech differ; all such variations, taken together, make it hard to recognize a word. A critical period is reached when children begin to attach semantic significance to speech. From nine months, they are aware that words have meaning, and their principal aim is now to understand—to recognize words and connect them with meanings. A radical change thus occurs in the processing of words with the constitution of the first verbal repertoire. Children become attentive to meaning and seek to memorize and represent the forms to which they can attribute significance. This entails a redistribution of the capacities of attention and representation. It may be assumed that from now on, children's primary interest and greatest pleasure will be to recognize familiar words as often as possible, to give them a meaning—and thereby to focus their linguistic capacities.

Recognizing Familiar Words

Experimentation allows us to investigate infants and young children—strangers of many talents who are capable of reacting to the most subtle variations in speech sounds. Now, when our interest turns to the learning of words—how words are extracted and their meaning discovered—experimentation falters. Children are no longer the precision machines they once were, sensitive to every characteristic of speech sounds. They now have narrowed their choices and modulated their capacities for response. The perceptual abilities of infants are henceforth placed in the service of another end—extracting meaning. Following them in this quest is not easy. The first step is to investigate the form in which children memorize words.

To examine how babies begin spontaneously to encode words, it is necessary to determine when, independently of any context and beyond the confines of experimental training, they come to prefer words frequently heard in their linguistic environment. Pierre Hallé and I (Hallé and Boysson-Bardies, 1994) selected twelve words with which we supposed babies to be familiar, for they belong to the repertoire frequently used by French adults with children—among them, the first words said by French babies. Words such as *biberon* (baby bottle), *chaussure* (shoe), *chapeau* (hat), *gâteau* (cake), *lapin* (rabbit), and *ballon* (ball or balloon) have a strong chance of belonging to the linguistic universe of the child's family circle. One may tentatively assume that these words have a meaning for children since they accompany contexts that are stable with regard to form and situation.

For this particular test of preference, then, the children received no prior experimental training. In devising the experiment, care was taken to eliminate influences of intonation and context. The mother listened to music through headphones so as not to interfere with the child's responses. The child, seated on her knee, heard the list of familiar words in one ear, emotionally charged words such as *papa* and *mama* having been excluded. In the other ear the child was presented with a list of French words of the same phonetic complexity but whose rarity in everyday language made it likely that the babies had seldom, if ever, heard them: *caduc* (obsolete), *bigot* (zealot), *volute* (scroll), *busard* (harrier), and so on. The listening time for each list was taken as a sign of preference indicating the recognition of words.

In our experiment, a clear preference appeared in children between the ages of ten and eleven and a half months: of the sixteen children tested, twelve preferred to listen to the list of familiar words. These children therefore extracted and coded words they heard frequently in their everyday linguistic environment, forging in this way long-term representation that could provisionally be regarded as constituting the basis of their early lexical repertoire (see figure 4.3).

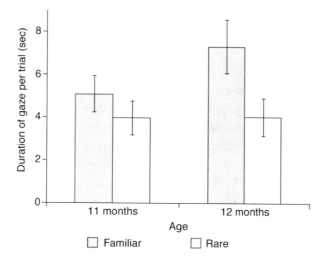

Figure 4.3 Time spent listening during the presentation of familiar words and rare words. At eleven months, children display a preference for hearing familiar words, and the preference increases at twelve months (from Hallé and Boysson-Bardies, 1994).

But this method for testing preferences did not, of course, allow us to say what meaning the children attached to words. Certain of their reactions while listening to the list of familiar words clearly suggested, however, that recognition is indeed connected with meaning. Many children, for example, looked at their feet on hearing the word *shoe*.

The Mental Representation of Words

For a word to be recognized, there must exist a mental representation that corresponds to this word. In adults, each of the various pieces of information that serve to characterize it—acoustic spectra, meaning, syntactic category, particular connotations attached to it by each speaker—is represented and provides access to the word in the speaker's lexicon, or mental dictionary. Lexical access has been the object of many psycholinguistic studies in adults. So great are the obstacles presented by the subtlety and diversity of the human mind, however, that how it works is not yet understood precisely. In fact, the various processes involved in accessing the lexicon not only involve different levels of representation and different stages of processing but also vary from language to language depending on its form (Cutler, Mehler, Norris, and Segui, 1983).

In seven-month-old infants, only the formal aspect enters into the recognition of verbal forms. In the next few months infants demonstrate early understanding of words. They are able to do this because the information that specifies these words, though no doubt highly incomplete, associates one or more meanings or a particular connotation with an acoustic form. By ten or eleven months, the child has encoded a certain number of words. How are these words represented in this initial lexical repertoire? How do children access this repertoire when they hear a word?

As we have seen, infants possess a sophisticated system of phonetic processing that rests on acoustic-phonetic mechanisms of an analytical character. Can these mechanisms, which permit discrimination between phonemes and syllables, account for the representation of the child's earliest words? In adults, access to the mental dictionary for purposes of comprehension is facilitated by the representation of a word as the unique combination of a small number of units whose nature varies with the structure of their native language (Mehler, Segui, and Frauenfelder, 1981; see also Mehler, Dupoux, and Segui, 1990). These intermediate units of representation include the syllable in French, the foot in English (a metrical unit that captures the stressed and unstressed contrast between successive syllables), and the mora in Japanese (a unit smaller than the syllable but larger than the phoneme). Organization into units also plays an essential role in the perception (Bertoncini and Mehler, 1981) and production of early words (Ferguson and Farwell, 1975).

In processes of segmentation, however, the role of the prosodic and phonotactic organization of speech units seems essential when it comes to understanding words. In the context of everyday speech reception, the representation of words is coded in a somewhat more holistic form that takes into account the elements of prosody—for the most part, at the expense of detailed segmental description. This hypothesis has been proposed by psycholinguists who have studied the productions of children (Menn, 1978; see also Macken, 1979). For them, the first representations of words in infants do not include a complete segmental description but instead assume the form of a prosodic word—a global, syllabic structure in which certain articulatory features are noticed. Against this position, it may be objected that the simplifications found in the earliest words stem from various constraints on programs for the realization of words. One may also wonder whether the representations used to access words are the same as those used for the production of words and whether the production of words is valuable for understanding the form of the coded representations in children's first verbal repertoire. These long-debated questions have not yet been clearly answered.

The representation of a word emerges from traces left in memory by the different examples of this word that have been heard up to a given moment. The form represented in the child's lexicon is necessarily more abstract than any individual trace, since it must answer to each and every one of them. Accepting the equivalence of forms uttered in different ways by different people—in a father's deep voice, a little sister's high-pitched voice, a country uncle's dialect, or the voice of a mother suffering from a head cold—or simply the equivalence of forms pronounced in different ways in different sentences demands that words be represented in an idealized or schematic fashion rather than in the form of an exhaustive and detailed description. Doing this means abstracting from speech in a way that preserves what is pertinent for present purposes—recognizing and encoding words in the early acquisition period, when a mental lexicon of the adult type is not yet established. An underspecified encoding no doubt suffices for recognizing words when this repertoire is limited, without a great many similar forms (Charles-Luce and Luce, 1990)—which is in fact the case with the repertoire of one-year-old children.

To test the form of coding words known in the early receptive lexicon, it is first necessary to verify that word recognition withstands modification of a segment. If children could be shown to recognize these words despite the modification of a consonant, this would demonstrate a qualitative difference in the ways in which children of seven months and children of eleven months code and identify words. Indeed, we have seen that younger children, trained on words they do not understand, cannot identify words so modified.

Our inquiry thus needed to be taken a step further (Hallé and Boysson-Bardies, 1996). The familiar words used in the recognition experiment were modified along two phonological dimensions. First, the voicing feature of the first consonant was systematically inverted. Thus, the French word *biberon* became "piberon", *gâteau* became "kateau", *chapeau* became "japeau", and so on. Disregarding such modifications, children of ten to eleven months continued to be more interested in these words than in the rare words. What is more, when the list of modified words was presented together with the list of unmodified familiar words, no difference in listening times was found. Identical results were obtained when the manner of articulation of the first consonant was modified. Thus *biberon* became "viberon", *gâteau* "jateau", *chapeau* "kapeau", and so on. Despite the phonological significance of this transformation, the children paid as much attention to the list of transformed familiar words as they had to the original list and did not show a preference for the list of original familiar words when this was contrasted with the list of transformed familiar words (see figure 4.4).

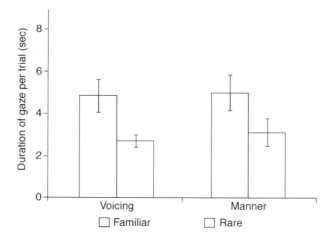

Figure 4.4   Time spent listening to familiar words with alterations of the initial consonant and to rare words. In the altered familiar words, the first consonant was replaced either by *(a)* a corresponding voiced consonant (/b/, for example, by /p/) or *(b)* a consonant differing with respect to the mode of articulation (/b/, for example, replaced by /v/). In both cases, the eleven-month-old children continued to prefer words altered in this way to rare words.

The representation of words is therefore not sufficiently specified in the child's memory for a feature change in the first consonant of words to prevent recognition. These experiments thus suggest that the perceptual representation of words in children's early repertoire does not specify a sequence of phonemes but rather a sequence of more global, less analyzed units. These units no doubt depend on the structure of the language. In French, the syllable plays a fundamental role in structuring words. If the first consonant of a familiar word is suppressed, children no longer register a preference for such words. It therefore seems that they represent the first syllables of words in consonant + vowel form without, however, precisely coding the consonant.

A related study by Christine Stager (1995) shows that in experiments in which children are taught to associate a word with an object, children of fourteen months have trouble with words that are phonetically very similar. They do not differentiate between such words, whereas they are successful in this task when words have clearly distinct forms. This result was anticipated in earlier studies by

David Barton (1978), who observed that discrimination between words that differ by a single consonant (such as the French words *boire* and *poire*) proves to be too difficult a task for children until the age of twenty months.

The results of these experiments show that young children's representations are not detailed enough to distinguish between phonetically similar words. At first sight, such results seem to contradict the data on word recognition in younger children, but in fact they make it possible to follow the organization of different levels of speech processing. They reveal a reorganization of the child's capacities as increasingly high-level invariants come into play—in this case, the link between sound and meaning. To comprehend and speak, children abandon a representation of sound units that is at once too detailed, universal, and disorganized. They adapt themselves to the dazzling discovery they have made: words have meaning. This now focuses their interest.

We do not yet know within what limits the global representation of a word suffices for it to be recognized. What degree of transformation can children tolerate and still map a spoken form to a word in their repertoires? This certainly depends in part on the structure of the words in a child's native language and on the number of phonetically similar words in the child's repertoire: when these become too numerous, this method of representation no longer works. We shall see how children then begin to reorganize their lexicons and how they code words. For the moment it would be interesting to know what inclines them to maintain the equivalence between a word and a transformed representation of it, and under what conditions they are led to distinguish two words whose forms are similar. Thus, researchers slowly learn about the upheavals the child undergoes during this period—upheavals in speech processing and cognition that will manifest themselves through the emergence of understanding and the production of the child's first words.

Understanding Words

In everyday life, young children extract various sorts of linguistic information—phonetic, prosodic, syntactic, and contextual—that help enable them to grasp the meaning of words. Children have also learned by this point to communicate. Weeks, sometimes months, before adults recognize them as producing words, children dispose of a panoply of gestures and particular forms of verbal expression that allow them to communicate with adults and to express their emotions. Children of nine to ten months point, wave their hands to say goodbye, turn their heads away to signal refusal, and use a series of gestures, both personal and socialized, to express desires, interests, and disinclinations.

On the other hand, babbling by the end of the first year is not random, and systematic correspondences can be discovered between certain expressions and certain situations. It has been shown that the child pairs particular vocalizations with demands, manipulations of objects (arranging blocks, for example), and movements such as sitting (Blake and Boysson-Bardies, 1992).

Studies based on the observation of children and questions put to parents show fairly clearly that comprehension precedes the production of words. In a study dating from 1979, Helen Benedict proposed an age of nine months for the first understanding of words. However, her study, like most of those bearing on the comprehension of words in infants of less than twelve months, did not separate the comprehension of words from the comprehension of nonlinguistic clues. We have seen how children of nine months respond to a "no" and a "yes" pronounced in the same circumstances with the same intonation. Simple observation suggests that, toward eight or nine months, they begin to recognize words as sequences of sounds that go together with a particular situation.

It is difficult to distinguish the recognition of objects and the circumstances surrounding comprehension from the words that accompany them—a problem that complicates the study of lexical comprehension in the very young child. Experimental methods attempt to eliminate the influence of particular situations and customary cues to determine whether a given verbal form is understood independently of context. Until a few years ago, most of the tasks used to test the comprehension of words rested on a relationship between a command and a visual object. The experimenter would present the child with three or four objects and say, "Pick out the truck," "Give me the book," and so on. In other tasks, the child had to point to an object whose name had been mentioned; the name of the object then was inserted in a sentence and one looked to see whether the child was still capable of pointing out the object. Most of these tests proved to be disappointments. Making a one-year-old child understand what one has in mind is not a simple matter, and children are not always ready to obey when one asks them to pick out the object that one names. They do what they please and pick out the object that seems the most attractive. Mistakes are difficult to interpret, and successes are sometimes a matter of luck.

All studies, however, indicate an important change between eleven and thirteen months. The ability to memorize—at least for a brief time—the names associated with unknown objects emerges toward eleven to twelve months. Sharon Oviatt (1980) calls this phenomenon *recognitory comprehension*. It requires recognition of a linguistic form, the association of this form with an event in the environment, and the awareness of a link between the linguistic form and its referent. However, this recognitory comprehension is distinguished from symbolic comprehension. The latter requires that the word refer to an object in its absence—that the word take the object's place. More recent experiments use the duration of the child's gaze rather than the picking out of objects. They show that an understanding of words begins to develop toward thirteen to fourteen months. Roberta Golinkoff, K. Hirsh-Pasek, K. Cauley, and L. Gordon (1987) (see also Golinkoff and Hirsh-Pasek, 1995) tested the comprehension of nouns and verbs in children at the beginning of the second year with a procedure relying on duration of visual attention. The children were seated on their mothers' knee and, from a speaker situated between two television screens, a woman's voice was heard asking "Where is the truck?" Images then simultaneously appeared on the two screens—on the left screen, a truck; on the right screen, a shoe. The woman's voice then said, "Find the truck." Each pair of objects was presented twice; in all, six pairs were presented in the course of thirty-six trials (see figure 4.5).

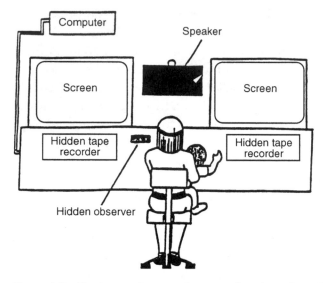

Figure 4.5 Device used to test the compehension of words and sentences by a method of visual preference (from Golinkoff and Hirsh-Pasek, 1995).

For the object corresponding to the command, times of fixed gaze were longer, and latency periods were shorter. Nine of thirteen subjects had higher scores for images that agreed with the command. However, in certain pairs, the responses were skewed for no apparent reason. An experiment of the same type done with verbs gave similar results. A number of small scenes were presented in the course of the experiment, acted out by a woman who mimed various actions— drinking a cup of coffee, dancing, blowing on a piece of paper. The gaze time for actions that agreed with the command was longer, and eleven of twelve children scored higher on actions that corresponded to what they heard. Experiments done with short sentences yielded similar results as well. But it was not before thirteen months that certain children looked longer at the object whose name had been mentioned and not before sixteen months that responses to verbs became generalized. All the experiments showed that, even with good preparation, just one child in ten between the ages of nine and eleven months looked more or less systematically at objects whose names had been given, and five in ten between twelve and fourteen months looked when animals were involved. It was only between fifteen and seventeen months that this behavior was found in eight of ten children.

The results obtained through experiment did not agree with the impressions of parents and illustrate the discrepancies that are liable to be found between observations of children in a natural setting and under laboratory conditions. It may be that in an experimental setting the instructions given to the child go too far in dissociating the reference of a particular word from the intention to refer. Early words acquire their linguistic value from communication with other persons interacting in a shared world. When words do not occur in the context of some usual process of communication, the child no doubt has a harder time recognizing them. Some minimum number of cues must agree for the child to be able to access a word and recognize its meaning. This explains why later the child sometimes has difficulty detaching the meaning of a word from the context in which it was learned.

Can the size of a child's comprehension vocabulary in a natural setting be estimated in this case? A systematic study conducted in the United States by Elizabeth Bates, P. Dale, and D. Thal (1995) with the parents of 1,600 children was based on parents' estimates of the number of words their children understood (see figure 4.6). The parents reckoned that, on average, children understood fifty-eight words at ten months, 126 words at thirteen months, and 210 words at sixteen months. As always, individual variations were important. Some children were credited with 183 words at ten months, while others were supposed to understand only eight words. The methods for collecting data in this study gave free rein to subjective estimation: parents were asked to check off, on specially prepared lists, the words that they thought their child understood. Parental love sometimes leads to illusions, and so it is not surprising that this type of study tends to overestimate children's capacities for understanding words.

The same test administered to French parents, who are less inclined to see their offspring as prodigies, would probably yield less spectacular results. In this respect the cross-cultural data are quite interesting. Nonetheless, an average of forty to fifty words understood at the age of twelve months, when these occur in pertinent

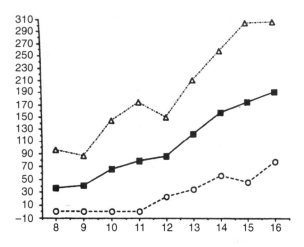

Figure 4.6   Estimate of the number of words understood by children between eight and sixteen months. The upper line indicates the performances of the most advanced 10 percent, the middle line the performances of the majority of the children tested (80 percent), and the bottom line the performances of the least advanced 10 percent (from Bates, Dale, and Thal, 1995).

situational contexts, may reasonably be assumed. This figure has been advanced by a number of psycholinguists.

In A.D. 400, Saint Augustine (1960, pp. 50–51), speaking of the way in which he learned to talk, wrote the following: "Grown up men did not teach me by presenting me with words in any orderly form of instruction.... But I [taught] myself, with that mind which you, my God, gave me.... I pondered over this in memory: when they named a certain thing and, at that name, made a gesture at the object, I observed that object and inferred that it was called by the name they uttered.... That they meant this was apparent by their bodily gestures, as it were by words natural to all men, which are made by change of countenance, nods, movements of the eyes and other bodily members, and sounds of the voice.... So little by little I inferred that the words set in their proper places in different sentences, that I heard frequently, were signs of things."

All the things that help the child to understand the meaning of words are mentioned in this passage. At the end of the first year, not all of them have the same weight; context at this time plays a much greater role than syntax. This situation will evolve in the course of the second year, and other sources of linguistic information will come to acquire their full importance.

At the age of one year, children have learned communicative gestures, extracted forms from the linguistic environment, and begun to control their articulation. For the first time, they associate sounds with events, persons, and objects. They have said their first words. But what, in fact, is a word—and how does it come to have meaning—for a child?

The First Lexical Steps: Eleven to Eighteen Months

There are words that I see and other words that I do not see.
—A child

The Words for Saying It

What, then, is a word? From the point of view of morphology, it is a structure that obeys rules. As a unit of meaning, it is, in Steven Pinker's (1994, p. 157) definition, "a pure symbol, part of a cast of thousands, rapidly acquired because of a harmony between the mind of the child, the mind of the adult, and the texture of reality." Because both philosophers and linguists have trouble defining what a word is—beyond saying what it is not—we might as well work with this definition.

The acquisition of a mental vocabulary touches on a special domain—namely, our knowledge of the world. The phonological system and the syntactic system are conventional systems; the lexicon that the child must learn, on the other hand, directly involves the texture of reality. The words that we employ map conceptual divisions of objects and actions onto phonological forms. These mappings are not arbitrary: they are in fundamental agreement with the ways in which the world itself is divided up.

Thus, we call the extremity of the arm—consisting of the palm and five fingers and ending at the wrist—the hand. Beyond this, as everyone knows, is the forearm, which goes from the wrist to the elbow. The words correspond here to areas that are well defined by joints. We do not have a word for "hand + the forearm as far up as the middle of it." This category does not exist. The physical structure of the body governs the naming of it, and the names given to the parts that constitute the body conform to this structure.

How do children learn that the word *hand* is applied only to the extremity having five fingers and not to the whole appendage that their mother waves to show her hand? The explanation often proposed—that children simply relate the sound form that they hear with the object that is presented to them—can be sustained only in very specific cases of name learning. This simple association is generally not a reliable method; in particular, it cannot hold for the learning of verbs. To be sure, babies remain highly dependent on their perception of the world. However, in usual situations, they are confronted not with isolated sound-object pairs but with sound forms in contexts where several actions and several objects are found simultaneously related. Thus, at lunchtime, the child may be brought into the kitchen and seated in a high chair, where a bib is tied around his neck, and a plate put in front of him. His mother sits next to him, takes a utensil in her hand, and puts it in his mouth, which then becomes filled with something hot and delicious. This scene incorporates objects and actions that are found every time the event occurs but that are only parts of it—independent entities. How does the child extract the meaning of the words said by his mother on this occasion—*eat, chair, spoon, hot, bib*? The child must learn to distinguish well-determined referents that designate not the whole of an event but parts of it, such as the chair, the spoon, and the bib. The infant knows that the spoon and plate of baby food are distinct objects: their contours are not contiguous, and their spatial displacements are independent of each other. In the same way, the sounds can be isolated into blocks—words and sentences—that end at certain moments.

Children can therefore discover the correct meaning of a word by having an intuition about the link between divisions in the external world and divisions in the acoustic forms they hear. The first question we need to ask is what knowledge they have of the world and how the connection with words is made.

The World and the Baby

The conceptual partitioning of the world by human beings—categorizing material objects and apprehending persons as others—is to a large degree predetermined. We live in Euclidean space, in a world ruled by physical principles. These physical principles permit us in most cases to separate actions and objects and to attribute to them stable characteristics that preserve their identity and allow them to be represented and categorized.

The question of whether the system used to represent and categorize the objects and actions of the world is constructed with words or, rather, precedes words has long been the subject of passionate debate. It is now known that children's knowledge about how the world is divided up is both instinctive and learned and that they form categories based on reality well before learning the linguistic signals that correspond to it. As Pinker (1994, p. 154) says, the baby's brain sculpts the world "into discrete, bounded, coherent objects and into the actions they undergo." This dynamic aptitude for categorizing the phenomena of the world is another one of the gifts that children receive at birth. But while they are capable of making—indeed, are innately constrained to make—predictions about the world and to carve up the world into categories of objects and categories of actions, interaction with the environment is once again necessary if they are to be able to apply names to categories, natural or learned.

When and how is the relationship developed between, on the one hand, the knowledge that the child possesses and will go on acquiring about the world and, on the other hand, the growing awareness that sound forms have meaning? We have seen that children's processing of language is initially more acoustic than linguistic. Subsequently, in a second stage of development, the recognition and production of early words show them to be aware that sound forms have meaning. Children have established a relationship between sound forms and events and objects. They have understood the intentions of people around them in using words to refer to objects or situations or to communicate meaning and information. In a third stage, some months later, the rapid growth of vocabulary corresponds to the discovery not only that words denote concepts but that they may be learned on the basis of the concepts that children have at their disposal. There is a word for each thing that the child can perceptually extract as an object or action. Sound forms thus emerge as a new system that channels the processing of reality. Giving a label to a set of physical parts therefore guarantees a conceptual unity of these parts.

Is the Baby a Physicist?

The experimental approach to infant cognition has managed to show that the physics of material objects—the principles that explain the concept of movement and underlie the geometry of space—can help the child in the first months of life to structure the world. According to Elizabeth Spelke (1982; see also Spelke, 1991), children are born with certain intuitions about the nature and behavior of objects. For Renée Baillargeon (1991), children instead are born with highly constrained mechanisms that guide their reasoning about objects. Experiments show that, at three and a half months, the infant represents a physical object as subject to constraints of continuity and solidity in space. To question infants about their intuitive grasp of physics, researchers compare reactions during the presentation of normal and anomalous physical situations. If children do, in fact, have certain expectations about the physical nature of objects, an event that violates these certainties will provoke their surprise and, correspondingly, evoke longer periods of visual attention than the presentation of a normal event.

In Spelke's (1991) experiment, babies are comfortably seated in chairs and visually track an object that moves slowly along a horizontal plane. At a certain moment, the object is made to pass behind a screen. If, by a conjuring trick, the object is modified in such a way that it comes out on the other side having a different size or appearance than when it passed behind the screen, the babies manifest a strong reaction of surprise. Infants expect the same object to come

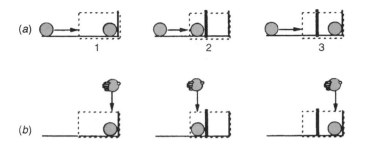

Figure 5.1 Device for testing the notions of continuity and solidity in two-and-a-half month-old babies: *(a)* the experimental situation, *(b)* the control situation. The dotted line indicates the screened area. The child is familiarized with situation 1. The ball rolls and disappears behind the screen, which is raised to reveal the ball stopped by an obstacle. The child is next presented with situations 2 and 3. One expects the child to look longer at situation 3, which violates notions of continuity and solidity. *(b)* shows the control situation with respect to which the gaze times of children in the course of the experiment were interpreted (from Spelke, 1991).

out again. To satisfy this expectation, the object that was momentarily hidden must return to view with its size and shape preserved. In other experiments, Spelke showed that notions of solidity and continuity exist in babies by the age of two and a half months.

Figures 5.1 and 5.2 show the types of situations studied. In the first situation, babies were familiarized with a ball introduced from the left side, which rolls and disappears behind a screen. The screen is raised to reveal the ball on the right side next to an obstacle. In the experimental situations, the obstacle is at the center of the device, and the raised screen reveals the ball either in front of the obstacle (normal situation) or on the other side of it to the extreme right (anomalous situation). The babies systematically looked longer at the situation that violated their intuitive notions of continuity and solidity. In the experiment presented in figure 5.2, Spelke tested the notion of gravity in the same fashion. Somewhat later, between four and six months, children show that they expect the hidden object to continue to fall until it encounters a solid surface. At five to six months, the principles of gravity and inertia allow babies to predict the motions of objects: a falling object ought to fall according to the laws of gravitation.

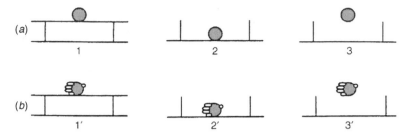

Figure 5.2   Device for testing the notion of gravity in six-month-old babies: *(a)* the experimental situation, *(b)* the control situation. The child is familiarized with position 1. The gaze times for positions 2 and 3 were compared. The child looked longer at the third situation, which violates the notion of gravity (from Spelke, 1991).

In a fascinating series of experiments, of which we have mentioned only a few examples, Spelke and Baillargeon managed to show that babies, like adults, assign properties to objects in three-dimensional space: a solid object cannot pass through another solid object, two surfaces belong to the same object if they touch each other and move together, the partial concealment of an object does not imply the loss of the hidden part, an object cannot remain stable without support, and so on. The perception of objects is therefore guided by a certain conception of physical properties that entails certain constants in the behavior of objects in space.

The distinction between living and nonliving things is also made very early. Infants expect animate and inanimate objects to move according to different laws. They intuitively separate the motion of inanimate objects, which obey physical laws, from that of animate objects, which move intentionally.

Infants represent inanimate and animate physical objects and reason about their displacement in accordance with the constraints that rule the physical world. Thus, the physics of material objects, the geometry of space, and the intuition peculiar to human beings combine to shape infants' attempts at categorization and allow them to make deductions about the world well before they speak their first words.

Later, of course, children appeal to other types of knowledge. It will be a long time before they know that virtual objects do not exist in the way that solid objects do, and, like adults, they will often be fooled by the "reality" of a computer-generated image. But that is another story. Children's cognitive apparatus permits them to have a basic conception of the structure of the surrounding physical world. This enables them to organize reality and to divide it into delimited entities that remain stable over time.

However, neither what is given to all human beings at birth for language acquisition nor what is common to the structure of all the world's languages exempt children from the need for experience with a particular language. All children have to make the acoustic forms of their native language—that is, speech sounds as they are carved up in a particular language—correspond with actions, events, and objects in the world.

Objects and Words

Animated by a desire to communicate and armed with a certain knowledge about the world and about the structure of language sounds, the child has still to relate sound patterns to representations of objects, actions, and events.

Is it as simple as that?

It is clear that children bring their own representations to bear on the physical, linguistic, and cultural data supplied by the world. The question is how they manage to do this. Given a series of events, how are they able to extract the meaning of a word, make a correct generalization, and dismiss interpretations that may be coherent with observations but are incorrect in predicting future events? What Willard Van Orman Quine (1960, p. 29) called "the scandal of induction" is relevant in this connection.

Quine's classic example in *Word and Object* (1960) involves the word *gavagai*. Would a linguist who hears this word uttered in a foreign country when a rabbit runs past be able to conclude that the word means "rabbit"? It might mean any number of other things: "it runs," "there it is," "let's catch it," and so on. In the case of young children, let us take the word *dog* as an example. The child may have heard this word while seeing a basset hound gnaw a bone, watching a German shepherd run after a ball, or hearing and being frightened by a barking noise. He knows his aunt's white poodle and his father's dog, which is black and called "Fido" rather than "dog."

How does the child extract the meaning of the word *dog* from the diversity of forms and events related to his hearing this word produced by adults? The word *dog* denotes a particular species of animal. How does the child avoid generalizing the word to all four-legged animals? At the same time, why does he not focus on some part of the dog—say, the tail—and think that the word *dog* is a label for this part rather than the whole? In fact, why does the child assume that the sound sequence he hears designates an object in the world and not an action, such as barking? Metaphorical uses of the word may also get him off on the wrong track. A child who knows that the word *dog* refers to a particular animal is liable to be confused when his father, looking out the window, says, "It's raining cats and dogs"— without there being a dog in sight.

Will the child privilege similarities of form or of function? Most of the time a word occurs with enough indeterminacy that the child has to choose a meaning. However, ontological constraints—the early knowledge of the world that children possess—lead them to make a limited number of hypotheses. And most of the time, in fact, children's predictions will turn out to be correct, or at least reasonable. The word *dog* will be applied to something that moves, whose shape is characterized by such things as four legs, a tail, and a head, and whose method of making sounds is barking. Only an object having all or some of these characteristics is recognized in different scenes. Of course, generalizations (or, alternatively, certain restrictions on the use of the word) remain possible and are, in fact, relatively frequent. In ordinary language, the word *dog* denotes a particular species of four-legged animal, but children may generalize this concept and begin to think that the word *dog* is applied to every animal with four legs and fur. This type of generalization rests, however, on a conceptual foundation. The deductions are not wrong, but by setting aside one or several of the object's attributes the child is led to select a supercategory—mammals—rather than a subspecies of this supercategory, dogs. One child we studied, Guy, at seventeen months used the word *dog* for all mammals—and also for dinosaurs. He used the word *hen* for all birds and the word *fish* for all sea creatures. In

Guy's partitioning, supercategories received the name of an element of a particular category (if one disregards the mistake with dinosaurs). But even some adults are apt to be misled by the physical appearance of a diplodocus or a brontosaurus and might classify them among the mammals rather than reptiles. In fact, children's guesses are generally correct. Most of the time they succeed in calling persons and things by their actual names.

The child's first words are typically attributed to preexisting representations of objects, actions, and events. However, the same approach, founded on both pragmatic and ontological constraints, is used for new words corresponding to new concepts as well as for the generalization of known words to new objects belonging to the same category.

Let us follow Guy a bit more as he learns his first words. He knows the word *oreille* (ear) and knows how to point to his own ear and to that of another person. He does not have a dog and has never played with one. He has seen dogs from a distance, as well as in his picture book. Finding himself one day in the presence of a real dog, a spaniel with floppy ears, he was not frightened: to the contrary, he was delighted. Since Guy had a little routine of pointing to his ear and that of his father, he was asked to point to the dog's ear. Without hesitation, Guy lifted up the dog's ear. Is this such a trivial thing? Do a spaniel's ears, covered with silky fur, resemble human ears? Guy's generalization could have been made only on the basis of an implicit knowledge of the parts of the body and their function, in humans and in mammals.

One of the constraints that guide children's word-mapping hypotheses directs them to suppose that new words will refer to new objects. They are cautious, however, in extending their meaning to other objects. A bit later, they quickly learn that an object may have several labels: a physical dog may be labeled *dog* and at the same time be called "Fido" or "Rover." This does not seem to pose a problem for children. They recognize that a father is also a man who may be addressed as "sir," but who may also be called "Peter" or "Paul" or "my darling." It has sometimes been supposed that, when a baby calls all men "daddy," it is through an error of overgeneralization. One must be wary of this kind of interpretation: it is not necessarily a case of mistakenly generalizing a name intended for a particular father, who alone is qualified to bear it, but rather could be a generalization of his function. When children know how to use articles, they say, "This man is a daddy." The role of men as paternal protectors and providers is part of the imagination of little children. In the Middle Ages, in France, as still today in Italy and Spain, baby food was called *papa*, thus indicating the symbolic role of the father in feeding the child.

Of course, the child's task may be facilitated by adults—for example, when they point out objects or mention the name of an object particularly frequently. However, this type of learning is not the rule and, in fact, is virtually nonexistent for certain children or for children in certain cultures. Until children are able to ask the definition of a word, they must guess its meaning with the help of their knowledge of the world and relations with others. On the one hand, children are helped in their guesswork by the physical or abstract constraints that restrict the possible referents of a word and limit its scope and structure. The agreement of external cues with linguistic cues (which may be phonetic, prosodic, semantic, and syntactic) and the reactions of adults assist the child in relating words to objects, actions, and feelings. Very quickly, the child comes to understand that a series of words corresponds to a complex event. Toward thirteen to fifteen months, well before entering into a much more advanced phase of language production—and without having to wait for this phase—children understand relatively complex sentences. Little by little they are able to free themselves from external cues and to rely on the syntactic analysis of sentences.

First Words

The date of the child's entry into the domain of words is highly variable. The age at which the first words are pronounced, their form, and the rate at which vocabulary develops vary from child to child. Culture, social environment, and the child's temperament and birth order all influence the age at which the first words appear.

Certain general tendencies are worth mentioning, however. The first words of children are most often heard by adults between the eleventh and fourteenth months. The growth of early vocabulary is very gradual. Children take, on average, five to six months to arrive at a vocabulary of about fifty words (Vihman and Miller, 1988). This vocabulary is remarkable not only for the length of time needed to acquire it but also for its variability. At times, the child is no longer able to employ certain words used previously, and the pronunciation of a particular word may vary. Furthermore, words are used in restricted contexts and are not generalized to other situations.

Elizabeth Bates and her team (Bates et al., 1994; see also Bates, Dale, and Thal, 1995) conducted an inquiry with 1,803 parents, asking them to mark off words said by their children on lists that had been prepared in advance, in order to chart the evolution of English-speaking children's vocabulary from the age of eight months until thirty months. The results of this study show an enormous variability and stunningly rich lexicons in the case of certain children. At eleven months, the number of words uttered by children, according to their parents, ranged from zero to fifty-two with an average of six words. In the course of the second year, children's expressive vocabularies may vary: some say only a few words, while others have an effective production vocabulary of more than 500 words, the average being about 300 words at twenty-four months. The number of words spoken by the children in the study by Bates and her colleagues is much higher than the number recorded in other studies. Katherine Nelson (1973), in a study of children aged fourteen to twenty-four months, gave an average of fifty words at twenty months and 186 words at twenty-four months (the variation at two years running from twenty-eight to 436 words). Applying stricter criteria, Larry Fenson (Fenson et al., 1994) proposed averages of ten words at thirteen months, fifty words at seventeen months, and 310 words at twenty-four months. This is consistent with the performances of the children that my colleagues and I have studied. These children, aged fifteen to seventeen months, produced between thirty and forty words in a session. Nor did their mothers reckon their vocabularies to be much larger. Among Swedish and Japanese children one finds comparable averages. In all these studies, however, the variability among children's performances is quite sizable.

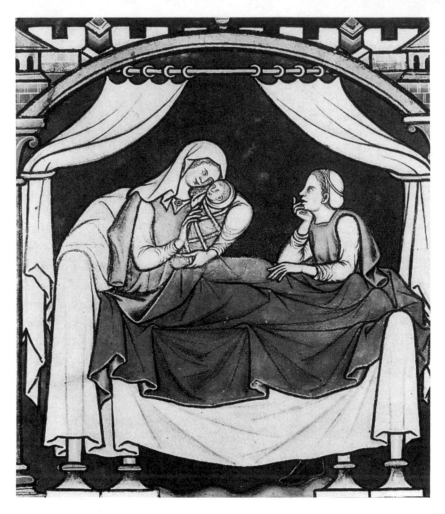

The Birth of Samuel, Maciejowski Bible, M 638, F. 19 v, France, 13th century (The Pierpont Morgan Library, New York).

In this illustration from the thirteenth century, one sees the magnetizing exchange of looks between a mother and her newborn child—a loving first moment of communication.

PLATE I

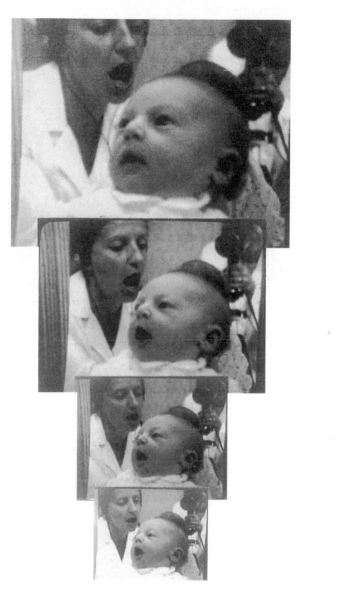

Photographs from author's personal collection.

Imitation is one of the infant's first interactions after birth. In this sequence of photos, a four-day-old newborn imitates the experimenter's opening of the mouth.

PLATE II

View of a Flemish bourgeois interior, about 1500 (*The Holy Family*, anonymous master, Royal Museum of Fine Arts, Antwerp).

The gesture of pointing is an example of joint attention. At first the young child directs the adult's attention to what interests him; later, the child will point at the object in order to learn its name.

PLATE III

The Holy Family at Work, from the Book of Hours of Catherine de Clèves, Utrecht, M 917, p. 149 (The Pierpont Morgan Library, New York). (Photo by David A. Loggie)

The child's language develops within the framework of family and culture.

PLATE IV

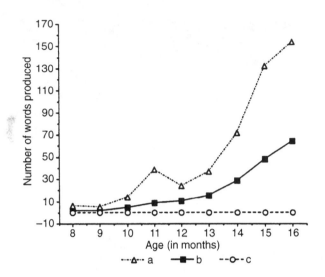

Figure 5.3   Evolution of the repertoire of words produced by children between eight and sixteen months: *(a)* the most advanced 10 percent, *(b)* the average (= 80 percent), and *(c)* the least advanced 10 percent (from Bates, Dale, and Thal, 1995).

The divergent results of the study of American children by Bates and her colleagues (Bates, Dale, and Thal, 1995) suggest that the method of collecting data from parents, using lists prepared in advance, unduly encourages the imagination of certain parents. Nonetheless, a very considerable range of variation is observed, and a certain precociousness does indeed appear to exist. But, as the averages indicate, it is rare for children to have more than fifty words at twelve months or more than 300 words at sixteen months.

Figures 5.3 and 5.4 show the development of the expressive repertoire of the most advanced 10 percent of the children studied by Bates, the least advanced 10 percent, and the other 80 percent whose performances made up the average.

The increase in expressive vocabulary is particularly noticeable between sixteen and twenty months, after the four- or five-month period during which the first fifty words are acquired. After this first and relatively laborious stage, expressive vocabulary grows regularly and rapidly. In the four months that follow the acquisition of the first fifty words, children acquire on average another 120 words, then

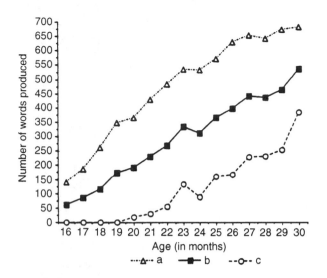

Figure 5.4 Evolution of the repertoire of words produced by children between sixteen and thirty months: *(a)* the most advanced 10 percent, *(b)* the average (= 80 percent), *(c)* the least advanced 10 percent (from Bates, Dale, and Thal, 1995).

another 140 in the four following months, and another 260 by the beginning of the third year.

The number of words produced does not greatly depend on age. In fact, in children under eighteen months, age accounts for only 22 percent of the variation observed. In older children, age becomes a more pertinent variable, accounting for 46 percent of the variation. Until the third year, then, variations in the number of words in children's vocabularies are due more to personal factors than to age.

Variations as considerable as these may seem surprising. Are the sizable lags observed all pathological? Do the signs of precocity predict future good pupils? Certainly not. Difficulties in understanding words have a much stronger predictive value than the number of words produced. Bates, Dale, and Thal (1995) compared children who were far below the average in expressive vocabulary (but who, with respect to vocabulary comprehension, fell within the normal range) with children whose comprehension, like their production, was below the norm. A year later, the first group of babies had caught up with the average group with regard to number of words produced;

most of the others caught up with this average only at the age of six years. Among children displaying precocity in production, comprehension was below average in some cases. This observation reinforces the notion that comprehension and production in very young children are partly dissociated.

There may also exist dissociations between the level of vocabulary and levels of syntax and verbal memory, so much so that a large vocabulary at eighteen months does not predict early development of sentences. No doubt many children who have a large vocabulary at an age when others say only "papa" (or "dada") and "mama" have a good chance of becoming fluent speakers some years later. These are children who like to talk. But a delay in the production of words is not an indicator of a relative lack of intelligence or failure in school any more than a precocious vocabulary allows the contrary to be predicted. Einstein, one of the greatest minds of the century is said to have begun to talk only at the age of five. While one must be vigilant in keeping an eye out for language problems in children, it must be realized that a delay in the production of the first words is not necessarily a sign that a deficit exists. Parents need to be particularly attentive to problems of comprehension, however.

It must be kept in mind, too, that Elizabeth Bates's experiments relied on reports by parents who had been given lists of words to be checked off depending on whether they thought their child had produced these words. Imitations were accepted: children who were good imitators—in particular, ones who were good at imitating animal sounds—were therefore apt to be wrongly credited with knowledge that they did not yet possess. Word form was not taken into consideration, though the different sorts of correction to which children's pronunciation was subject varied a good deal as well. The willingness of parents to accept a more or less deformed version of a target word as an instance of that word is, to a large extent, a cultural phenomenon. This kind of survey approach is liable to a certain underestimation or overestimation on the part of parents, depending on the importance they attach to children's early performances. Overestimation is found with particular frequency in the United States, where competition, even in this domain, begins quite early. The precociousness that Bates recorded is unquestionably related in part to this problem of estimation. "Vocabulary illusion" remains very strong in certain cultural settings that favor a referential approach to language learning and aim at teaching children the greatest possible numbers of words. Comparative studies, that we will look at later, have shown that French and Japanese mothers are much less anxious than American mothers to promote early speech in their children. But the studies by Bates and her colleagues do, in any case, permit us a glimpse of the extraordinary individual variability in children's production vocabulary between the ages of eight and thirty months and help us to clarify our thinking on this subject.

Trials and Errors

Producing a word involves several steps. One must first select the appropriate word in the repertoire, then find the phonetic program that allows it to be realized, and finally give a sequence of commands to the various articulators to arrive at the pronunciation of the word.

How are these processes actually carried out by the child? We have evidence that the adult begins by programming words in a metrical form that supplies specifications for syllabic rhythm and, in the case of some languages, stress and accent as well. When this framework is constructed, it is filled with segmental material (consonants and vowels, or syllables) and, perhaps, again depending on the language, tonal material. In the child, we have seen that in most cases the metrical framework is only partially filled up by segmental material. It is therefore on the basis of a framework adapted to the specific metrical elements of the language—syllables or feet—whose content is unspecified, that articulatory gestures will be programmed. In certain children, the only salient features that are present are those of the intonation contour. All of us are familiar with the phenomenon of having a word "on the tip of the tongue" when we try to recall a rare or foreign word or a proper name. We may know, for example, that it contains three syllables (the frame), that it begins with a /g/ and ends in something like /ol/ or /or/. We have coded the metrics as well as an ending (vowel plus lateral consonant), but the segmental filling of intermediate syllables is missing, preventing us from correctly producing the word *glycerol*. The child runs up against

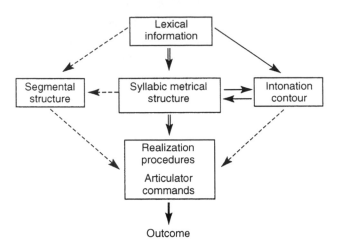

```
                    ┌─────────────────┐
                    │     Lexical     │
                    │   information   │
                    └─────────────────┘
                              ⇓
┌──────────────┐    ┌─────────────────┐    ┌──────────────┐
│  Segmental   │ ◀--│ Syllabic metrical│ ─▶ │  Intonation  │
│  structure   │    │    structure     │ ◀─ │   contour    │
└──────────────┘    └─────────────────┘    └──────────────┘
                              ⇓
                    ┌─────────────────┐
                    │   Realization   │
                    │   procedures    │
                    │                 │
                    │   Articulator   │
                    │    commands     │
                    └─────────────────┘
                              ↓
                          Outcome
```

Figure 5.5   Model for the production of words in young children. Children rely on the metrical structure and intonation of words without necessarily programming the whole segmental structure.

problems of this type. Phonetic patterns only vaguely specify the appropriate succession of syllables and segments (see figure 5.5).

Adding to these difficulties is the fact that, at the end of the first year, the child's control of the articulatory system is still uncertain. This system, responsible for executing the phonetic program in the form of a series of complex neuromuscular instructions, is not ready to produce all possible programmed sounds. Mastery of the supralaryngeal articulators has not yet been acquired. Thus, a beginning of the type /fl/ may be correctly coded without the child being able to produce it. Most children under the age of two years are incapable of producing consonant groups such as /gr/, /pr/, /fl/, and so on. All these factors explain why the form of children's words typically differs from that of adults. The principal studies on this topic are due to the group at Stanford led by Charles Ferguson (Ferguson and Farwell, 1975; see also Vihman, Ferguson, and Elbert, 1986; Stoel-Gammon and Cooper, 1984). His group found that early words exhibited many of the same formal characteristics as the productions of babbling: syllables are most commonly of the consonant + vowel type and are introduced by labial or dental occlusives. Words that end in a consonant are rare; when they do, the terminal consonant is more often a fricative than an occlusive. For the most part, there is no discontinuity between the forms of babbling and those of early words: certain children thus give the impression of choosing their first words from among the babbling sounds that they like to produce (Vihman, Ferguson, and Elbert, 1986).

Let us take the example of a French baby we studied, Émilie, whose babbling favored syllables introduced by velar consonants such as /g/ or /k/. She chose the majority of her first fifteen words from among those introduced by a velar occlusive. Sometimes such words are unexpected in so restricted a vocabulary—words such as [kje] and [kuja] for *cuillère*, [ke] for *clef* or the name Mickey, [ka] for *sac*, along with [kaka] for *canard* and [gogo] for her stuffed animal (a dog). This behavior, while frequently encountered, is not invariable: some children show a marked independence with regard to their babbled forms when they enter the domain of words.

Because first words involve programming with reference to a target and therefore require an additional cognitive investment on the part of the child, they often take simpler forms than the last productions of babbling. In an effort to produce a sequence of non-random syllables, children tend to reduce the articulatory demand, which leads them to simplify the forms of these syllables. They tend to choose disyllabic words with repeated syllables or to reiterate one of the syllables of a disyllabic word. They further strengthen their propensity to produce labials (Boysson-Bardies and Vihman, 1991). As mentioned earlier, labial phonemes are the ones favored by young children—particularly young French children.

These early tendencies are constant features of first-language acquisition. By the thirteenth century, Aldobrandino da Siena (1911/ 13th c.) had observed the ease with which children produced words with labial occlusives and repeated (or similar) syllables. He remarked also that the words belonging to the universe of young children are built up in this way: thus, in French, *papa, maman, bébé, poupée*. To this list of words must be added the forms thought of as typically childlike, descended perhaps from the stuttering recommended to nurses by Bartholomaeus Anglicus (1994/13th c.): *bonbon, mémé, lolo, dodo, bobo, popo, wouah-wouah* (the last, in English, the canine *woof woof* or *bow wow*).

In babies younger than twenty months, one finds suppressions of syllables or segments, substitutions of easy phonemes for ones that demand complex coordination of movements, such as the fricatives /s/, /z/, and /ch/ or the laterals /r/ and /l/.

Syllables seem, however, to be a fundamental unit of speech, particularly in French. Considering all the early words of French children, it is rare to find syllables omitted in disyllabic words; omissions amounted to about 8 percent of the total in our studies. Such omissions are a bit more frequent in the first trisyllabic words: [efa] for *éléphant*, for example. But, more often than not, the child uses a technique of filling up or reduplicating syllables that allows the number of syllables to be preserved: [tetefan] for *éléphant*, [papapo] for *paletot* (jacket). The suppression of the first consonant is found in about 7 percent of the productions of French children: [apo] for *chapeau* (hat), [apin] for *lapin* (rabbit).

In English-speaking babies, syllabic omissions in disyllabic words are much more frequent (about 23 percent of the total number). The child keeps only the first syllable of the word, that on which the stress falls. The structure of languages modulates the form of first words very early, such that the types of errors found in the pronunciation of first words do not appear with the same frequency in English, French, and Japanese, for example. Though all children have a strong tendency to omit final consonants—French babies, for example, say [zosy] for *chaussures* (shoes), and [kala] for *canard* (duck)—the structure of English leads anglophone babies to produce more of them and sooner. The systematic reduction of consonant groups is fairly general —[bawo] for *bravo*, and [ke] for *clef* (key). Errors due to phonemic substitutions mainly involve the substitution of occlusives for fricatives, whose production is more difficult—[to] for *chaud* (hot), and [tal] for *sale* (dirty). The distinction between fricatives such as /v/, /s/, /ch/, and /z/ remains difficult for many children until they are five or six years old.

Many children at this stage produce truncations or innovations of words based on coherent strategies. Marilyn Vihman (1978) and Marlys Macken (1993) have studied two kinds—harmonic patterns and melodic patterns. Harmonic patterns consist in assimilating the first consonant to the second consonant of the word (consonant harmony or consonant assimilation), particularly when the latter is a labial occlusive—[papo] for *chapeau*, [papẽ] for *sapin* (pine tree), [tato] for *gâteau* (cake), and [kako] for *Jacquot*. Consonantal harmonizations are frequent in early words. More common than instances of vowel harmony (or vowel assimilation), they also persist much longer.

Melodic patterns indicate constraints of another type that involve specific syllabic schemas. Vihman (1992) gives the example of Alice, whose speech at fourteen months exhibits a canonical and well-established consonant-vowel-consonant-vowel pattern: [baji] for *bottle*, [taeji] for *daddy,* [baeji] for *bunny*, and [ma:ni] for *mammy*. The melodic organization of Alice's schema affects the beginning of the word as well as the rhyme of the second syllable.

Léo, one of our subjects, organized a certain number of productions around /l/, a sound that generally is rare in children of this age. For a brief time he crystallized his productions around a consonant-vowel-consonant-vowel form: [pala] for *pas là* (not there), [bala] for *ballon* [ball], [kola], the name of a stuffed penguin; [kola] for *cuillère* (spoon); [delo] for *de l'eau* (some water), [walla] for *voilà* (there it is), but also [pala] for *brosse* (brush) and [kala] for *canard*, words normally without /l/ in central position.

With many children, however, errors in pronunciation during the first half of the second year remain random, and realizations of a single word vary in the speech of the same child. In the course of a single session, the word *gâteau* was said seven times by Noël in various ways, with only the second syllable holding constant—[tato], [eto], [geto], [kato], [Həto].

In the second half of the second year, children's errors are less erratic. One finds regularizations of certain forms that, while not always correct, show that the child, having acquired the phonetic system, is now in the process of crystallizing the phonological system of his language.

Two Lexicons?

We have seen that children understand more words than they produce. Does this mean that a comprehension lexicon exists that is

distinct from a production lexicon? Does the child have one representation for word recognition and another representation for word
production? The initial lexicon is supposed by definition to contain
the child's knowledge of a word. In young children, this knowledge
is weak: grammatical features and a good deal of information regard-
ing segments and their combinations are absent. It may be that these
phonetic representations and metrical patterns make it possible to
find words but do not give enough information to reconstruct a
word's form. Children therefore would need a production lexicon
that consists of a collection of forms that they recognize, know how
to pronounce, and apply to words exhibiting certain similarities. This
hypothesis might explain why children's comprehension exceeds
their production, why they have a greater facility for imitating than
producing words, and, finally, why their vocabulary increases only
slowly during the first months of production. It might explain why
some children are late talkers: perhaps they demand a more precise
phonetic specification of the lexicon to pronounce words.

But it may not be necessary to suppose the existence of two
lexicons to square these facts with each other. It may be that a single
lexicon has different access routes for perception and production.
These access routes develop at different rates, thus accounting for the
lag of production behind comprehension. The appeal of this alterna-
tive view is that it assigns responsibility for the productions of young
children to the perception lexicon. Indeed, children must recognize
the words they produce. Many examples show that there is a relation
between the choice of the first words and children's favorite production routines. Children are more attentive to words that include
forms that they have practiced during babbling, which often serve as
reference points and models (Ferguson and Farwell, 1975).

Building the First Vocabulary

Among the words of the child's early vocabulary, nouns are plentiful,
while predicate forms (verbs and adjectives) are relatively rare. Certain
studies, particularly ones done in the United States, have insisted on
this predominance of nouns. Even if, among the very first words,

social words such as *hello* and *goodbye,* and function words such as *there* and *more,* are frequent, the majority of the fifty first words are names of objects and animals. Katherine Nelson, J. Hamson, and L. Kessler-Shaw (1993), Helen Benedict (1979), and Elizabeth Bates, I. Bretherton, C. Shore, and S. McNew (1983) have found that nouns make up more than 70 percent of the early vocabulary of American children. According to Bates, however, nouns account for 45 percent of the total when children have a vocabulary of fewer than fifty words. But because this figure included neither personal names (numerous in the speech of American children) nor the animal sounds children use to name animals, she claimed to have substantially underestimated the proportion of nouns in the vocabulary of children. In the same group of children, few verbs were found (3 percent). This is the same percentage that we found in our own studies of English-speaking children in the United States. We will see later how important it is not to generalize these data to children in other linguistic environments. Of the first fifty words produced by French children of the same age and linguistic level, 13 percent were verbs. In fact, depending on the structure of the mother tongue and children's styles of language acquisition, the composition of vocabulary exhibits sizable variations in the proportion of verbs, social words, and nouns.

It is fairly generally the case, however, that there are few verbs in the early vocabulary of children: their meaning is less easily grasped than that of nouns, which are more easily identified in the actual world. As Leila Gleitman (1990) has shown, the learning of verbs depends, at least in part, on the possibility of understanding sentences: syntactic structure constrains their meaning. A sentence such as *The baby is smiling* calls for interpretation of an action that has no object, unlike *The baby picks up a toy* or *The baby gives a ball to her mother.* French, Swedish, and Japanese children, who, in our studies, acquired a fifty-word vocabulary somewhat later, clearly produce more verbs than English-speaking children, no doubt because, being older, their comprehension of sentences is better.

Non-noun forms regularly increase when vocabulary passes from 100 to 600 words. Language gradually moves, then, from simple reference to predication and grammar.

The percentage of names in children's vocabulary may vary considerably, however, as a function of their style. In certain children, almost the whole vocabulary before twenty months is composed of nouns. Their style is called *referential*. For others who use an *expressive* style, one finds a balance between nouns, on the one hand, and predicates and words of the closed class (including adverbs such as *more* and *there*, and sometimes pronouns, articles, and copulas), on the other. These children often use expressions that American authors describe as fixed (such as *gimme* and *allgone*). These utterances are perceived and coded as wholes, and their constituent words are not used productively in other sentences. These formulas are particularly numerous in an acquisition style that favors prosodic division. In other children, who favor syllabic division, they are less often encountered.

"To live is to be different," said Blaise Cendrars (1983/1926). The diversity found in the acquisition of language by children springs from their differing styles. We shall see the various choices made by young French children as they prepare for their entry into language. But diversity is fed also by the variety of languages, places, and cultures in the world, and we shall also look at the differences among children that emerge in foreign climes.

To Each Baby His Own Style

6

From primitive mammals to humans, the genetic envelope opens to more and more individual variability.

—Jean-Pierre Changeux

All the Same and All Different

All human beings share certain instructions, inscribed in the code of their genetic inheritance, that determine the characteristics of the human species. Newborns are all destined to see themselves develop the distinctive marks of their species—upright posture, the faculty of abstraction and generalization, articulate language. They are all genetically programmed to learn to speak. Some researchers have sought, for theoretical reasons, to separate the study of the encoding of language capacities in the human biological system from the study of the implementation of language capacities in the course of development. In recent years it has been fashionable to treat as negligible, if not actually uninteresting, the various effects that differences of language or individual style are liable to produce in paths of acquisition. However, the study of the innate language system and that of the role and limits of variation in this system as a function of experience are complementary and ought not to be separated. The interplay of the possible and the actual in the human being is often much more powerful than some researchers suppose. By ignoring—or denying—

the heuristic usefulness and charm of such differences, they forget Ilya Prigogine's (1987) not-so-provocative suggestion that "universal constants always express a limitation in our manner of doing experiments and seeing nature."

Following Charles Darwin (1871)—who noted that language, though not a true instinct, yet does not merely involve the learning of an ordinary art—we may regard language acquisition as involving an instinctive tendency to acquire a very particular art. The term *art* thus corrects whatever may seem inadequate or insufficient about the term *instinct* so far as human language is concerned.

Armed with a powerful and adaptable device, babies will be able to acquire articulate language no matter what the characteristics of their linguistic environment may be. But artistic variations will appear. Languages are very diverse. Though universal rules no doubt account for the common fundamental features that underlie individual languages, their realizations nonetheless differ greatly. Children learn the language spoken in their environments. They do this in the ways, and within the limits, provided by the genetic determinants of the human species. But this approach also bears the mark of personal choices and experiences with the specific clues furnished by language and culture in realizing an instinctive tendency to acquire the art of speaking.

The diversity manifested by the ways children begin to speak is therefore of the greatest interest, whether it issues from the individual styles of children, their experiences of the language spoken in their environments, or cultural models.

Though they are all alike in their humanity, babies are all different as well: their hair may be blond, brown, or black, curly or straight; their eyes may be blue, brown, green, or gray; their heads may be full of hair or hairless; there are big babies, funny and romantic babies, chubby ones, too; some are easygoing, and others are strong-minded or affectionate or obsessive. All of them are capable of speaking, and each arrives at language in his or her own individual way. The imagination, creativity, and cleverness with which they use their common linguistic tools are fascinating. Some styles of approach are particularly evident among infants. The structure of children's native language, the influence of culture, the ways in which they communicate with their parents, and most especially their own individual style bring us into the domain of choice. It is as though the babies, on hearing language, find themselves in the course of the first year faced with the need to choose from among a series of rival enterprises: "What should I extract from the speech I hear? What should I train my attention on? What are the most important features of adult speech? Which of them can I reproduce? Which of them must I reproduce?" These are the sorts of questions babies might ask when confronted with both their own limitations and an enormous body of linguistic data.

The choices that children are able to make are, fortunately, limited. Their choices gradually lead them to master the pronunciation and basic grammar of a language before the age of six. But from the end of the first year and on into the second year, the choices are still open enough to influence the child's style and performances in quite particular ways.

The age at which the first words are spoken, the number of words produced by the age of two, and the character of early vocabularies vary significantly from child to child, as we have seen. But a still more essential difference is seen in the strategies of production. These suggest that infants have not all noticed the same aspects of the language during the course of the first year.

The attention of certain babies is devoted almost entirely to phonetic elements and the structure of syllables. These babies tend to break up the speech stream into words and select the syllabic structures that they know how to produce. It is on the basis of these units that they build their vocabulary. Their first productions consist of isolated, often monosyllabic words. Their early vocabulary is composed almost exclusively of names of persons, animals, and objects. The style of these children is called *referential* or *analytic* by *Anglo-American* authors such as Katherine Nelson (1973), Lois Bloom (1975), Ann Peters (1977), and Elizabeth Bates, P. Dale, and D. Thal (1995), who, along with others, have inquired into individual differences in the acquisition of language. Opposed to these children, one finds others whose style is called *holistic* or *expressive*. These children concentrate their attention more on intonation contours and the syllabic rhythm of words and sentences than on their phonetic structure. They produce long sequences that resemble sentences with coherent intonation patterns and filled-in syllables. They have fewer nouns in their early vocabulary and more predicates (verbs, adjectives) and ready-made expressions (or formulas). Other children use mixed strategies. Still other children, finally, enter into spoken language only after having first noticed its systematic aspect and having organized their lexical entries phonologically. The differences between referential children and expressive children are particularly clear at the very beginning of language. They progressively weaken—and the gap between the number of nouns and predicates almost disappears—by the time children arrive at a vocabulary of 600 words (Bates, Dale, and Thal, 1995). A comparative approach, which takes into account the structure of different languages, somewhat modifies the definitions of styles proposed by Anglo-American authors. Depending on the native language to be learned, their effectiveness is not, in fact, always the same. But the universality of these two basic tendencies, the referential and the expressive, is confirmed.

They may be illustrated by means of a few examples.[1] There exist many variants, with some modes of access being more extreme or more marginal than others, but the individual styles examined here correspond to the most common strategies found in children between the ages of one and two years.

Émilie, Sean, and Timmy: The Minimalist Strategy

Émilie is a lively little girl, always in motion, who loves to dance and move about but also enjoys looking at picture books. Her mother is attentive to her behavior, which already shows signs of impishness, and calls her "my little clown." She takes care of her daughter herself and attaches great importance to her linguistic progress. She teaches Émilie the names of objects by trying to have her name them in actual situations; she does not, however, correct the child's pronunciation. Émilie willingly takes part in these games and readily agreed to the ones we proposed for the purpose of collecting samples of her vocabulary. We monitored her progress from the age of ten months until fourteen and a half months. She then said twenty-five words in the course of the half-hour we spent recording her. Of the French children whom we studied, she was the first to acquire a twenty-five-word vocabulary. To enter into the world of words, she had adopted a simple and effective style.

In her babbling, Émilie avoided long, intonationally modulated productions. Monosyllables represented 61 percent of the babbling productions observed between ten and thirteen months, as compared to an average of 40 percent for the other French children. She strongly favored occlusives. These represented 60 percent of the consonants in her babbling, whereas they represented only 49 percent of the consonants in the babbling of the other French children.

These same tendencies were found in her first words. Émilie paid particular attention to the articulatory information in words, privileging the syllables and consonants that she had already produced in babbling. She thus systematically selected adult words that contained one of the two most frequent articulatory patterns in her babbling. Her technique was thus simple and consistent:

1. Choose words including a syllable introduced by an occlusive, either velar (/k/) or labial (/b/ or /p/).
2. Shorten disyllabic words to monosyllables by keeping only the syllable that begins with an occlusive. The position of the syllable in a given word does not matter, and only this syllable is reproduced, whether it occurs at the beginning or the end of the word.
3. Preserve the pertinent vowels, thus allowing homophones to be avoided.

A bit later, she added another rule:

4. If necessary, reduplicate a syllable when it is reduplicated in a word or when this word is disyllabic.

Until the acquisition of a twenty-word vocabulary, Émilie's vocabulary was therefore largely composed of monosyllables made up of a consonant—either /k/, /b/, or /p/—and, in general, the vowel that follows this consonant in the word of the language, in this case French. It included the following forms:

Mickey	[kχ]
canard	[ka]
clef	[ke]
cuillère	[kkɪ]

sac	[ka] or [qa]
balle	[ba]
bouton	[bø]
bébé	[bebe]
chapeau	[po]
pomme	[pɔ]
pépé	[pɛ]
papa	[papa]
petit pot	[popo]

A little later, at the stage when twenty-five words had been reached, she was to augment her disyllabic productions, either by introducing certain words with a supporting vowel /a/:

à boire	[Abɥa]
poire	[abɥa]
brosse	[abɔ]
tortue	[æɦy]

or, more generally, by reduplicating the syllable:

babar	[baba]
pompon	[pupu]
cuillère	[kokoa]
canard	[kaka]
lapin	[papa]
voiture	[ɦity]
gogo (name for a stuffed animal)	[gogo]

At twenty-eight to thirty words, 40 percent of the occurrences were disyllabic and 8 percent had more than two syllables. On the other hand, dental occlusives (/t/ and /d/) had begun to appear, but no fricatives or laterals were yet found. Émilie's vocabulary remained quite concrete, formed exclusively of nouns. The thirty words that she now said were all names of objects, animals, or persons.

With Émilie one sees routines prepared in the production of babbling serving as first words. Indeed, she accentuated the phonetic tendencies of her babbling in these words. Occlusives grew to comprise 88 percent of her consonants, as against an average of 55 percent for the other French children. When, toward fourteen months, disyllables came to be added to monosyllables, the majority of them were words composed of repeated syllables. This type of word represented 64 percent of Émilie's disyllables, as against an average of 35.6 percent in the other French children. Along with frequent reduplications, one finds many omissions of syllables—14.7 percent as against an average of 6.6 percent for the other French children.

Émilie's technique of production reveals other characteristics that show how hard she tried to operate simply and efficiently, naming things with the least possible articulatory effort. This profitable strategy allowed her very rapidly to develop a vocabulary that, despite the poverty of its consonantal repertoire, contains relatively few complete homophones. In fact, words could be distinguished by their vowels. Moreover, these words were easily spotted by adults, for Émilie had mastered their production and pronounced them only in contexts that eliminated ambiguities.

In parallel with the cross-linguistic research we conducted into the acquisition of phonology in young children, Marilyn Vihman and R. Miller (1988) analyzed the first productions of English-speaking children in the United States. Many of them were found to exhibit a minimalist strategy of Émilie's type. In certain individuals, this strategy was pushed to the limit.

Sean produced 77 percent of his words in the form of occlusive consonant + vowel monosyllables. He selected his targets: 71 percent of the words he attempted were monosyllabic. When he risked disyllabic targets, he reduced them to monosyllables in 65 percent of cases. He even avoided the simple expedient of reduplicating syllables. Only 12 percent of his word productions were of this type, the lowest percentage found in the productions of the twenty children in the various linguistic groups we studied.

The repertoire of Sean's fifteen words included the following forms:

ball	[bʌ]
bear	[be]
book	[bu]
bowl	[bʌ]
baby	[peːp]

bike	[pæ] ou [bæ]
cat	[tæ]
duck	[da]
dog	[dɔ]

One sees that the first productions are monosyllabic homo-phones or near-homophones. Sean's phonetic patterns are comparable to those of Émilie. The words are constructed around two schemas. The first consists in a simple consonant-vowel syllable with a labial occlusive /b/ or /p/ and a vowel; the second consists in a consonant-vowel syllable introduced by a dental occlusive /t/ or /d/. Sean's vowel inventory, like that of Émilie, is rather varied: /a/, /æ/ and /o/, /e/, /i/.

The development of Sean's repertoire did not proceed by the introduction of disyllables but by attempts to produce words ending in a consonant. The consonant Sean added was always the velar /k/, in final position:

block	[ba:k]
clown	[kəæ:k]
bug	[bʌ:k]

Sean's repertoire, even at twenty-five words, was still composed for the most part of very simple forms, demanding only a minimum in the way of articulatory gestures and remaining quite close to the initial consonant-vowel combination. As with Émilie, Sean's first words were principally names of specific objects, animals, and persons. Sean is a good example of the referential, or analytic, style.

To see the law of least effort pushed to an extreme, let us look at Timmy, another American child of the group analyzed by Marilyn Vihman. His productions were characterized by a rigid ideal schema that served for all adult words without exception. Two types of consonant-vowel syllables formed the base of his vocabulary. The vowel was always /a/. The two consonants were the labial occlusive /b/ and the velar occlusive /g/. Timmy's words beginning with /b/ corresponded to adult words beginning with /b/, but his words introduced by /g/ are words that, in adult speech, contain a velar, either at the beginning or end of the word.

The rigidity of his vowel pattern places Timmy apart from the two first children. Émilie and Sean varied their vowels while Timmy stuck with only one, /a/. At sixteen months, he produced fifteen words, all pronounced either [ba] or [ga]—all of them, therefore, perfect homophones. Timmy utilized [ba] (or [pa]) for *bell, ball, block, box, bird, boy,* and *goodbye* and [ga] (or [ka]) for *car, kitty, quack, cup, cow,* and *girl.* It was only at seventeen months that a few timid variations in vowels were found, as well as disyllables, generally the result of reduplications of the primitive consonantal pattern. The vowel pattern of the disyllables was likewise rigid—the first vowel was /a/ and the second one /i/:

please	[pai:]
cookie	[kaki]
bottle	[babi]
coffee	[gagi]
daddy	[da^{d}di]
goodbye	[gabi]

Adult words whose phonetic structure is very far from the ideal schema were completely reorganized as a function of this schema:

| light | [iga] |
| lizard | [ɹaɪɹa] |

For Timmy, the minimalist strategy was not profitable: at seventeen months, his repertoire remained very poor.

What influence do native languages and maternal practices have on children's styles? Comparative approaches allow us to relate the frequency of different strategies in learners of a given language to the prosodic organization and phonological system of this language. Since the segmentation cues of the native language affect the form of representations, it makes sense to look for their effects on children's productions. The frequency of monosyllabic words in English, and the alternation of strong and weak syllables, favor the production of monosyllables in English-speaking children. The rapid development of vocabulary in many American children is connected with the choice of monosyllabic targets as well as the energy that mothers devote to teaching nouns to their children. They are very indulgent in the case of a syllabic schema that yields many homophones, and they accept these homophones as distinct words. It would be interesting to know how far such indulgence accounts for the persistence of quite incorrect pronunciations, as with Timmy. Most of the French mothers whom we met showed themselves to be more demanding about pronunciation and would not count as words forms that were as rigid and as generally used as those tolerated by American mothers. This may perhaps explain why Émilie, though she produced only quasi-homophones, abandoned her particular ideal schema more rapidly than her American peers abandoned theirs.

Simon, Léo, and Marie: The Charms of Conversation

At eighteen months, Simon is credited by adults with only a few words. And yet he talks. How he talks! His conversation is as charming as it is interesting. He delights everyone with his way of joining in the discussions of guests during meals. He intervenes with long "sentences" to signal his agreement with some general idea or to put "questions" to one person or another. The intonation, the phonetic and syllabic rhythm of his "sentences" are so characteristically French that a foreigner would marvel at their linguistic maturity. Similarly, on the telephone, he can hold polite and altogether pertinent conversations. Simon is a very funny, cute, and sociable little boy, with plenty of cheek.

We monitored his progress over ten months with pleasure, since he made us laugh a great deal. In the course of ten sessions, between the ages of eighteen and twenty months, we recorded 2,554 vocalizations. Simon was very much at ease during these recording sessions and spoke almost incessantly. He commented on everything he did, holding forth while arranging and putting away the toys that were regularly given to him, which occasioned many soliloquies. But he also conversed with the experimenter, replied to questions, and made demands. Most of the time it was impossible to find a correspondence between his productions and words or sentences in adult language. It is difficult to describe these productions. Did they amount to a kind of private language? Certain syllabic sequences, which were very stable from the phonetic point of view, were related to well-defined situations in the outside world, but for the most part the sequences he produced were too irregular for any correspondences with external events to be detected. Simon spontaneously produced a few words but not many; on the other hand, he willingly imitated others when asked. In any case, he understood perfectly what was said to him, which did not surprise us.

His sentences consisted most frequently of sequences of three, four, or five syllables; sometimes longer sentences were found (7 percent of the total). Disyllabic utterances were predominant, representing one-third of Simon's productions.

Simon seems to have concentrated his full attention on the prosodic form of adult speech, but he also had a large syllabic repertoire. The peculiar character of his entry into speech, however, depended on intonation and rhythm. He chose an intonation contour corresponding to a group contour of words or sentences and filled it with various well-articulated syllables. His choices of intonation contours were quite diverse and well suited to French. In monologues, as in his dialogues with adults, he varied slightly rising contours, sharply rising contours (interrogatives?), and falling contours in pertinent ways. Rising contours made up the majority, a circumstance favored by the intonation of French and typical of the speech of most French children. But in dialogues, when the adult's questions invited a declarative response, Simon's replies were characterized by a flat or falling contour. Thus, in response to the question "What are you doing?," his contours were found to be flat or falling 80 percent of the time, whereas such contours represented only 45 percent of his productions as a whole. In the case of his soliloquies, however, a majority of his contours were found to be rising, though it also happened that Simon sometimes contrasted two successive intonations, giving the impression that he was questioning himself (see figure 6.1).

Figure 6.1 Example of an intonational schema with contrasting contours produced in the course of a monologue delivered by Simon at nineteen months.

When Simon pointed and added a "ça"—the demonstrative pronoun *that*, one of his only comprehensible words—at the end of
sentences, these were almost always (in 92 percent of cases) characterized by an important vocal variation—either a significant rise in
intonation, which seemingly indicated a question, or a significant fall,
which could be interpreted as a comment (see figure 6.2).

In fact, Simon must have known and used more words than
adults recognized at this stage, but his strategy of filling in functional

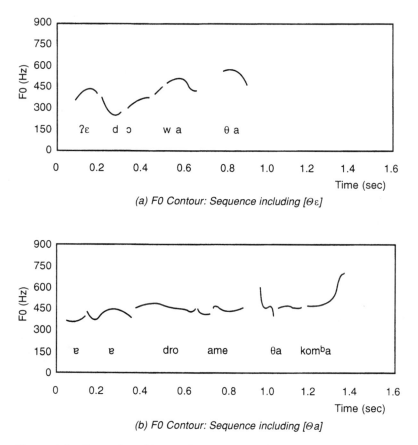

(a) *F0 Contour: Sequence including [Θε]*

(b) *F0 Contour: Sequence including [Θa]*

Figure 6.2   Examples of intonation contours of productions of the "comment"
type made by Simon at nineteen months: *(a)* intonation ending with the
demonstrative *ça*, *(b)* intonation including the demonstrative *ça*.

intonation contours with syllables masked whatever words he may have been using. From time to time, adults guessed a word or even a sentence of several words, but in the course of the first two months during which we recorded him (between the ages of eighteen and twenty months), most of Simon's speech was incomprehensible, if not uninterpretable.

The syllables that he used to fill in intonation contours were well formed according to the rules of French. Moreover, the distribution of his consonants and vowels reflected the phonetic distribution of French. If Simon was speaking a private language, it was a very French one.

And were his comments really incomprehensible? No doubt for us they were, but not for him. Eight months later, we had him listen to the comments that he had made at the age of twenty months. His reaction was wonderful. Delighted, he nodded or shook his head in approval or disagreement as he listened, commented on what he heard, laughing or looking cross. In short, Simon at the age of two and a half recognized his own melodious speech at twenty months and reacted to it with pleasure, even enthusiasm.

We followed Simon for ten months. Throughout he adhered to this intonational strategy while tending toward realizations more in keeping with adult models. Though he augmented his production of isolated words, he nonetheless did not give up producing sentences, which over time became more and more comprehensible. He entered into language with sentences.

His strategy was not effective if the number of words understood by adults is taken as the index of linguistic development. But it was eminently profitable from the social point of view. In any case, it did not prevent Simon, at three years of age, from having a language that was quite articulate, well adapted, and very rich.

Simon pushed the expressive style to the other extreme, privileging prosodic and rhythmic components while subordinating the phonetic component. As a practitioner of this style, he displayed an unrivaled brilliance and panache.

Pushed less far, the expressive style seems fairly common among French children. In fact, the prosodic organization of French facilitates division not into words but rather into larger prosodic groupings or into clauses. The intonation contours of French are marked, as we have seen, by the lengthening of terminal syllables and, frequently, by a rising contour indicating the continuation of speech. These cues are clearer at the boundaries of groups of words or sentences. Stress contrasts, which structure the segmentation of words in pitch languages, do not exist in French. On the other hand, unlike English words, French words are more often than not disyllabic. French children are therefore encouraged by prosody and the other properties of their language to carve up adult speech into units larger than the word. We observed this tendency in Simon and also in two other children whom we studied, Marie and Léo. Like Simon, they have an expressive style in which the prosodic component plays a great role, without, however, excluding a phonetic component well adapted to French.

Marie is the fifth child in her family; her brothers and sisters range in age from four to seventeen. In this company she alternates between solitary games in which she becomes deeply absorbed and games with others in which she is an eager participant. Like Simon, Marie is in the habit of delivering monologues. At eleven months, again like Simon, she willingly imitates, and this gives rise to games in the course of which Marie repeats sounds and syllables spoken by her mother. This greatly amuses her and makes her laugh. These games can go on quite awhile, causing her mother to remark, "It's as though one is having a real conversation with her." Indeed, at the age of one year, one did have the impression that Marie responds to questions.

Mother: Do you want to go beddy-bye? What do you want to do?

Marie: (with a resolute and falling intonation): baegm:gmba:yae weo jajaja: m:: bam.

However, sentence-type productions correspond more frequently to soliloquies. Marie produces many polysyllables (75 percent of the words she produces are disyllables or polysyllables).

At thirteen months, Marie said five words in one session:

ça	[ta]
bravo	[babθ:]
poupée	[bøβə]
nono	[nɛno]
maman	[mamæ̃:]

Already one finds a majority of disyllables but no special phonetic pattern. It was only at seventeen months that we heard fifteen words in one session. As with Simon, the words were buried in sentences of four to seven syllables (34 percent of her productions), which hampered their recognition. Let us look at Marie's repertoire at fifteen to twenty words:

attends (wait)	[ættæ]
bateau (boat)	[hatø]
bébé (baby)	[bebe]
dodo (sleep)	[dodo]
c'est beau (it's nice)	[təbɔ]
c'est beau ça (that's nice)	[ebotsa]
Jacquot [name]	[ɹæko]
poupée (doll)	[popi]
Tintin [name]	[tat̃ɜ]
tartine (toast)	[ta:tinn]
Ludovic [name]	[ado]
papa (daddy)	[papa]
non (no)	[næ̃]
Nono [name of a teddy bear]	[nonɔ]
maman (mommy)	[memæ̃]
Mimi chat [name of a cat]	[hemɹetsA]
papillon (butterfly)	[papɨdʐA]
voiture (car)	[voaɟy]

Although consonant-vowel-consonant-vowel forms predominate, this repertoire reflects an indubitable phonetic and semantic variety. The target words are mono-, di-, and trisyllabic. Marie has succeeded in carving out, as it were, expressions and groups of words such as *c'est beau*, *c'est ça*, or *Mimi chat*. The variety of forms is surprising. Only five words exhibit a pattern of reduplicated syllables; in the others, the vowel and/or consonant varies. If one counts all the occurrences of words (instead of counting each word in the repertoire a single time), one finds a large percentage of disyllables (48 percent) and productions containing three or more syllables (30 percent). Marie uses the principal vowels in French: *a, é, e, ou, o, i, u*. She favors occlusives, with the exception of velars, but also produces words beginning with nasals—/m/ and /n/—and fricatives—/v/. The only consonants still missing are laterals, but in a session fifteen days later, at the age of seventeen and a half months, Marie said twenty-five words, among them several words (or expressions) containing /l/:

houlà [emotive expression]	[ʊlla]
là (there)	[halla]
c'est là (it's there)	[əlla]
l'eau (water)	[ɛ:llo]
elle la met (she puts it)	[haləme:]

Marie has certainly not chosen a minimalist strategy. There is a great difference between her performance and that of a child such as Timmy, credited at the same age with only fifteen words and displaying only two phonetic forms, with targets selected for these forms. It is probable that Marie, like Simon, had for a certain time produced more words than we were able to identify. Marie's pronunciation being clearer than Simon's, we later noticed the presence of embedded words such as *poupée* in "panichi*papé*nedla"—a word immediately confirmed by Marie, who clutched her doll and again said "pepé". The same was true for the expression *c'est beau ça* in the series "a:én*ébo*cha" and for the word "chapeau" in "deneda*apo*."

From the age of seventeen months, Marie, while continuing to produce many sentences of five to six syllables interpretable by adults, said enough isolated words for one to be able to see that her vocabulary was growing rapidly. She pronounced true sentences of two or three words: "*e poupé la amoua*" (it is my doll), for example.

Her repertoire of meanings was also much more varied than the repertoires of Émilie, Sean, and Timmy. In addition to names of objects, Marie used verbs, adjectives, pronouns, expressions such as *c'est beau* and *houlala* that signal emotions, and made comments about others, such as *elle la met*. She used the pronoun *moi* (me).

Marie's expressive style led her to enter language with small sentences and expressions having very pertinent intonations. This choice no doubt delayed the appearance and recognition of her first words, but they were there, having been prepared before being heard, and enabled Marie to develop a varied vocabulary, a rich space of linguistic representations, and a sparkling phonetic palette.

This strategy for language entry was also adopted by Léo, with some personal variants. Léo is a lovely first-born child. He is sociable, serious, and sensible; he likes music and happily hums to himself. His mother speaks to him in a very adult way, using relatively long sentences. When she looks at a book with him, she not only names the images but comments on them at length. Léo is looked after at home by a nanny who speaks French.

He was only ten months and eighteen days old when seven words were noticed in his productions. This is very early. His words referred to demands or otherwise were terms of social interaction:

allô (hello)	[ɔ:ɟlo]
donne (give)	[do]
tiens (take it)	[ta]
eau (water)	[ʎɔʎɔ]
encore (more)	[hælo]
papa (daddy)	[papa]
maman (mommy)	[mamɛ̃]

Two peculiarities characterized Léo's choice of words. He privileged disyllabic words and, surprisingly, ones containing an /l/. His productions were long. At this age, as in the case of the words that were to follow, 73 percent of Léo's babbling productions contained more than two syllables, and certain sequences included up to eight or nine syllables.

At fourteen months, Léo was credited with fifteen words. These words occurred either in isolation or as part of sentence. Thus "*allô*," already found in the course of preceding sessions, was now pronounced [ele] and included in the sequence [elodija], which Léo said on picking up the telephone.

It was only at seventeen months that twenty-five words were heard in a session. But these words were varied and, most of the time, embedded in expressions:

Donne, donne-le (give, give it)	[dɔ̃]
là (there)	[la]
allô (hello)	[ʔɜlɜ]
bébé-poupée (baby doll)	[baba]
coucou (peek-a-boo)	[kukku:]

maman (mommy)	[mamɛ̃]
papa (daddy)	[papa]
Koko [name for a stuffed penguin]	[kokɔ]
bouton (button)	[tʉtʉ]
manger (eat)	[məmɒ:]
ballon (ball)	[ba:la]
Didier [name]	[ɟyty]
pas là, parti (not there, gone)	[pəla ǂpɜdli]
petits trous (little holes)	[tʰɨtʰɔ]
non non non (no no no)	[nɛ̃ nɛ̃ nɛ̃ nɛ̃]

Words and expressions—numerous in the vocabulary of twenty-five words—illustrate the pattern he favored in babbling and first words. It consists in putting the consonant /l/ in medial position in consonant-vowel-consonant-vowel and vowel-consonant-vowel words:

allô (hello)	[alo]
de l'eau (some water)	[dəlo]
voilà (there it is)	[wallaʰ]
cuillère (spoon)	[kola]
brosse (brush)	[pʌla]
canard (duck)	[kwala]
Koko [name for a stuffed penguin]	[kolɛ̃]
chapeau (hat)	[bølo]
là la dame là (there the lady there)	[ləlɪdala]
canard dans l'eau (duck in the water)	[balaᵈdalo]

Léo often adds "là" (meaning "there") at the end of a word. Why this choice of a phoneme that is difficult for most children? Several explanations can be advanced—the influence of Léo's name, which begins with /l/, for example—but this is pure speculation. Only Léo could tell us.

As with Marie, the semantics of Léo's first words are multiple and not limited to concrete words. One finds expressions, verbs, and adjectives. Léo began to produce some sentences, however, in which unidentified syllables survived. Thus, the sentence "tato ya pae reXka pélla" answered the question "Est-ce que tu veux un gâteau?" (Do you want a cake?), when there were no cakes in the room.

Conversation first! The strategy that seems connected with the charms of conversation assigns a particular weight to the intonation and rhythms of utterances. It favors expressivity and the choice of semantically more varied words than those usually found in the vocabulary of children this age. Expressions and small sentences appear even before the child has a vocabulary of more than fifty words.

Acquisition sometimes takes place at the expense of segmental fidelity, as in the case of Simon. But the sequences parodying sentences of the language are spoken with ease. The intonation contours and phonetic filling are pertinent and could pass for possible sentences in the language. But are the filler syllables really put in at random? On closer examination, productions that seemed unintelligible sometimes revealed surprises when placed in context. It became clear that children did, in fact, produce stable forms—interpretable words and expressions—but their role appeared so secondary by comparison with the overall expressivity of these productions that they were not recognized as such. Such utterances can also hide the early production of actual sentences, such as in Léo's preceding example. The expressive style may delay the development of the lexicon (in particular, of nouns), but it favors social integration and entails the development of a more varied lexicon than the minimalist strategy.

The style of another child, Minh, a little English speaker studied by Ann Peters (1977), displays the same characteristics as those of Marie and Léo. The structure of languages guides, rather than determines, children's choices, and individual differences persist that are not reducible to external constraints.

Learning strategies that are more global and more expressive are frequently encountered in French children. Anglo–American authors take a dim view of such strategies. They regard expressions as fixed formulas and maintain that the expressive style involves less variety in lexical categories and less rapid vocabulary development. The prosody of French naturally encourages global segmentations, however, and in fact the style of French children is often richer and far more productive than the picture of it found in the English literature. On the one hand, it appears to favor future grammatical acquisitions and sentence production, and, on the other, its allegedly fixed formulas are not so fixed as they may seem.

Marc had learned the expression *y a quelqu'un?* (is someone [there]?) that his brother used when he could not manage to open the door to the lavatory. Marc, in his turn, tried to open it saying "*yakéqun?*" Fixed expression? It looks very much like one. One day an adult passed Marc on his way to the lavatory and teasingly said to him, "*Yaquéqun?*" "*Non,*" Marc replied, "*ya pas quéqun!*" (No, there's no one [there]). So this expression was not absolutely fixed. A negation could be correctly introduced in it.

Children who choose this style, and the members of their families have certain characteristics in common. Their mothers speak in elaborate sentences that often are longer and more adult than those used by other mothers. These children are frequently more attracted by music and show a precocious talent for it. Thus, Marie, who is now eight years old, is an excellent cellist. Ann Peters concluded her analysis of Minh's productions on a speculative note, proposing that his love of music (singing and piano playing) suggests the Gestalt strategy of language production may be related to the development of his right hemisphere, while his analytic strategy is related to left-hemisphere development. In this form the proposition remains highly speculative. A more nuanced formulation may correspond to a certain linguistic reality, however.

Charles, Noël, and Others: The Middle Way

The middle way is wide. Some of the children who follow it wander about and dawdle; others walk quickly and straight ahead. Many children mix the analytic style and the expressive style, while displaying a measure of moderation that places them nearer the former than the latter. Their strategy is not as reductive as that of Sean or Timmy or as systematic as that of Émilie or as flamboyant as that of Simon or Marie. Taking the word as their basic unit, these children seek to reproduce its constitutive syllables. Omissions, syllabic reduplications, and preferential schemas are encountered, of course, but none of these techniques is able by itself to account for their first productions.

Charles is a well-behaved first-born child who goes to a daycare center. He busies himself with his blocks and his toys, but, having a sociable disposition, took time to assist us in our inquiry into first words. His first words were heard at twelve months:

au revoir (goodbye)	[awa]
boum (boom)	[ba]
non (no)	[nɛ̃:]
donne (give)	[da]
manger (to eat)	[ʔæm]
beau (nice)	[bø:]
maman (mommy)	[mɒmɒ̃]
papa (daddy)	[pəpʌ]

Charles's words are generally monosyllabic but varied. Among the ten first words there were none for objects or things, but they did include terms necessary for satisfying vital, fundamental needs. At fourteen to fifteen months, Charles disposed of a vocabulary of fifteen to twenty monosyllabic and disyllabic words, fairly varied on the phonetic level. The usual labial and dental occlusives are found along with nasals, fricatives, and laterals:

bravo (bravo)	[bʌbo]
poupée (doll)	[bɛpʌ]
boire (to drink)	[bʌ]
gâteau (cake)	[toto]
canard (duck)	[kʌ:nɒ]
maman (mommy)	[mɒmɒ̃]
non non (no no)	[nɛno]
au revoir (goodbye)	[awʌ]
assis (seated)	[aʃ]
chaussures (shoes)	[tʃetʃu]
ours ([teddy] bear)	[ʒo]
ça (that)	[taʰ]
chaud (hot)	[øʃø]
allô (hello)	[alo]
caméra ([video] camera)	[mʒmãʀa]

One finds names, adjectives, and relational words in this list but no expressions or formulas. Charles sought to produce the principal features of each word and did not hesitate in the face of dental fricatives /s/–/ʃ/, which are generally very rare in children's first words.

He produced /l/s and /r/s. He carefully preserved the number of syllables in words—no reductions, even when presented with a tri-syllabic model. By contrast, the initial consonant was sometimes omitted:

chapeau (hat)   [apo]
lapin (rabbit)   [apA]

However, more often than not, he respected as far as possible the syllabic and phonetic structure of the target word.

Charles was to go on, sensibly enough, adding to this simple and well-balanced vocabulary. At fifteen and a half months, he said more than twenty-five words per session, all quite understandable. Calmly continuing on his way, already by the age of sixteen months he had achieved a sizable vocabulary without giving in to the temptations of truncation or to grand flights of incomprehensibility.

Noël is a third child and holds his own with two sisters, both of whom have sharp and lively minds. His five first words were found at thirteen months:

manger   (to eat)
papa   (daddy)
poum   (boom)
wouah wouah   (woof-woof)
coucou   (peek-a-boo)

He produced fifteen words in a session at the age of sixteen and a half months, and twenty-five at seventeen months and twenty-three days:

pas là   (not there)
poupée   (doll)
paletot   (jacket)
lapin   (rabbit)
pomme   (apple)
pain   (bread)
l'eau   (water)
biberon   (bottle)
banane   (banana)
gâteau   (cake)
main and "pas main"   (hand and "not hand")

Noël's production is significant because he repeated words several times. His vocabulary, like that of Charles, contained monosyllables (38 percent) and disyllables (59 percent), but few polysyllables (3 percent). Noël reduced some syllables and consonants. In this there was no apparent system—no expressions and little syllabic reduplication. It was a repertoire essentially based on occlusives. It seems that Noël sought efficiency but without adopting a minimalist strategy. His vocabulary contained many names of objects (particularly words for food) but also verbs, adjectives, and social terms.

Comparing the approaches of Charles and Noël, on the one hand, and that of Émilie, on the other, we see that they share certain characteristics. Nonetheless, Émilie's approach was clearly more systematic. Simon, Marie, and Léo exhibited a very different approach. The styles of these children stand in contrast to the others with respect to length of productions, intonation, percentage of words with repeated syllables and syllabic reductions, frequency of production of expressions, percentage of names of objects, and, in general, choice of targets.

Henri: Stepping Back to Move Forward

Parents of children who are alert and understand quite well what is said to them but who refuse to speak—while their little cousins the same age are already "talking a lot"—should be reassured to recall that Einstein did not speak until he was five years old. But let us be careful not to generalize too far: not all children who begin to talk late are geniuses, and in the case of some, alas, it is a sign of more or less profound problems. Even so, one should not worry too much when children do not speak before the age of two and a half years. It must be established first that the child hears correctly, understands what a child of his age ought to understand, and has no other behavioral problems. Given this much, one must wait until the child decides that he can speak. Certain children decide this only when they have already worked out a highly structured system. In such cases, one witnesses more often than not a kind of triumphal entry into speech that leads the child to acquire a vocabulary of more than

200 words, and of sentences made up of two words or more, in only a few weeks.

Henri is an example. He did not babble—or babbled very little. His hearing was then checked; it turned out to be completely normal. A quiet child but lively and attentive, he began to walk early and showed signs of a teasing spirit that revealed a capacity for subtle observation. Everything around him he found of great interest. His principal pleasure was being read to. From the age of ten months he "asked" adults to read the books he brought to them and stayed put for quite a long while, listening to them describe pictures and tell stories—already for several hours at a time when he was twelve months old, according to his mother. He indicated which things he wished to know the names of by saying "hein" with a rising intonation. Though he repeated animal sounds, he never said a word and never let himself be tricked into saying one. In the following little game, adults were always the losers:

Adult: The dog goes "woof."

Henri: Woof.

Adult: The cat goes "meow."

Henri: Meow.

Adult: The turtle dove goes "coo."

Henri: Coo.

Adult: The child says "auto."

Henri: *(no reply but a small half-smile).*

At thirteen months, Henri recognized the form of words, for he pointed to pictures of things whose names he was told. He knew their meaning: he said *vroom* for motorcycles and sniffed and pretended to cry when shown the picture of a little girl crying. He understood quite well what he was asked, while nonetheless remaining quite silent. He did not say a word, much less speak a sort of private language as Simon did. At the age of sixteen or seventeen months, finally, two or three words were noticed. They were seldom spoken and then with caution.

Papa, maman, and *non* were the only words he habitually employed until the age of eighteen months. At twenty months, Henri suddenly came out with all his accumulated vocabulary: more than thirty words for animals and objects and more than fifteen relational words, such as *dedans* (inside), *là-haut* (up there), *attends* (wait), *encore* (more), *a pas* (hasn't), *ça y est* (that's it), *donne* (give), *tiens* (take it), *regarde* (look), *allô* (hello), *au revoir* (goodbye), and so on. At twenty-two months, there was an explosion of words. In one half-hour session, Henri displayed a vocabulary of more than 150 words and spoke genuine two- and three-word sentences.

No general patterns were detectable, but it was clear from the beginning that a system of complex rules governed the structure of his words. Henri could pronounce every phoneme, but only so long as they occurred in certain places within a word; if not, he worked out a system of regular substitutions.

Thus /m/ was perfectly spoken in medial position and in initial position before /a/. But in initial position before another vowel, /m/ was replaced by /b/ if the second consonant of the word was voiced and by /p/ if the second consonant of the word was unvoiced. Henri kept the labialization of the initial consonant but denasalized it:

musique	(music)
maison	(house)
messieurs	(sirs)
méchant	(mean)

Similarly, /s/ in initial position was replaced by the consonant of the following syllable (consonant assimilation):

serpent	(snake)
sapin	([fir] tree)

but it is correctly reproduced in medial or final position:

messieurs	(sirs)

The development of Henri's language then continued very rapidly. At thirty months he had a vocabulary containing rare and sophisticated words, and his sentences were syntactically very elaborate.

He had entered into the phonological stage almost immediately. Clearly, he had stored words but used them only when their encoding had been specified within a system. He refused the approximative productions of minimalist strategies and the flights of the conversational strategy. Somehow he had managed to jump over the period of the first fifty words that is associated with a more global process of encoding in order to begin producing words on the basis of already well-specified representations.

Although Henri may not have attempted to produce sounds during babbling, his productions were from the outset well articulated and quite comprehensible. The idea that babbling is a necessary articulatory exercise finds itself refuted in this case.

Late speakers have not been studied much, but in most of the nonpathological cases mentioned in the literature, one notices that by the time the late-talking child does begin to speak, an elaborate and coherent system grounding the structure of the first words is already in place.

Are these children perfectionists? Are they shy—or scientific? Why do they make this radical decision to refuse to use words so long as they have not been structured by a system? Is it a matter of waiting for the left hemisphere to develop further, refusing in the meantime to make use of the global data provided by the right hemisphere? The experimental field remains open to such speculations.

They Are the Ones Who Choose

Children's styles or modes of accessing language show themselves to be incredibly different. How can this be explained on the basis of common mechanisms?

The tools that children possess allow them to segment and recognize words and sentences, no matter what the structural features of the language may be or how great their complexity, variety, and subtlety. However, the capacities of attention, the cost of carrying out perceptual and cognitive calculations, and the limitations of memory impose constraints. Children choose to privilege certain hypotheses. In doing this they adopt a personal approach to language. Their choices determine a style. The more restricted the vocabulary and the more limited the modes of expression, the more pronounced the style will be.

Several reasons may be given to explain the differences among children's approaches. First, each child has a particular focus of interest in his or her environment. Children who are intrigued by external objects and inclined to analytical thought will tend to adopt a referential style. Some of them, as we have seen, will be particularly systematic and organized in their productions. Their vocabulary, based on information supplied by the physical environment, will be almost exclusively made up of names of objects—nouns.

More extroverted children, who like to express themselves and to feel part of a sphere of social communication, adopt the expressive style. Their approach is more global, and they are more sensitive to the music of the language than to phonetic precision. Children who have a gift for music, or who show a special interest in it, probably choose a style influenced by intonation contours.

The influence of the right and left hemispheres with their respective affinities for prosody and music, on the one hand, and for analysis, on the other, probably underlie the preferences of children in processing the prosodic and phonetic components of speech. Language functions rest on the interplay of processing components that may be lateralized in one or the other hemisphere. Studies in this domain have only just begun.

The child's intellectual capacity is not at issue in any case. Perhaps the future degree and form of intelligence and imagination can be guessed at, but young children have far too much undisclosed ability and far too much creativity for us to confine their potential within the limits of premature predictions.

Their mothers' style also plays a certain role. Mothers who teach words, name objects, and wait for the child to do the same channel the child's choice toward a referential style, whereas a more personal, affective manner steers a child toward an expressive style. If the mother's language is impoverished, the child may adopt a restricted mode of speaking or speak a sort of private language. The style of the child and the style of the mother are not interdependent: sometimes they influence each other without either one wholly determining the other.

Another factor plays a crucial role in the choice of styles for approaching articulate language, and that is the particular language the child hears. Languages in which word order is essential to the meaning of a sentence and that have few inflected variations, as well as pitch languages that favor individual words as the unit of segmentation, may dispose the child toward the referential style. By contrast, languages whose prosody divides speech into phrases and sentences may more readily elicit holistic styles. No large-scale study has yet been undertaken, however, that would make it possible to understand the respective shares of these factors in shaping the ways in which spoken language is acquired during the first years.

Let us venture a comparison. If the engine that guides the development of language is indeed the same for all children—if languages and cultures, like the chassis, tires, and suspension, influence the mode of driving—then infant strategies represent the individual style of the driver, who displays verve or cautiousness, risk or care and forethought. The engine is robust, in any case, and, barring accident, all drivers reach their destination. Likewise, all children reach their destination—the acquisition of their native language—no matter which strategy they adopt at the outset.

Languages, Cultures, and Children

7

Diversity is a way of dealing with the possible.
—François Jacob

Language and Socialization

Socialization is the greatest force for language learning there is. All children have fundamental needs that manifest themselves in certain forms common to early vocabularies. But to communicate with the people around them, every child must be recognized as a speaker—that is, each child must speak the language of his or her environment and conform to certain formal and social customs imposed on both the language and the culture. Children's vocabulary grows out of contact with the adult language, which, from the outset, dictates the objects in the world that must be seen and learned, the manner in which these objects are to be spoken of, and the modes of expression that allow children to be recognized as speakers and understood.

Language is not taught. Mothers wait impatiently for their children's first words, however, and most of them wish to assist, or rather accelerate, the beginnings of speech in their children.

Learning to talk does not have the same meaning from culture to culture. The expectations of parents differ, as do the objects of speech. Thus, the Kaluli (Papuans of New Guinea) reckon that children know how to speak when they know how to say *no* (mother) and *bo* (breast) (Schieffelin, 1986). Words that might have been said previously are scarcely heard, and Kaluli mothers speak little to their infants for they think that they have no comprehension. This attitude is extreme, but, even in cultures nearer our own, depending on the country and social milieu, the modes of interaction and the content and forms of mothers' speech are still very dependent on the image of the child in the culture and on parents' expectations.

American mothers encourage their child to talk and, above all, to name. They want their child to be early in everything, while French mothers think that the child has plenty of time to learn. French mothers do not watch for linguistic performances, feeling instead that the child ought to be happy and well behaved and should play a great deal. Thus, too, German mothers expect their children to speak later than do Costa Rican mothers. One could multiply examples of the discrepancy in expectations of mothers in different cultures and consequently of discrepancies in parents' hearing children's first words. But these words depend also on the structure of each language.

The linguistic and conceptual organization of the world is manifested in languages by the forms and images that are peculiar to them. The pragmatic and efficient cultures of the West are oriented to a greater or lesser degree toward the production of nouns: "Each thing is to be called by its name," as the French popular saying has it. English, with its exceptionally rich vocabulary, is altogether remarkable in this respect. The reverse is true in certain Asian languages, such as Korean and Japanese, in which verbs and adjectives are used to refer. It is not necessary for a Japanese speaker to mention an object when it is present or when the subject of conversation is understood by an interlocutor. Thus, one can say "is cracked on the edge," without specifying what one is talking about, if the general subject of conversation concerns Heian vases, for example, and an example of such a vase is in the room. Similarly, someone who has just received a bouquet of roses can say "smell delightfully good" without having to mention the flowers themselves. Japanese and Korean are languages that take the role of interpersonal relations particularly into account in the mode of expression. One may therefore expect the lexical schemas of Japanese and Korean children to be different from those of children whose language requires explicitly nominal reference.

Among Western languages, it is also possible to predict different vocabulary patterns. Word form (length and syllabic structure) is highly monosyllabic in English, whereas in French and Italian words are for the most part disyllabic or trisyllabic. There are also marked contrasts between languages in which word order grounds meaning (most notably English) and languages in which word order is freer and relations are indicated by morphological inflections (such as Russian and Turkish). Additional sources of variation include the percentage and form of nouns in the language, the proportion of grammatical words, the presence or absence of inflections, the function of auxiliaries, and many others.

Cultural Milieus and First Words

If you ask an American mother whether her little girl of thirteen months speaks, more often than not she will exclaim, "But of course. She knows at least fifty words." What might be called *vocabulary illusion* is very strong among American mothers. Put the same question to the mother of a little French girl the same age, and she will usually tell you, "No. Apart from *papa* and *maman*—and even these are not yet clear—she doesn't say any words. But she has plenty of time."

Small American children are not all linguistic geniuses. Why, then, do French and American parents respond so differently?

The strategies that parents use to direct their infant's attention to the physical environment and to encourage participation in the social world are differentiated early on. At three months, the characteristic style of interaction in a culture appears in the relations between infants and the members of their family circle (Fernald and Morikawa, 1993; see also Toda, Fogel, and Kawai, 1990; Bornstein, Tamis-LeMonda, Pêcheux, and Rahn, 1991).

These styles are reflected in the ways in which mothers react to their children's first words. Let us compare how they present words to their children while looking at a picture book together. We go first to San Francisco. Mary, the mother of Sue, is seated next to her little daughter of fourteen months.[1] They are looking at a book and come across a picture of a cat:

Mary: Look at the cat. It's a cat. Look at the cat. Cat.

Sue: [a].

Mary: Good girl. You say "cat, a cat." Good girl.

Mary's encouragement of her daughter comes through loud and clear. The next picture is one of a dog:

Mary: Look at the dog. A dog. Say, "Dog, dog."

Sue: [ʌ].

Mary: Good girl. You say "dog." Say "dog."

Sue is credited by her delighted mother with two words, *cat* and *dog*.

Several studies have shown the highly didactic tendency of American middle-class mothers. They try to draw the child's attention to objects in the immediate environment and to have the baby name them. The learning of names of objects and also of persons (television characters, for example) occupies a large place in mother-child exchanges, which rest on typical naming-game questions ("What is this?," "Who is this?," "Who is she?," "Can you say 'juice'?") followed by the correct answers ("That's your toe," "That's your bottle," "It's a butterfly," and so on). Throughout, the little boys and girls are very strongly encouraged—and congratulated, no matter what the result of their attempts.

We go now to Paris, to Marie's house. She points out images in a picture book to her son, Léo:

Marie: Look at the cat, Léo. It's black with a little pink tongue. It's a nice cat. You see the cat?

Léo: a.

Marie: Yes, it's a cat. It drinks milk and goes meow.

Léo is not specially encouraged in his productions. His mother laughs at the idea that Léo's "a" might be considered a word. But Léo has no doubt learned something about cats.

There is no forcing here and no insistence that the child repeat words. French mothers are not concerned with performance; they are concerned to bring out details in stories by commenting on the pictures—even with very young children. They use a more adult language with the child and are less interested in adapting themselves to his whims than in preparing him to "speak nicely."

Most French mothers accept a production as a word only if it is relatively well pronounced. The sound [ta] for *chat* ("cat") is not always accepted (or even understood), especially if the child uses this form to refer to other things. Minimal pronunciations are much more readily accepted by American mothers used to words being underarticulated. Timmy, for example, had a recognized vocabulary of fifteen words revolving around the two forms—[ba] and [ga].

Let us now go to visit with a Japanese mother, Fusako, and her son Taku. Fusako points to a picture and asks: "That one?" Taku says nothing. After a time, his mother resumes:

Fusako: Oh, there, there, the baby does not talk. Taku, where is the car?

Taku: Bubu (car).

Fusako: Bubu, oh good. It's a car, yes. Isn't that a pig there? Oh, this book is difficult! There are many people!

The mother puts herself in the child's place and formulates the sorts of comments he might make. She also questions him about the picture, but without insisting and often without giving the answer when the child does not reply.

For the Japanese, the baby's approach to language is therefore very different. The Japanese mother intervenes much less often in the baby's learning of names and comments less frequently on the baby's exploration of his surroundings. But she insists more on the quality of her communication with the child and on his integration as an individual in the social group. Rules of politeness, attention to the feelings of others, and the ways in which one communicates one's own impressions to others are much more highly valued in the language. The attitude of Japanese parents will change drastically with school-age children, but with young children it is sensitive and noninterventionist.

Most English-Japanese intercultural studies find that Japanese children acquire words late (Fernald and Morikawa, 1993). But one detailed study shows that their first words are systematically longer and correspond to more varied semantic forms. All this counts more than being able to name the greatest possible number of objects, which is considered by Japanese mothers to be secondary in comparison with the quality of expression.

Of course, these behaviors cannot be generalized to all mothers. But many studies show that the concern with early performances, whether verbal or motor, is much greater among parents in the United States than in France or Japan (Tamis-LeMonda et al., 1992; Bornstein et al., 1992; Morikawa, Shand, and Kosawa, 1988). In these latter countries, the approach is more personal and more poetic.

The use of words in remarks addressed by mothers to children reveals much about the style of adult discourse and the topics of interest to which it attempts to draw the child's attention. Analyses of the remarks of French, American, and Japanese mothers illustrate this point in particular. Thus, the use of nouns in the speech of American mothers is 35 percent, compared with 25 percent in that of French mothers (Vihman et al., 1994). In another study, nouns were found to make up 40 percent of the comments made by American mothers to their children, as against 20 percent of the comments by Japanese mothers (Fernald and Morikawa, 1993).

Subjects of Conversation of French, American, Swedish, and Japanese Children

How do such different attitudes manifest themselves in the first vocabulary produced by the child? Among the babies whom we recorded in large modern cities—Paris, San Francisco, and Stockholm—certain categories were found to be constant in the vocabulary employed. These included names of familiar people whom the children call by name (mothers, fathers, and often grandmothers) and names of objects necessary to survival—(foods, drink, the utensils used to feed them, such as bottle and cup, the clothes they put on and take off before and after a walk, such as shoes, and so on). We also found names of certain household objects, particularly ones that make noise and attract attention (such as the telephone) or that are movable and ride on wheels (toy cars and trains, for example). In all the vocabularies studied, great importance was accorded to animals and what they say: the sound that an animal produces often serves to name it. Thus a dog is a *bow wow*, a duck is a *quack quack*, and so on.

One of the great needs of the human species, play, is also manifested in early words. Probably every language in the world has a name for the game of hide-and-go-seek, the playful mimicking of appearance and disappearance. We found it among the first words of all the children of the different linguistic groups that we studied. Finally, another aspect of infant behavior revealing identical fundamental preoccupations in different cultures is that of social communication: words for saying *hello* and *goodbye* are found in most early vocabularies.

Individual variations, the influence of culture, and the structure of the language already affect the choice and distribution of the child's first words, however. Examining the behavior of our French, American, Swedish, and Japanese toddlers in relation to the language and culture of their maternal and social environment, as manifested in their first words, we see how persistent cultural variations are and how far away Valéry's "time of the finite world"—an age when the world has been completely explored and standardized—remains.

Consider the distribution of types of words in the early vocabulary of these children, from the time they uttered their first word until they produced twenty-five words in a session (which corresponds to a vocabulary of between thirty and fifty words, depending on the child) (see table 7.1).

Despite a certain community of words reflecting general needs and universal language categories, and beyond individual variations, characteristics specific to each group began to emerge in our babies.

First, a bias exists toward producing nouns (see table 7.2).

In addition to their propensity to produce nouns, whose referents are concrete and stable, rather than verbs, the children tackled other grammatical categories. These categories are particularly sensitive to the structure of the language.

Table 7.1. Distribution of the types of words in the vocabularies of French, American, Swedish, and Japanese children having fewer than fifty words.

	People	Animals	Objects
French	9	23	44
	8.1%	20.7%	39.6%
American	16	24	51
	13.1%	19.6%	41.8%
Swedish	12	18	44
	11%	16.5%	40.3%
Japanese	7	20	29
	6.3%	18.2%	26.3%

The Hedonism of French Babies

Between ten and eighteen months, nouns accounted on average for 64 percent of the productions of the French babies, and verbs accounted for 24 percent. If, like Swedish babies, they were clearly less sociable than Japanese or American babies, they seemed to be the most hedonistic. Although the number of types of words relating to food was comparable to that of the Americans and Swedes, the French babies used them markedly more often (15 percent of their productions being food related as against 4 to 6 percent for the other groups). They also had more terms to designate clothes but fewer to designate other objects in the surrounding environment. The variety of their verbs was less great than that of the Swedish children, although the frequency of verb productions was the same. The French verbs referred to agreeable activities or states (reading, drinking, eating, giving) rather than to energetic physical actions, as in the Swedish samples. Expressions such as *That's nice* were common among French children, as well as relational terms such as *more*. Surprisingly, moreover, this latter word, used by all the French children studied, was not found among the Swedish or the Americans and was used by only two of the five Japanese.

Table 7.1 (*continued*)

Verbs and Adjectives	Onomatopoetic Forms	Social Expressions	Number of Words
24	2	9	111
21.6%	1.8%	8.1%	
11	5	15	122
9.0%	4.1%	12.3%	
25	1	9	109
22.9%	0.9%	8.2%	
26	15	13	110
23.6%	13.6%	11.8%	

Table 7.2. Relative production of nouns and verbs (and other grammatical categories) in the vocabulary of French, American, Swedish, and Japanese children.

	Nouns		Verbs and Others	
French	76	68.5%	35	31.5%
American	91	74.6%	31	25.7%
Swedish	74	67.9%	35	32.1%
Japanese	56	50.9%	54	49.1%

The Pragmatism and Sociability of American Children

American children are pragmatic: they name the people around them as well as the characters of English nursery rhymes (Humpty-Dumpty, for example) and of modern American cartoon mythology. We found three times more proper nouns in their speech than in that of Japanese children. They also name animals (in this respect, our subjects did not differ from the members of the other groups) as well as objects of everyday life (which accounted for 36 percent of their productions).

[*Memi*]—money—was the reply of one sixteen-month-old American baby when his mother showed him coins. Certainly the child did not yet understand their use, but the word already belonged to his vocabulary.

We found surprisingly few verbs and adjectives in the early vocabulary of American children: verbs made up 9 percent of the total (compared with more than 21 percent in the other three groups). This figure agrees with the findings of most authors who have studied the distribution of first words among children in the United States.

The American children we followed were as sociable as their Japanese counterparts and were more so than French and Swedish children: 15 percent of their productions took the form of greetings.

A number of reasons may be advanced to explain the high percentage of nouns in the vocabulary of small American children—the importance of word order in English, the frequency of monosyllables, stress patterns, and the tendency of American parents to encourage their children to name people and things.

The Taste for Action of Swedish Children

Like the French, the little Swedes we studied were unsociable in their speech. But they were the most active of the lot, at least to judge from the number of action verbs in their vocabulary: *ga* (to walk), *hoppa* (to jump), *dansa* (to dance), *gunga* (to sway or rock), *sitta* (to sit), *tanda* (to light), *rita* (to draw), *tanka* (to fill up with gas), *backa* (to back up), *klappa* (to applaud). They were more interested than the French, Japanese, or even the Americans by household objects: words such as *klocka* (clock), *lampa* (lamp), *pall* (stool), *dörr* (door), and *stuga* (cottage) were found in several children. Thus, Swedes at the age of eighteen months were active and interested in their homes.

The Aesthetic Sense of Japanese Children

The group of Japanese children was distinguished by the preponderance in their productions of words belonging to a grammatical category other than nouns. It is interesting to see how the civilization that young Japanese children grow up in, which expresses itself through a use of language quite different from that in the West, marks their early vocabulary in spite of fundamental similarities due to the common abilities and needs of all young children. The Japanese language is often structured, as we have seen, around verbs that it puts at the end of sentences—a position that is particularly salient for all children.

The five Japanese babies that we followed had a more restricted vocabulary than the babies of the other groups for personal names (7 percent versus 15 percent for the Americans) and for nouns denoting toys, foods, and so on. They displayed a slight environmentalist or poetic tendency, which led them to mention elements of nature rather than household objects: *rain, cloud, leaf, sun,* and *moon*. They had a more extensive vocabulary in other grammatical categories that already betrayed the concern, peculiar to their culture, for one's relations with others. They made the most frequent use, of all the children, of social terms such as *hai* (hi), *haro* (the English loan word hello), *dozo* (please), *arigato* (thank you), *akushu* (let's shake hands). Japanese mothers are careful to ensure that children use polite phrases.

Many of the forms recorded reveal the importance attached to communicating with others and mentioning "states" and impressions: *atta* (I found it, here it is), *totte* (can you give it to me?), *are* (what is the matter?), *jatta* (I did it), *owatta* (it's done), *aishi* (delicious), *kire kire* (very pretty), *kawai* (cute).

In addition to this vocabulary, one finds a set of adverbial forms peculiar to Japanese, especially onomatopoetic forms. These are not reserved to infantile language, as in Western cultures. They permeate the sensibility of all Japanese, being commonly found in poetry and works of literature (Shibatani, 1990). Encountered in everyday life as well, they reflect physical sensations—visual and auditory sensations as well as more subtle feelings and complex concepts. Japanese babies are very fond of saying *jaja* to express the sound of a water fountain, *picha picha* for the splash of icy water, *kon kon* for the bang of a hammer, *goto goto* for a knocking sound, and *liko liko* for a gentle tapping. Even the noise made by people when they sleep—*gu gu*—and the sparkle of light—*kira kira*—have their place in the early vocabulary of Japanese children. These expressions will therefore represent more than 50 percent of the productions in the typical thirty-word vocabulary of Japanese children and give it a very different coloring than that of English-speaking children.

But All the Children of the World

Only nineteen words, or 12 percent of the total, were found to be common to the lexicons of the French, American, Swedish, and Japanese children (that is, were said by at least one child in each of these groups). To calculate this proportion, words having an equivalent function were grouped together, even if they did not correspond to precisely the same transcription—for example, *eau, juice, saft* (lemonade), and *jusu*, the basic drinks for the four groups of children, respectively. It comes as a surprise that terms having common functions or references for the four groups should make up scarcely more than a tenth of their total vocabulary, considering how many fundamental needs children share in common.

Fifteen of the nineteen words found to be common to all the groups are names of people and animals and social terms. Rounding out the list were a deictic (a term that serves to indicate or point out, such as *this* or *that*) and a negation. In English, these words were *daddy, mommy, baby, eyes, dog, duck, bird, bear, juice, cake, ball, shoes, car, there* or *that, not there, peekaboo, no*, and words of the type *goodbye* and *hello*.

Cultural practices therefore strongly orient the semantic choice of children's first words. If the groups are considered independently, one notices that 30 to 40 percent of the words used are common to at least two children in the same group. Individual preferences thus contribute less to variability than does membership in a linguistic and cultural group.

A certain minimum in the way of favorable conditions is enough in most cases to guarantee that children, being endowed with specific faculties, will begin to utter words between the ages of one and two years. However, they need to make use of all the resources at their disposal if they are to succeed in achieving command of the language. Taking into account the phonetic, prosodic, and syntactic structures of their language, as well as the available methods for transmitting these structures, children choose a mode of accessing speech that suits their temperaments, but the opinions and expectations that adults project onto children will also affect their choices.

Speech Becomes Language:
Eighteen to Twenty-Four Months

8

A German scholar has said that every child acquires in his first three years a third of the ideas and knowledge that, as an old man, he will carry to the grave.

—Fyodor Dostoyevsky

A New Stage

A few months after they have begun to speak their first words—between eighteen months and two years for the majority of them—children enter into a new stage. Important modifications occur in their language behavior. Their expressive vocabulary suddenly increases, the pronunciation of words becomes less erratic, and utterances composed of several words appear. Parents have the impression that children are now really beginning to speak, and not without reason: the grammatical system of the adult language is perceptible in the linguistic productions of the child.

The mention of grammar usually causes adults to shudder, and one may wonder what relationship tiresome school lessons have to the combinations of two or three words produced by young children. But we are not Molière's Monsieur Jourdain: we know that the grammatical competence that allows us to produce sentences does not depend on grammar lessons. The essential elements of grammar are known before they are taught, for they are an essential part of our capacity to express ourselves. But how can we follow the structuring of grammar through the end of the second year?

A grammatical system is a vast entity that takes in phonology, vocabulary, morphology, syntax, and the functions of communication that are made possible by these aspects of language. Between eighteen and twenty-four months, each of these aspects evolves while children learn the grammatical principles that govern language. Children do not construct fairly complex sentences until after the age of two years, when we finally can follow their successive acquisition of the grammatical rules (or syntactical and morphological principles) of the language. But by the end of the second year, children have entered this last stage, following the stages of babbling and first words, in which their grammatical talent flowers.

The Explosion of the Lexicon

At this point the child says only some fifty isolated words or expressions. How does the beginning of this new stage in the lexicon—the pronunciation and combinations of words—manifest itself?

When children attain an expressive vocabulary of about seventy words—which corresponds to a recognition vocabulary of more than 200 words—a veritable explosion occurs: suddenly they say four to ten new words a day. This growth in vocabulary entails a reorganization of the systems responsible for representing and producing words. The child's vocabulary is transformed into what is called a *phonological lexicon*.

At the beginning of the second year, the first spoken words are represented in the child's repertoire as units whose construction is relatively unanalyzed (Ferguson and Farwell, 1975; Macken, 1979). In all likelihood, they are recorded only with reference to prosody, syllabic structure, and a few articulatory features. When the number of memorized words increases, this method of representation is no longer sufficient. Such undefined representations do not allow the items of a large vocabulary to be distinguished, stored, or produced. Children must therefore somehow put their lexical house in order, so to speak, by arranging words in a systematic way that guarantees rapid and reliable access to the various elements of their vocabulary. This arrangement involves a more precise analysis of both the phonetic segments of words and their combination and also grammatical information. It is now a question of integrating in the lexicon the phonological rules that control the pronunciation of words and the morphological rules that govern their construction.

The Discovery of Phonology

Phonology is the part of grammar that accounts for the knowledge speakers have of the sounds peculiar to their language and of the specific organization of these sounds in it. More simply, phonological rules govern the production of words. Up to this point we have seen children discover the phonetic system of their language—to notice and learn how to generate the sounds necessary for producing the words of the language. But it remains for the child to master the rules that organize the relations among sounds as they are pronounced—the adjustment between neighboring sounds and within each particular pattern of tone, stress, and intonation. Each language possesses its own particular phonological system, and the rules of this system are complex.

The words in a lexicon are necessarily organized according to the sounds in a phonological system. A word in a language is not a ready-made form that can be recognized or produced as a whole; it is a form that must be reconstructed. Accordingly, its rules of construction must be known. The sound–based word substitutions that young children actually make show the complexity of the information necessary to reconstitute and produce a word. Slips such as saying "pony" instead of "mommy" supply evidence that speakers assign phonemes within a strict framework according to a definite order and that, in doing so, they are liable to make attribution errors. On the other hand, because the forms of pronunciation for words and series of words obey relative, rather than general, rules, they are complicated. In English, for example, one says *cat=s* but *dog=z*, *Pat=s* but *John=z*. In French, the [t] in the middle of the word is pronounced but not the final [t] in "*petit*" if one says "*le petit chat*"; the final [t] is pronounced, however, in the phrase *le petit enfant*, while the silent [d] at the end of *grand*, in a phrase such as *un grand éléphant*, is pronounced as a [t], and so on.

To understand and pronounce words, adults therefore refer to a lexicon, or mental dictionary, containing a series of lexical entries. These give the meaning of a word—that is, what it signifies as well as information about its sound form and its grammatical properties. The information about sound form supplies the order of succession of phonemes and the rules of their combination. The grammatical component determines the syntactic and morphological properties of the word. It indicates the word's category (such as noun or verb), affixes and inflections (singular or plural markers and verb endings that, in languages such as French, specify tense and mood), gender (masculine and feminine), and so on. In these markers, syntactic and semantic information meet. They specify the meaning of the word and the ways in which it may be combined with other words in constructing sentences—in short, how it is to be used, together with its sense and reference.

This encoding appears at the end of the second year. By this point children know how to articulate sounds in the form of syllables. They have selected the most frequent phonetic patterns of their language. They now turn to the formal system that organizes the combination of sounds in their language and connect it with the grammatical features that permit them to produce sentences.

The reorganization of the system for producing words is therefore characterized first, as we have seen, by a sudden growth in vocabulary. Whereas earlier it took children five or six months to go from one to fifty words, it now becomes possible for them to regularly learn between four and six new words per day.

This growth of vocabulary is accompanied by a change in how children produce forms of words. Production becomes more regular, if not more correct. New forms are the principal beneficiaries of the changes brought about by the new rules of pronunciation. Children often resist reorganizing the pronunciation of words previously acquired and continue pronouncing them in the old way, which has been strengthened by frequent repetition. With new words, however, children manage to pronounce correctly the phonemes that they continue to avoid or alter in the words of their early vocabulary.

The study of errors illustrates the construction of the phonological system, in the course of which segments acquire their value, which is as much individual as relational. Children first look for regularities in pronunciation and display a tendency to systematize them. In doing this, they generalize certain regularities and so are led into error. A classic example is the little boy studied by Lise Menn (1971). Daniel initially produced the words *down* and *stone* as [doewn] and [don], respectively. Later he came to have a nasal harmony rule and pronounced *beans* as [minz] and *dance* as [nans]. He began, then, to generalize this rule and to pronounce the first two words, which previously were correctly introduced by an occlusive, as [noewn] and [non].

Our little friend Henri provides a good example of the search for systematization and harmony in French. At twenty-two months, he used complex rules that changed the first consonant of a word introduced by /m/ (followed by a high or midhigh vowel) into an occlusive, voiced or not depending on whether the second consonant of the word was voiced. In *monsieur* [møsjø], which he pronounced [pøsjø], and *méchant* [meʃã], pronounced [peʃã], /m/ was replaced by /p/, an unvoiced occlusive, since the /ʃ/ is an unvoiced fricative; whereas in *musique* [mizik], which he pronounced [bizik], and *maison* [mezõ], pronounced [bezõ], /m/ was replaced by /b/, a voiced occlusive, since the fricative /z/ is voiced.

This search for harmony among the consonants of a word shows that the child no longer refers to a global form but to relational structures: the articulatory features of a segment are related to those of other segments of the word. These transitional forms last only for a brief time, however. Increasingly, productions become adapted to those of adult speech.

Of course, the phonetic aspects of pronunciation—those connected with the physiology of the vocal apparatus of the child—do not disappear in this reorganization. Certain difficulties of pronunciation that we had seen in the first fifty words survive, sometimes persisting until the age of four or five years. Consonantal groups and the production of the liquids /l/ and /r/ will pose problems for certain children for a long time yet. Final devoicing sometimes survives in children's productions: it is easier to say [pat] than [pab]. The distinction in the word *chaussette* between the fricatives /ʃ/ (as in *chaud*) and /s/ (as in *saucisse*) is an articulatory pitfall still encountered by French adults if they try to quickly say a sentence like *Les chaussettes de l'archiduchesse sont sèches, archisèches*. In the history of the Gauls as retold by Uderzo and Goscinny, the creators of the famous series of *Astérix* comics, Obélix carries menhirs rather than obelisks, though his name as pronounced by children would seem better suited to the latter objects. The pronunciation of [ix] remains a major difficulty for children until the age of five and longer. Beyond these, individual errors persist. It is really not before the age of six or seven that the temporal organization of articulatory features catches up with that of adults.

Children's behavior thus suggests a profound reorganization of their capacities for processing language. Can physiological correlates for this behavior be detected?

The Modification of Cerebral Responses

The present state of our knowledge suggests that speech is processed during the first two years of life according to a dual system: an analytical form of phonetic processing is reserved for phonemes, and a more global form is used to handle words. According to this hypothesis, neither the course of maturation nor the functional development of the associated neuronal systems occurs at the same rate with regard to syllables and segments, on the one hand, and intonation contours, on the other. The increase in vocabulary and the emergence of regularities in word production, which manifest themselves between eighteen months and two years, result from the integration of these two systems. Indeed, the phonological encoding of words requires processing that is more specific than that of speech segments and more analytical than that of holistic forms. Does the emergence of this mode of processing and the encoding of words involve other cerebral systems than the ones involved in the encoding of holistic forms? Does the neuropsychological approach make it possible to confirm hypotheses formulated on the basis of analysis of behaviors?

Recent studies by Debra Mills, S. Coffey, and H. Neville (1993a, b) have sought to measure the potentials evoked in response to presentations of words that are known and unknown to children as well as to recordings of words that are played backward and so do not correspond to speech sounds. These event-related potentials (ERPs) were collected at eight sites in the brain—the frontal, temporal, parietal, and occipital lobes of both the right and left hemispheres. After having rigorously controlled for the lexical knowledge of their subjects (that is, number of words understood and number of words produced), the authors separated the children into groups. In the first stage of the analysis, they were grouped according to age. One group consisted of twenty children between the ages of thirteen and seventeen months, and the other of twenty children between twenty and twenty-four months. In the second stage, the grouping was done not by age but as a function of the number of words the children had.

The cerebral responses to the three types of stimuli (known words, unknown words, and backward words) was characterized by series of positive and negative deflections: a positive peak (P100) and two negative peaks (N200 and N350). The P100 peak was registered by all the stimuli and represented the acoustic response to the physical parameters of the signal. The N200 and N350 peaks were observed only with words, whether known or unknown. They differed in localization and amplitude from group to group. For the youngest children and for those who produced few words, the negative peaks N200 and N350 were more significant for known words than for unknown words, but this difference in amplitude was the same for both hemispheres and for all sites. In those children whose vocabulary was weak, the cerebral responses were therefore similar in the two hemispheres. There was no preferential hemispheric lateralization for processing known words (see figure 8.1).

The data obtained with children who possessed a more extensive vocabulary are radically different. The N200 and N350 variations are more significant in the temporal and parietal sites of the left hemisphere for known words. These words were therefore preferentially processed by the left hemisphere.

These results indicate that in children of twenty months, known words are processed by specialized systems of the brain, at the level of the temporal and parietal lobes. A degree of hemispheric special-

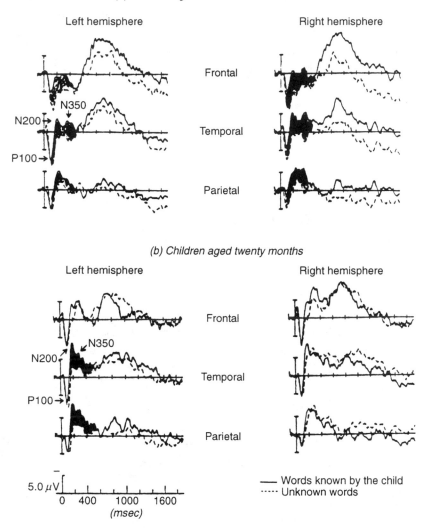

(a) Children aged thirteen to seventeen months

Left hemisphere   Right hemisphere

Frontal

N350
N200 →
Temporal

P100 →
Parietal

(b) Children aged twenty months

Left hemisphere   Right hemisphere

Frontal

N350
N200 →
Temporal

P100 →
Parietal

5.0 μV

0   400   1000   1600
(msec)

—— Words known by the child
····· Unknown words

Figure 8.1   EEG responses of the left and right hemispheres in children of *(a)* thirteen to seventeen months, *(b)* twenty months to the presentation of known and unknown words. It is only at twenty months that there is a noticeable difference between the two hemispheres at the parietal and temporal sites during the processing of known words (from Mills, Coffey, and Neville, 1993).

ization with respect to the processing of words therefore emerges at twenty months or after the acquisition of roughly 100 words. Before this stage, the processing of words is distributed over both hemispheres.

Can one go further in interpreting these data? We have said that caution must be exercised in extending adult results to children, but this does not rule out looking to the findings of adult neuropsychology in search of support for hypotheses being investigated by psychologists and neuropsychologists specializing in child learning. Studies in adult psychopathology show that although the right hemisphere can acquire words and their associated meanings, it cannot actively make use of this knowledge. The static lexicon of the right hemisphere cannot furnish the complete signification of the stimulus required by a phonological lexicon (Hannequin, Goulet, and Joanette, 1987). The left temporoparietal cortex is involved both in the phonological encoding of words and in the accessing of a form of lexical organization that includes the grammatical class of words (Caramazza and Hillis, 1991). The first indications of focalization in children's processing of known words, in the left temporal and parietal sites, would account for the emergent organization of a lexicon with phonological and grammatical components. The behavioral data, showing an abrupt increase in vocabulary, change in the pronunciation of words, and the first combinations of words thus present a picture of the left hemisphere taking over responsibility for processing speech. Prior to this stage, the hemispheric nonspecialization of very young children reflects a system of unanalyzed representations, a partial processing of words, and a lack of flexibility in their use—all characteristics that we have noticed in children's early vocabulary.

Collaboration between psycholinguists and neuropsychologists holds great promise. It will be interesting to see precisely where in the brain babbling and the production and comprehension of first words have their starting points. Such delicate and difficult studies have so far not been undertaken for very young children.

Other, later behavioral stages in the psycholinguistic development of children have been corroborated by neuropsychological studies. It has been shown that when syntactic processes become more automatic, at about ten years of age, the investment of the anterior areas of the left hemisphere in the processing of sentences becomes larger. These areas, including Broca's area, do indeed specialize in the automatic processing of syntax, whereas Wernicke's area (in the left temporoparietal cortex) is capable of syntactic judgments but without the temporal constraints of rapid and automatic processing (Friederici, 1993).

First Sentences

The transition to combinations of words occurs at around twenty months. Variability among children's performances cannot be overemphasized, however, particularly in the case of boundary zones, where it is not yet known whether one may call certain juxtapositions of words sentences or not (see figure 8.2)

As with first words, the discrepancies in children's ages when they produce their first sentences may be considerable. Certain children concentrate on vocabulary before attempting to combine words,

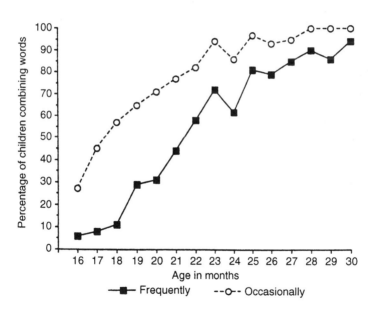

Figure 8.2 Word combination by age: *(a)* percentage of children occasionally combining words, *(b)* percentage of children frequently combining words (from Bates, Dale, and Thal, 1995).

while others seek to put words together very early. Children who are slow to say their first words often make up for it with early first sentences. At the end of the second year, however, most children have begun to combine words. May one therefore speak of sentences?

Before eighteen months, particularly in children having an expressive style, one finds formulas—ready-made expressions such as *est là* (is there), *a pas là* (isn't there), *c'est beau* (that's nice), *veux pas* (don't want)—that might be counted as several words were it not for the fact that they appear to have been learned as whole units. Psycholinguists tend to be cautious in analyzing such productions and, in this case, prefer to speak of formulas or fixed expressions rather than combinations of words. From sixteen months, however, one finds such expressions combined with words.

On the other hand, and very early, children often add particles —neutral elements—to their first words—/a/s and /e/s—whose referents are not clear. Thus,

a main   (Émilie, 12 months, 17 days)
a poire   (Émilie, 12 months, 17 days)
é chat   (Marie, 17 months, 1 day)
é poupée (Marie, 19 months, 26 days)

Examples of this sort are numerous in the productions of children between the ages twelve and twenty months. It is tempting to interpret them as articles or demonstrative pronouns, and, indeed, the coherence and stability of their use is striking. But it may simply be that children have coded ready-made article + word forms such as [lavjo] for *l'avion* (airplane) or demonstrative pronoun + word forms such as [ʃa] for *c'est le chat* (that's the cat). The fact that words are also found in the child's vocabulary without neutral elements does not prove that these added signs are independent. But even if one is unwilling to accept that the grammatical adaptation of the article is already underway by the first part of the second year, it is nonetheless reasonable to suppose that these signs are in the process of becoming articles or demonstrative pronouns.

Two-word sentences gave rise to a voluminous literature during the 1970s. Psycholinguists at the time were greatly interested in the first combinations of words, limited for the most part to utterances of two juxtaposed terms, without articles or prepositions. Productions of this type were said to exhibit a "telegraphic style." Eminent psycholinguists such as Martin Braine (1963), Roger Brown (1973), and Lois Bloom (1970), relying on the distribution of words in these sentences, highlighted sequences composed of two classes of words: (1) operator or pivot words that were frequently used and appeared regularly in combination with a great number of terms and (2) words belonging to a so-called open class, including nouns, verbs, and so on. This second class grows more rapidly than the first. The two principal types of construction characterizing child language are pivot word + open-class word, and open-class word + open-class word.

Constructions of the first kind—such as *more cake*, *no dog*, and *bye-bye boy*—allow the child to construct many sentences by varying the words associated with the pivot words *more*, *no*, *there*, *isn't*, and so on. This type of sentence is used most often to express the presence or absence of objects, recurring events, questions, and refusals.

Constructions of the form open-class word + open-class word— such as *daddy bike*, *drink juice*, and *mommy sleep*—typically express actions and belonging.

The regularity and frequency of these forms in the productions of American children led psychologists in the 1970s to suppose there exists a specific and universal grammar that is peculiar to the child at this age, independent of adult grammar, whose principles regulate the distribution of words. Fairly quickly this analysis encountered reservations among critics, who were able to show that it was neither specific nor universal enough.

High frequency and regularity in two-word productions are not found in all children, nor are they found in all linguistic groups. Word order is guided not so much by a specific grammar as by the syntactic structure of the locally spoken language. Thus, the French baby says *chaussures papa* (*shoes daddy*) to indicate his father's shoes, while the English child says *daddy shoes*. On the other hand, the role of the semantic component in the analysis of these first sentences was underestimated.

The idea of a grammar peculiar to two-year-old children having been dismissed, might one yet suppose there is such a thing as a semantic grammar? It is hard to imagine what the principles of such a grammar might look like without referring to grammatical structures. In fact, though all languages must express conceptual structures of the same type (such as the relation between the agent and the object of an action, membership, temporal relations, and so on), they divide up the structures into different categories and organize the various relations among the words of the language into particular orders. Babies, as we have seen, form concepts before speaking. Their apprehension of external events permits them to work out notions such as an action requires an agent and an object. To be able to speak their language grammatically, however, children must classify the concepts they have formed, classify the words that translate those concepts into categories specific to their language, and then express relationships among the concepts in terms of the ordering rules (or syntax) of their language. Do children have to pass through a stage of inadequate grammar before arriving at this syntactical stage? Why not posit, more simply, that children have a grammar that is incomplete but already adapted to their language, on which later grammatical development is founded? This is what experiments on comprehension seem to show, as well as comparative studies of utterances by children from different linguistic backgrounds and recent studies of bilingual children.

The experiments on comprehension confirm the thesis that children recognize grammatical categories and word order early. Toward sixteen months, American children are already aware of these things. Tested with the preferential methods described previously, they are capable of associating transitive or intransitive verbs with the corresponding situations. They are also capable of interpreting variations in word order, on the condition, however, that the prosody, syntax, and semantics of the sentences presented agree (Golinkoff and Hirsh-Pasek, 1995; see also Hirsh-Pasek and Golinkoff, 1991). Other experiments by Lou Ann Gerken, B. Landau, and R. Remez (1990) show that function words (articles, prepositions, and the like)—which children of this age do not use spontaneously in their productions— nonetheless help them to segment and analyze the sentences that they hear. These experiments suggest grammatical competencies may be masked by the limitations imposed by the programming and realization of speech during the second year.

Studies using comparative cross-linguistic methods reinforce this thesis, showing an early adaptation on the part of children to the structural principles of their maternal language. Virginia Valian (1991) set out to determine whether children, when they are very young, are sensitive to the structure of sentences and, particularly, to the mention of the syntactic subject. English, unlike Italian, requires that the subject be mentioned before the verb. The sentences *Io sono bravo tato* and *Sono bravo tato* are both correct in Italian, whereas only the sentence *I am a good kid* is correct in English. Suppressing *I* makes the sentence *am a good kid* incorrect. Do American children realize that the mention of a subject is necessary in their language? A comparison of the productions of American and Italian children aged twenty to twenty-four months revealed a disparity in the proportion of nominal and pronominal subjects mentioned. There were twice as many nominal and pronominal subjects in the utterances of the American children than in those of the Italian children. Valian concluded from this that the American children had begun to learn, before the age of two, that in their language it is necessary to mention the subject of a verb.

The most recent work on the acquisition of language by bilingual children suggests that these children keep separate the grammatical systems of the two languages to which they are exposed. When they begin to combine words in one or the other language, they respect the order proper to each language (Meisel, 1995). This early separation of grammatical systems is confirmed when sentence order becomes more complex.

The First Sentences of French Children

We found numerous instances of word combination in children under the age of twenty months. Two-word utterances were frequent but hardly accounted for all the productions of children under the age of two.

Two-word combinations more often than not group words of the operator type with content words. Between sixteen and twenty months, most of the examples we recorded were made up in this way, but the style of such combinations is not therefore necessarily telegraphic: articles were often present. The order was not fixed but varied from situation to situation while usually respecting the canonical order of French.

Léo, from late in the fifteenth month until seventeen and a half months, produced sentences such as the following:

la dame là	the lady there
encore de l'eau	more water
plus l'eau	no more water
donne l'eau	give water
canard dans l'eau	duck in the water
de l'eau	some water

The last expression cannot be considered to be fixed since the addition of a negating or localizing element causes the partitive article to disappear. The following forms were also found:

moi là	me there [in a photo]
c'est moi	that's me
chapeau moi	hat me [used when asking to be given his hat]
papa parti	daddy gone
pas là parti	not there gone

Marie, between seventeen and twenty months, also favored operator + content word forms. These forms were quite varied:

nounours là	teddy bear there
voilà papillon	there is butterfly
y a poupée	[there] is doll
c'est Grégoire	that's Grégoire
pots dedans	jars inside

Already more complex combinations were found as well:

poupée là moi	doll there me
où est poupée?	where is doll?
où est chapeau?	where is hat?
dedans on le met	inside it is put
attend elle le met	wait she puts it

In the utterances of these two children, isolated words were often preceded by an article or marker—"è" or "a".

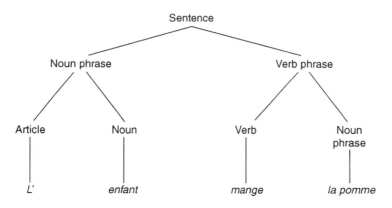

Figure 8.3 Structure of the sentence *The child eats the apple* in French.

Few examples were found combining two content words:

bébé beau	nice baby (Charles, 17 months, 11 days)
mange poupée	eat doll [= the doll eats] (Marie, 19 months, 12 days)
moto papa	motor[bike] daddy (Henri, 21 months, 5 days)

From twenty months, sentences become more structured. Can young French children help illuminate this adaptation to the grammar of the adult language? We shall see that certain utterance structures are quite specific to French children and are related to the grammatical characteristics of spoken French.

The structure of a simple French sentence such as *L'enfant mange la pomme* ("The child eats the apple") is analyzed as shown in figure 8.3. For the syntactic subject *l'enfant*, a pronominal subject *il* may be substituted.

In spoken language, and particularly in the forms used by adults when they address children, the overwhelming majority of sentences are constructed with a reduplication of the noun by a pronoun (called a *clitic subject*). Clitic subjects are not analyzed as noun subjects but as markers of person and number replacing the inflected verb suffixes that have almost completely disappeared from French today. They may duplicate the lexical subject, as in statements such as *Maman, elle t'a acheté un joli sceau pour jouer sur la plage* (Mommy, she bought you a pretty bucket to play with on the beach) or *Elle a de l'allure, cette voiture* (It's stylish, this car). Politicians often use this form. Laurent Fabius, the former French prime minister, used to rely heavily on it in his speeches: *Les français, ils n'accepteront plus que . . .* ("The French, they will no longer accept that . . .") or *Elles veulent enfin voir leurs droits reconnus, les femmes* ("They want to see their rights finally recognized, women [do]"). Ungraceful though these forms may be, they are very common in spoken language: they allow the subject or theme of one's remarks to be set off more clearly before saying what one has to say.

For French children, the structure of the verb phrase (verb + object) is from the start the same as that for adults: *eat yogurt*, *give water*, and so on. The noun or noun phrase indicating the subject is most often left in postverbal position. In this case, the verb is sometimes preceded by a clitic or a marker indicating the pronoun:

mange poupée	eat doll [= the doll eats] (Marie, 19 months, 12 days)
e [= il/elle] pleure bébé	he/she cries baby [= the baby cries] (Henri, 22 months)
e [= elle] pique a jambe Cécile	she pricks leg Cécile [= Cécile's pricking my leg] (Manon, 21 months)

A high proportion of postverbal subjects, with or without clitic subjects, is very characteristic of the first sentences of French children.

To better illustrate the evolution of sentences at the end of the second year, let us look at the case of Manon.[1] At the beginning of our recording sessions she was twenty-one months and twenty days, and at the end she was twenty-two months and twenty days. In the course of these sessions we collected more than eighty statements of several words. Manon understood that she was being recorded and showed herself to be very talkative. We used a tape recorder in which the tape could be seen winding and unwinding. One day Manon suddenly stopped talking and assumed a stern demeanor. I insisted on continuing the conversation. She pointed to the tape recorder and said, "It no longer goes around!" This little girl of twenty-two months was a precocious celebrity: she spoke in order to be recorded.

Indeed, her desire for stardom made her an excellent subject, and her many productions represented a good sample of the statements that a French child under the age of two is apt to produce. Though she was rather early to speak and, naturally, only one example among many, analysis of the productions of other children the same age revealed that Manon's preferred forms were quite common among her compatriots.

To indicate an action or a state and its agent, Manon, like many French children, tended to put the verb first, sometimes preceded by a pronoun, with the name of the agent being placed in final position.

In the case of a sentence beginning with the verb *to be*, the clitic subject was generally omitted:

est gentille Jacquie	is nice Jackie
est gentille la tortue	is nice the tortoise
est là le loulours	is there the teddy bear
est bon le yaourt	is good the yogurt

A few rare exceptions were encountered where the clitic subject accompanied the verb *to be*:

là i (= il) est loulours	there he is teddy bear

The (clitic) pronoun was present—with a postpositive noun subject—in the case of verbs of action:

elle pique Cécile	she pricks Cécile [where Cécile is agent rather than object]
i [= il] a tombé le camion	it fell the truck

With intransitive verbs, only the clitic subject was mentioned:

entend, elle parle	listen, she's talking
mais e [= elle] tourne, e(lle)	but [the tape] goes
tourne regarde!	around, it goes around look!

At the end of the twenty-second month, the syntactic subject was put in front and accompanied by a clitic in a few sentences constructed with intransitive verbs:

le chat i [= il] joue la balle	the cat he plays with the ball
ça tourne là	that goes around there

The pronoun *je* (I) was always placed in front:

je vois le chat	I see the cat
je veux pas	I don't want

The verb phrase is fixed, with the object always following the verb:

elle pique à jambe	she pricks leg
mange ma beurre le	eat my butter the spoon [= I eat
cuillère	my butter with a spoon]
veux un bonbon mamie	want a candy grandma

In negative sentences including a verb, *pas* always followed the verb, as well as the modal verbs *vouloir* and *pouvoir*:

non, veux pas	no, don't want
peux pas [at]traper	can't catch

or in injunctions:

[re]garde pas Cécile	don't look Cécile [= Cécile! don't look]

We have seen that the elements "a" and "e" before nouns are observed from fourteen to fifteen months. But between twenty months and two years, most children begin to mark gender and number. Nouns are preceded by definite, indefinite, or possessive articles, as we see in Manon's sentences. With her, however, definite and indefinite articles are always singular:

veux un bonbon	want a candy
y a pas là la balle	isn't there the ball
encore là / plus là le	still there / no longer there the
beurre	butter
est bon le yaourt	is good the yogurt

Errors, or transpositions, of gender were observed:

a pas là le balle	[la balle]
mange ma beurre	[mon beurre]
le cuillère	[la cuillère]

Although in certain of the previous sentences Manon had correctly said *la balle* and *le beurre*, this time she used the feminine possessive pronoun *ma* before the masculine *beurre* and put the masculine article *le* before the feminine nouns *cuillère* and *balle*.

French children typically specify number very early, using the form [adø] [= *a deux*] to indicate two (or more) things. This form is found in a great many children before the age of two. Thus, Marie at nineteen months, assembling a collection of small jars, used this phrase each time she added a new jar:

a de e[lle] le met   many she puts it [= she puts it with many others]

A child such as Manon makes it very difficult for us to speak of a telegraphic approach to speech, generalizing from those famous two-word sentences that led Derek Bickerton (1990)—in his eagerness to assimilate phylogenesis and ontogenesis—to assert that the first combinations of words are a form of protolanguage, similar to the gestures and utterances exhibited by chimpanzees. The sentences of children twenty to twenty-four months of age are distinct from those of Washoe, the chimpanzee who was taught sign language, as from those of its fellow creatures who were taught, less successfully, to express themselves in a human way. The sentences of children between twenty and twenty-four months display a coherent, nonrandom order, with numerous articles and gender markers. In these sentences, one finds regularities revealing specific constructions that correspond to linguistic categories. In the case of Manon, the position of the object and that of the particle *pas*, used to signal negation of the verb, were consistent with French practice and well respected by the child. In short, first sentences manifest a grammatical adaptation to the child's native language.

The child under two years of age can also express subtle semantic differences. Thus, at twenty months, Manon said *a pas nounours* ("isn't [there] teddy bear") or *a pas balle* ("isn't [there] ball") when these objects were removed from view, but *a plus musique* ("no more music") or *a plus toc-toc* ("no more knock-knock") when music or a noise ceased, already manifesting a distinction between the cessation of presence and the cessation of process. For her, *a pas* and *a plus* were not semantically identical forms but corresponded to differences in the nature of nonexistence. They were judiciously used as a function of the situation. As we have seen, the productions of two-year-old children reveal considerable grammatical knowledge. Of course, the rules manifested are incomplete, partial, sometimes personal, but nonetheless in accord with adult forms. At this age one does not find complex sentences of the *Mommy put on Daddy's hat to go to the beach* type, but when children wish to express this idea, they respect a coherent word order, even if some of the words are omitted. The limitations due to difficulties in realization mask the child's actual competence while allowing principles adapted to adult grammar to show through. Comparative studies of the first sentences of children from different linguistic environments thus support the view that the child has already begun to notice certain grammatical principles of the adult language.

Some psycholinguists have even proposed that children—like the goddess Athena, who sprang fully armed from the head of Zeus—are born fully equipped with linguistic knowledge. They discover the canonical order of words in the sentences of their native language by virtue of their recognition of grammatical relations. This immediate knowledge allows them to identify their native language as a language of the subject-verb-object type or of the subject-object-verb type. Other psycholinguists are less generous, and postulate a weaker degree of linguistic knowledge. On this view, children need the help of semantic categories constructing syntactic categories. But all psycholinguists seem to take it for granted that the grammar of children is of the same nature as that of adults, even though not all the principles that regulate adult grammar are realized in their productions. The rapid grammatical development that characterizes the linguistic achievements of the third year is based on this very incomplete, but not incorrect, grammar of the second year. In the course of the third year, the length, complexity, and variety of sentences grow very quickly, justifying Steven Pinker's (1994, p. 276) remark that, at the age of three, the child is a "grammatical genius."

In the first two years, thanks to the gifts given to all humans and the impetus provided by the linguistic environment, the newborn learns to process the sounds that constitute speech, to produce them, to work out how they are organized, and to discover their meaning. We shall not follow the rapid progress of our "young geniuses" further, but, on the threshold of their third year, take our leave of these children, to whom language has now come.

Conclusion

If while growing up they seem lacking in self-control and almost without reason, it needs to be kept in mind that it is knowledge of business and of all the subjects about which they must reason that is lacking to them rather than reason. This combined with the fact that the customs of the world, which make up all its wisdom, are often so contrary to what nature, being well ordered, requires of men that those who are born [into the world] need to live for several years to learn about things so far removed from what nature teaches.
—Géraud de Cordemoy

With the birth of a child, mothers are more interested in establishing physical and affective contact than in thinking about the biological and cognitive programs that will guide the child's development. Later, speaking comes so naturally that one is not surprised to hear children's first babblings and then their first words. One rejoices in these, makes fun of them, encourages them—but they seem altogether natural. Indeed, they are natural, because humans have been endowed with the ability to speak.

The little wonders whose delicate features and perfectly formed bodies are so admired by their parents are also endowed with minds designed to allow them to decode the world in which they live. At two months their vocal tracts are not yet ready to produce speech sounds, but their hearing is sensitive to them and their brains are suitably prepared.

In the course of phylogenesis a genetic system has been constructed that contains a large amount of knowledge. Because human consciousness and intelligence are embodied in a core of genetically transmitted predispositions, they may be seen as an extension of biological adaptation. Without this sort of preadaptation—without implicit knowledge about the basic forms that underlie all human languages—human beings would be incapable of learning language or speaking.

Can this preadaptation be shown to exist? If so, in what form? These two questions have guided the research of cognitive psycholinguists since the 1970s. In their search for answers, they sought first to establish the existence of very early and specific mechanisms for processing speech sounds. This inquiry then expanded to study how categorization and selection organize language processing. Researchers managed, finally, to show that children's language behaviors are consistent with the general principles governing the form of all languages, so far as linguists have been able to define such principles.

All these studies required an experimental approach. Methods based on the observation of babies reveal much about their behavior and development, of course, as well as about certain aspects of mental function in infants, but they do not enable us to identify the underlying processes of language processing. As adults, we are not conscious of the mental processes that allow a sound wave to be transformed into a meaningful sentence. The unconscious processes that make this transformation possible can be studied only by indirect means. To try to understand the how and the why of the unconscious processes that support the processing of speech while this is being acquired—processes that later will be integrated into the automatic processing of speech by adults—cognitive psychology insists on the experimental or analytical verification of hypotheses generated by theoretical models. This means rejecting any explanation that does not entail statements capable of being confirmed or disconfirmed. Accordingly, researchers dismiss conclusions based on general observations, on attribution of often poorly defined desires, or on inferences of repressed desires from the personal histories of individuals. Inferences based on this sort of analysis sometimes have a certain basis in reality and sometimes serve to stimulate reflection, but because they are neither directly verifiable nor generalizable, they cannot supply a valid method for investigating the bases of the mechanisms and processes that determine the faculty of language.

These remarks require some qualification, however. The quest for universality that animates work on human language capacities very quickly runs up against the fact that the acquisition of language is an interactive process. Thus, the course of linguistic development in children, despite the existence of common foundations, very soon finds itself subject to variability among languages, modes of transmission, and—in more subtle ways—individual styles. Neither underlying principles nor regularities in language behavior of universal import can be brought out by generalizing from insufficiently broad experimental data, whether these concern linguistic subjects or environments. Comparative analyses thus prove to be indispensable, both for verifying what aspects of cultural, linguistic, and individual variation are universal, and also for understanding the system of acquisition with its own aspects of variation and flexibility. Psycholinguists aim to discover the regularities imposed by innate structures. But they wish also to show the room for freedom and creativity that is allowed to the human species through its capacity for choice, invention, and imagination. We have learned much that is new about the child's first years, but much more remains still to be discovered. Even if we manage one day to work out what underlies the human aptitude for language, the part of it that springs from the babblings and words and commentaries of young children—all that is magical, charming, poetic, sad, and funny—will remain forever mysterious. But that will be the work of poets.

At birth, though the brain is prepared for spoken language, the baby's subjective experiences and states of consciousness are still quite rudimentary. Consciousness is built out of experiences issuing from perception, memory, the formation of concepts, and interactions with others, as well as from the relations among these experiences. In the course of the first year, the symbolic function—the capacity for representation and self-awareness—goes beyond the child's early knowledge and gives it structure. The child now imagines, rediscovers, and reinvents. The assistance provided by language, in its dual role as expression of thought and vehicle of communication, becomes ever more essential, as children manifest a desire to learn and to become acquainted with their surroundings. As part of the process of socialization, children will also have to conform to parental expectations and start to speak in appropriate ways. These cultural constraints, as Géraud de Cordemoy observed long ago, carry them far away from "what nature teaches."

Differences must—and indeed do—exist among children. For each individual, sensations, perceptions, and actual experiences follow a singular course, the result both of chance and of conscious intent. Through cultural and linguistic interactions, the mind creates certain aspects of reality. Very quickly, imagination and diversity come to support the behaviors of different children and of children in different cultures. In the course of the third year, the formal diversity of utterances grows weaker, however; they become more grammatical and more similar as children begin to speak their language more correctly. But diversity in both the modes and content of expression persists and indeed becomes more pronounced. One of the most striking characteristics of language is the creativity that it makes possible. When the degree of consciousness increases and a more evolved individuality appears, this creativity will become virtually unlimited. Of course, not all children will turn out to be Mozarts, Leonardo da Vincis, or Newtons, but, in each child, the personality we are able to glimpse in his first words will blossom. Experimentation has permitted us to discover a baby programmed for speech. Although this method remains the favored approach for the study of the development of language, it sometimes stumbles when the emergence of character, imagination, and humor in the course of children's development combine to make their personality more complex.

The child's first words owe their existence to the fact that they have been understood: so long as adults do not recognize them, the child is not supposed to have said them. Children's speech is transformed by the mysteries of listening and the projections of adults. Research teaches us how gifted children are at learning to speak and how robust the mechanisms of learning are when they are biologically intact. It also teaches us how normal it is to find substantial variations in the rhythms and forms of the development of language. Although parents and educators must be alert to deviations from the norm, they must take care not to be too normative. Careful study of the development of speech processing, as well as of the principles involved in the acquisition of syntax and morphology during the years ahead, is essential if we are to have a better understanding of problems in acquiring speech and language.

We now take our leave of the child who, on the threshold of the third year, has acquired speech but still has much to learn. Equipped with a universal grammar, children commit themselves further to the decoding of the grammar of their language. No matter which language this may be, it displays numerous subtleties, expressions of gender and number, verb aspects and tenses, inflections, relations, and so forth. The child entering the third year will know how to cope with them—not without trials and errors, of course, but, when all is said and done, with astonishing brilliance. This adventure is another fascinating story.

Appendix A
The Principal Stages in the Development of Speech from Before Birth to Two Years

	Perception	Production
Before birth	Reactions to voice	
	Recognition of changes in sounds	
	Preferential reactions to mother's voice	
From birth to one month	Categorical discrimination between speech contrasts	Cries, wails
	Recognition of, and preference for, mother's voice	Reactive sounds of comfort or uneasiness
	Recognition of, and preference for, native language	
	Sensitivity to prosodic and rhythmic cues	
From one to five months	Capacity for categorization	First expressions of laughter
	Ability to categorize speech sounds despite variations in intonation	Vocalizations with closing and opening of mouth
	Recognition of a syllable in different utterances	First "arrheu" with glottal sounds
	Capacity for detecting changes in intonation patterns	Vowel sounds
		Beginning of control of phonation at five months
From five to seven months	Preference for motherese	Vocalizations mastered
	Categorization of vowels according to native language	Play at varying sounds and imitating
	Detection of prosodic cues of clauses in different languages	Beginning of babbling at around seven months (mainly repetitive productions with rhythmic alternation of consonants and vowels)
	Possibility of establishing correspondences between vowels and movements of the mouth (intermodal perception)	

	Perception	Production
From eight to ten months	Detection of phrase boundaries	Production of vowels approaching those of native language
	Preference for word forms respecting stress and phonotactic constraints of native language	Variegated babbling
	Capacity for recognizing word forms in sentences after training on these words	Intonation contours influenced by native language
	Beginning of comprehension of words in context	Babbling of children identifiable according to different linguistic environments
From ten to twelve months	Detection of word boundaries	Selection of repertoires of consonants and syllables adapted to native language
	Reorganization of perceptual categories in accordance with phonological structure of native language	Varied babbling in long and intonationally modulated sequences
	Recognition of known words, independently of context	Appearance of stable production forms as a function of situations
	Comprehension of thirty or so words in context	First words
	Learning of words by association with referents	
From twelve to sixteen months	Comprehension of 100 to 150 words on average	Persistence of babbling forms with sentence intonation
	Understanding of idea of sentences and of simple sentences	Stable production forms as a function of situations
		Average production of fifty words at sixteen months, chiefly nouns
		Different styles of entry into language

	Perception	Production
From sixteen to twenty months	Comprehension of 200 words on average	Average production of fifty to 170 words
	Categories of words distinguished	Increase in production of verbs and expressions
From twenty to twenty-four months	Comprehension of relations	Rapid increase in vocabulary
	Comprehension of the syntactic order of words when context, semantics, and prosody are coherent	Average production of 250 to 300 words (some children may nonetheless still have a much more restricted vocabulary)
		Reorganization of the pronunciation of words
		Preparation for phonological lexicon
		First sentences of two or three words; still few articles but notions of gender and number beginning to be acquired

Appendix B
The International Phonetic Alphabet

CONSONANTS (PULMONIC)

	Bilabial	Labiodental	Dental	Alveolar	Postalveolar	
Plosive	p b			t d		
Nasal	m	ɱ		n		
Trill	ʙ			r		
Tap or Flap				ɾ		
Fricative	ɸ β	f v	θ ð	s z	ʃ ʒ	
Lateral fricative				ɬ ɮ		
Approximant		ʋ		ɹ		
Lateral approximant				l		

Where symbols appear in pairs, the one to the right represents a voiced consonant. Shaded areas denote articulations judged impossible.

CONSONANTS (NON-PULMONIC)

Clicks		Voiced implosives		Ejectives	
ʘ	Bilabial	ɓ	Bilabial	’	as in:
ǀ	Dental	ɗ	Dental/alveolar	p’	Bilabial
ǃ	(Post)alveolar	ʄ	Palatal	t’	Dental/alveolar
ǂ	Palatoalveolar	ɠ	Velar	k’	Velar
ǁ	Alveolar lateral	ʛ	Uvular	s’	Alveolar fricative

VOWELS

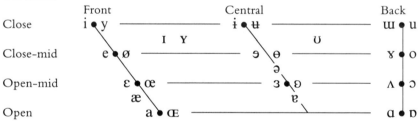

Where symbols appear in pairs, the one to the right
represents a rounded vowel.

OTHER SYMBOLS

ʍ Voiceless labial-velar fricative
w Voiced labial-velar approximant
ɥ Voiced labial-palatal approximant
ʜ Voiceless epiglottal fricative
ʢ Voiced epiglottal fricative
ʡ Epiglottal plosive
ɕ ʑ Alveolo-palatal fricatives

ɺ Alveolar lateral flap
ɧ Simultaneous ʃ and x
Affricates and double articulations can be represented by two symbols joined by a tie bar if necessary:

k͡p t͡s

	Retroflex		Palatal		Velar		Uvular		Pharyngeal		Glottal	
	ʈ	ɖ	c	ɟ	k	g	q	ɢ			ʔ	
	ɳ		ɲ		ŋ		N					
							R					
	ɽ											
	ʂ	ʐ	ç	ʝ	x	ɣ	χ	ʁ	ħ	ʕ	h	ɦ
	ɻ		j		ɰ							
	ɭ		ʎ		L							

SUPRASEGMENTALS

ˈ	Primary stress	ˌfoʊnəˈtɪʃən
ˌ	Secondary stress	
ː	Long	eː
ˑ	Half-long	eˑ
˘	Extra-short	ĕ
.	Syllable break	ɹi.ækt
|	Minor (foot) group	
‖	Major (intonation) group	
‿	Linking (absence of a break)	

TONES & WORD ACCENTS

LEVEL				CONTOUR			
e̋	or	˥	Extra high	ě	or	◌	Rising
é		˦	High	ê		◌	Falling
ē		˧	Mid	e᷄		◌	High rising
è		˨	Low	e᷅		◌	Low rising
ȅ		˩	Extra low	e᷈		◌	Rising-falling
							etc.

ꜜ	Downstep		↗	Global rise
ꜛ	Upstep		↘	Global fall

DIACRITICS

Diacritics may be placed above a symbol with a descender, e.g. ŋ̊

̥	Voiceless	n̥	d̥	Breathy voiced	b̤	a̤	Dental	t̪	d̪
̬	Voiced	s̬	t̬	Creaky voiced	b̰	a̰	Apical	t̺	d̺
ʰ	Aspirated	tʰ	dʰ	Linguolabial	t̼	d̼	Laminal	t̻	d̻
̹	More rounded	ɔ̹	ʷ	Labialized	tʷ	dʷ	Nasalized	ẽ	
̜	Less rounded	ɔ̜	ʲ	Palatalized	tʲ	dʲ	ⁿ Nasal release	dⁿ	
̟	Advanced	u̟	ˠ	Velarized	tˠ	dˠ	ˡ Lateral release	dˡ	
̠	Retracted	i̠	ˤ	Pharyngealized	tˤ	dˤ	No audible release	d̚	
̈	Centralized	ë	~	Velarized or pharyngealized	ɫ				
̽	Mid-centralized	e̽		Raised	e̝	(ɹ̝ = voiced alveolar fricative)			
̩	Syllabic	n̩		Lowered	e̞	(β̞ = voiced bilabial approximant)			
̯	Non-syllabic	e̯		Advanced Tongue Root	e̘				
˞	Rhoticity	ɚ		Retracted Tongue Root	e̙				

Notes

Introduction

1. For all technical terms, see the glossary following the Notes.

Chapter 1

1. On the relation between genetic determinism and phenotypic variability, see especially chapters 6 and 7 of Changeux (1997/1983, pp. 170–249).

Chapter 2

1. The Yoruba data were collected in Nigeria by Grégoire Lyon.

Chapter 3

1. Bartholomaeus Anglicus (also called Bartholomew de Glanville) wrote *De proprietatibus rerum*. This work, composed in the thirteenth century, was frequently quoted in the Middle Ages (see Riché and Alexandre-Bidou, 1994).

2. Aldobrandino da Siena (d. 1287) was an Italian physician of the thirteenth century who wrote in French; the quote here is taken from a modern edition of his *Régime du corps* (Landouzy and Pépin, ed., 1911).

Chapter 6

1. All the examples given below are taken from studies of language acquisition by French and American children: the study of the five French children was conducted by B. de Boysson-Bardies, P. Hallé, and C. Durand (1989, 1991, 1992); that of the five American children by M. M. Vihman et al. (1986, 1992). The example of Simon is taken from a study done by B. de Boysson-Bardies, N. Bacri, M. Poizat, and L. Sagart (unpublished).

Chapter 7

1. The examples of mother-child conversation that follow are taken from the collected transcripts of interviews conducted as part of a comparative longitudinal investigation into language acquisition among American, Swedish, French, and Japanese children. This research gave rise to international collaboration: C. Ferguson, M. Vihman and F. Arao studied the American and Japanese children; B. Lindblom, L. Roug-Hellichius, and I. Landberg the Swedish children; and B. de Boysson-Bardies, P. Hallé and C. Durand the French children (1992).

Chapter 8

1. For an analysis of the negative sentences produced by Manon, see Boysson-Bardies (1976).

Glossary

acoustic

Referring to the physical properties of sounds.

acoustic phonetics

The study of the acoustic parameters (energy and frequency of the sound wave) and phonetic parameters (identification of phonemes: consonants and vowels) in a sound production.

acoustic spectrum. *See* spectrogram

amplitude

Measure of maximum displacement of the air molecules in a sound wave as a function of the vibration energy of the vocal cords.

aphasia

A condition characterized by problems in comprehending or producing speech or by the loss of these functions as a result of a lesion to the areas of the brain responsible for language (due to hemorrhage, accident, or trauma, for example).

apraxia

Impairment of the ability to execute complex coordinated movements required for speech, without impaired use of muscles or senses.

arcuate fasciculus

Neural pathway conveying information from Wernicke's area to Broca's area.

articulators

The set of structures and muscles (tongue, lips, jaws, soft palate, and back wall of the pharynx) that, by their displacement or their movement, modify the trajectory of air in the vocal tract and thus allow different sounds to be formed.

auditory system

Neural pathways leading from the ear to higher cortical areas that underlie the perception of sounds.

axon

An extension of the nerve cell that transmits neuronal information.

behaviorism

Dominant school of Anglo-American psychology in the first half of the twentieth century that explained behavior by reference to the laws of stimulus-response conditioning. In its radical version, behaviorism denies the existence of mental states. In its methodological version, it considers such states to be too difficult to study and restricts itself to the study of behaviors.

bilabial consonant

A consonant that is articulated in a gesture in which both lips come together (such as /b/, /m/, or /p/).

Broca's area

Cortical area situated at the external face of left hemisphere in the lower part of the third frontal circumvolution.

canonical babbling

Term used for the relatively rigid forms of syllabification generally found at the beginning of the babbling (see Oller 1980).

categorical perception

Perception that consists in identifying objects or events in terms of discrete categories to which they belong and in ignoring intracategorical acoustic variations. *See* categorization.

categorization

The classification of sounds in a category illustrated by a prototype. A perceptual categorization thus makes it possible to recognize a particular vowel or consonant despite differences in realization.

cerebral cortex

The external tissue of the cerebral hemispheres containing the most evolved cell bodies—namely, neurons—and their mutual connections.

coarticulation

The overlapping articulation of speech sounds in the production of successive segments—sometimes even of nonsuccessive segments—of a statement. The effects of combination may be anticipatory or perseveratory.

cognition

The domain of representations and processes that make knowledge possible, including perception, language, memory, and reasoning.

cognitive sciences

The set of sciences that study the functioning of intelligence and, generally, how thought attempts to acquaint itself with reality (by means of reasoning, perception, language, memory, and control of movement). They include experimental psychology, linguistics, philosophy, and the neurosciences.

consonant

A phoneme produced with the vocal tract partly or wholly blocked. Consonants are classified according to their point of articulation (labial, dental, velar) and their manner of articulation (fricative, occlusive, and so on). They may be voiced (such as /b/ or /m/) or unvoiced (such as /p/, /t/, or /k/). See the entries for labial, dental, velar, fricative, occlusive, nasal, liquid consonant, and voicing lag.

consonant harmony

Refers to repetition of the consonant of a syllable in the following or previous syllable of a word. Often observed in adult speech errors (such as saying "popper" instead of "stopper") and in children's word productions while acquiring their native language.

content words

A syntactic class of words (such as nouns, verbs, adjectives, or adverbs) and some prepositions that express particular concepts in a sentence, as opposed to function words (articles, conjunctions, auxiliaries, pronouns) that specify only the information given by content words.

copulas

Words used to link a subject and a predicate (e.g., "is" in "The girl is nice").

cortex. *See* cerebral cortex

decibel

Measure of the intensity of a sound—that is, of the amplitude of the variations in the pressure of the air that form the sound. It is a relative measure, taking into account the comparative intensity of two sounds.

deictic

Element serving to relate a statement to the circumstances of its utterance (e.g., *I*, *there*, *yesterday*, etc.)

demonstrative pronoun

Pronoun that serves to designate or represent a noun, an object, or an idea (such as *this*, *that*, or *these*).

dental

A consonant (such as /t/ or /d/) that is produced when the tip of the tongue is brought into contact with the back side of the teeth of the upper jaw.

dichotic listening

An experimental technique that consists in presenting two different sounds, one to each ear. This method makes it possible to observe the functional asymmetry in the processing of language sounds (or musical sounds) by the brain, each ear being better connected with the opposing cerebral hemisphere.

diphthong

A vowel sound that changes between its beginning and end, as in *cow* or *buy*. Diphthongs do not exist in certain languages, such as French.

discrimination

The capacity for distinguishing between two stimuli.

distinctive feature

The system of distinctive features is constituted by the set of acoustic features that permit one sound to be distinguished from another with reference to a binary, or contrastive, criterion: thus, a sound may be voiced or unvoiced (/b/ and /p/), nasal or nonnasal (/m/ and /p/), and so on.

disyllable

A unit of speech composed of two syllables.

embryogenesis

The formation and development of the embryo.

endogenous signals

Signals coming from within an organism or a system of organisms.

engram

Trace left in the brain by a past event.

epiglottis

Elastic cartilage in front of the glottis that protects the glottis in swallowing.

exogenous signals

Signals that arise outside of an organism or a system of organisms.

event-related potential (ERP)

Electrophysiological response of a set of neurons in the brain, immediately following a stimulus, such as an auditory or visual stimulation.

F0 contour. *See* fundamental frequency and intonation

foot

A group of syllables forming an elementary measure in verse or a group of syllables marked as constituting a metrical unit in verse.

formants

Frequency bands within which the principal degrees of acoustic energy are concentrated. The first (lowest) three formants are considered to be important for the perception and identification of vowels.

formant transition

Rapid change in the spectral composition of formants generally due to the coarticulation of a consonant and a vowel.

fricative

A consonant in which the obstruction of air by the tongue is partial, producing a noise of friction (such as /v/, /f/, /s/, /χ/, and so on).

function words. *See* content words

fundamental frequency (or F0)

The frequency at which the vocal cords typically vibrate, which gives the pitch of the voice. The faster the vocal cords vibrate, the higher the pitch. Variations of intonation correspond to variations in the fundamental frequency and yield an F0 contour.

glissando

Rapid variations between two sounds.

glottal stop

Sound produced by tightly constricting the vocal cords against each other, which results in a complete obstruction of the flow of air up to the glottis. (The English expression "uh-oh" consists of two such stops.)

glottis

The space between the vocal cords.

harmony. *See* consonant harmony; vowel harmony

high-amplitude sucking (HAS)

An experimental method (developed by Siqueland and DeLucia, 1959) based on nonnutritive sucking in infants. When presented with a novel stimulus, infants increase their rate of sucking. When the novelty of the stimulus wears off, infants return to a baseline rate of sucking. This contigent technique has been used to study speech perception in very young infants.

hydrophone

A device used to detect acoustic variations that can be immerged in a liquid.

inflection

An element of a word that is added to the root to fulfill a syntactic function. Nominative inflection is found in languages where the noun is declined (Latin, for example): verbal inflection is found in languages where verbs are conjugated.

intensity

Sound intensity or power is related to the amplitude of the vibration of the air—that is, the energy transmitted along a sound wave, measured in decibels.

International Phonetic Alphabet (IPA)

An international system for classifying and transcribing vowels and consonants as a function of their type of articulation. In principle, it permits the sounds of any natural language to be captured in a consistent fashion by a combination of conventional and specially designed symbols, along with a restricted set of diacritics, that represent speech sounds that are phonologically distinct in all languages. See the chart in Appendix B.

intonation

The melody or contour of the pitch of the voice that accompanies the production of speech. Depending on the language, it may have a role in syntactical discrimination (such as distinguishing an affirmation from an interrogation) or lexical discrimination (in tone languages).

labial

A consonant articulated with the use of one or both the lips.

larynx

The organ essential to phonation, located in the upper part of the trachea. It contains the vocal cords (attached to two small cartilages), which open and close the glottis and thus cause a regular vibration of the air coming from the lungs.

lateral. *See* liquid

lexical access

A process by which a sound or a series of sounds leads to the selection of a word stored in a mental lexicon.

lexical entry

The set of items of information about a particular word (sound, form, meaning, syntactic marks) coded in the mental lexicon.

lexicon

A mental dictionary consisting of the set of phonological, syntactic, semantic, and orthographic representations of words that constitute the listener's intuitive knowledge of these words.

liquid

A voiced consonant produced with only partial obstruction of the air in the mouth. The group of liquid consonants includes the laterals /l/ and /r/ where air passes through both sides of the mouth.

magnetic resonance imaging (MRI)

Cerebral imaging through magnetic resonance. This measure is based on the study of cerebral blood flow (either by injecting intravenously a contrastive intravascular tracer, which allows the volume of blood in the brain to be measured, or by using ultrarapid acquisition sequences sensitive to the concentration of desoxyhemoglobin in the brain, which allows tissue variations following cerebral activations to be detected).

mental representation

A particular state of the cognitive system at a given moment in time (which may, however, become persistent) that reflects an aspect of reality external to this system.

module

A subsystem of the brain serving a specific function characterized by the automaticity and rapidity of its functioning and by its cognitive autonomy and impenetrability.

mora

A phonetic unit of time in certain languages, such as Japanese, that forms the rhythmic basis for pronunciation in the language. It may correspond to a short vowel, a nasal consonant, a vowel lengthening, or a reduplicated consonant. Thus *Nippon* (the Japanese word for Japan) is divided into four moras (*ni p po n*) and therefore takes as much time to pronounce as *kakemono*.

morpheme

The smallest meaningful unit into which the words of a language may be divided, including the grammatically significant elements of a word (such as the ending of a verb, the plural marker for nouns, and the inflection of an adverb— the *ly*, for example, in *kindly*). Many words are monomorphemic.

morphology

The study of the rules for forming words that describes the internal structure of words and the relations of kinship among words (such as *to flee, fleeing, fleeting, flight*).

nasal

A consonant pronounced by lowering the soft palate (such as /m/ and /n/), which allows air to pass through the nasal canal.

neurons

Cells of the nervous system. They are distinguished from other cells by their highly developed ability to communicate with one another.

nonnutritive sucking. *See* high amplitude sucking

occlusive (or stop)

A consonant pronounced with the complete obstruction of air in the oral cavity. Depending on the point of closure, the occlusive may be labial (/b/), dental (/t/), or velar (/k/).

onomatopoeia

A word or phase that phonetically imitates events, objects, or people (e.g., *bow–wow* for the sound of a dog barking)

onset

The quality of the first sound of a syllable (or of a word) given by the consonant or the consonant group preceding a vowel.

ontogenesis

The development of the individual from egg fertilization until adulthood.

palate

The roof of the mouth. The long anterior portion is called the "hard palate" and the posterior portion the "soft palate."

perceptual constancy

The ability to recognize phonetic categories despite irrelevant variations due to the speaker or articulatory context.

periodic and aperiodic sounds

The sounds of a language may be periodic, where there is a periodic vibration of the vocal cords at the level of the glottis (in vowels and voiced consonants), or aperiodic, as in the case of exhalations and where there is air turbulence at the points of constriction of the vocal canal (in fricatives; the occlusive consonants /p/, /t/, and /k/; and so on).

pharynx

Tube situated behind the larynx, mouth and nose, acting as a resonating chamber for the voice produced by the vocal cords of the layrnx.

phonation

The emission of language sounds by a set of mechanisms including the respiratory cycle, as adapted to speech, as well as the vibration of the vocal cords and the modulation of the voice by resonant cavities of the vocal tract (that is, the glottis and oral and nasal cavities).

phoneme

(1) An abstract unit of sound that forms words. (2) Contrastive unit of sound in a language: two sounds are distinct phonemes when their phonetic difference conveys different meanings (as, for example, *bed/led*, *bay/day*, *fine/wine*).

phonemic transcription

Representation of a word or connected speech in a particular language in terms of its constituent phonemes, neglecting phonetic detail; conventionally enclosed by diagonal marks or slashes (e.g., /word/). *See also* phonetic transcription.

phonetics

The analysis and classification of the production and perception of language sounds.

phonetic transcription

Representation of a word or connected speech at some level of phonetic detail, independently of a phonological analysis of the speech represented; conventionally enclosed by square brackets (e.g., [w ɜːd]). The International Phonetic Alphabet is standardly used in Europe, and increasingly in the United States, for this purpose. *See also* phonemic transcription.

phonology

A component of grammar that includes the inventory of the sounds of a language and the rules governing their combination.

phonotactics

The set of rules for the arrangement of phonological sequences ordering the structure of words in a language. For example, a word ending in /sd/ or beginning with /vlt/ is not possible in either French or English.

phrase (or syntagm)

Group of words having a unity within a sentence from the point of view of the grammatical analysis to which it gives rise. Thus, one distinguishes the noun phrase *the little girl* from the verb phrase *ran in the garden*.

phylogenesis

The mode of formation of species; development of species.

pitch

The pitch of a sound is determined by the frequency of the vibration of the vocal cords; the fundamental frequency F0 is measured in hertz (Hz).

planum temporale

A region of the upper surface of the temporal lobe that includes, in the left hemisphere, the classical speech area identified by Wernicke.

plasticity

Refers to the brain's capacity for adaptation. The brain puts the organism in communication with its environment and can organize or reorganize the transmission pathways of a nerve signal to adapt behavior in response to this environment.

prosody

The musical envelope of speech, exhibiting aspects of rhythm, tempo, melody, accent, and intonation. It may have a linguistic value (marking the boundaries of sentences or of words) or a nonlinguistic value (signaling an emotion, for example).

psychoacoustics

The study of the relationship between acoustic stimuli and accompanying psychological sensations.

psycholinguistics

The study of how language is perceived, acquired, produced, and understood.

quantity

In phonology, a term that refers to the duration of a sound; also called length.

retroflex

Sound produced by curling the tip of the tongue back behind the alveolar ridge.

scansion

Pronunciation that emphasizes the separations between phrases or words or syllables.

segment

The minimal unit of the speech chain of a language that allows it to be divided into distinct phonetic signs. Vowels and consonants are segments.

segmentation

The process of analyzing speech into its constituent parts, or segments.

semantics

The study of linguistic meaning, or the meanings of words and sentences.

sound intensity. *See* intensity

spectrogram

The graphic representation of the physical parameters of speech given by a spectrograph. The distribution of sound intensity is represented as a function of time (along the horizontal axis) and of frequency (along the vertical axis).

spectrograph

A device for measuring and analyzing speech sounds that registers the frequencies exhibited by a sound and their evolution.

spectrum

A graph displaying the relative amplitudes of frequency components of complex acoustic signals.

strategy

A conscious or unconscious decision procedure.

stress

Greater energy placed on an element or syllable of a word yielding a greater perceptual salience. In languages characterized by stress, accent has a linguistic value, its placement determining the meaning of the word: *canto* in Spanish means "song" when the accent falls on the first syllable and means "he sang" when the accent falls on the second syllable. English and Russian are examples of languages in which stress plays an important role.

syllable

Unit of phonological structure that varies according to the sound system of a language; constituted by a vowel nucleus, alone or preceded and/or followed by one or several consonants.

sylvian sulcus

Fissure situated on the lateral face of each of the cerebral hemispheres that separates the frontal and parietal lobes from the temporal lobe.

synapse

Junction between neurons; also between neurons and other cells, such as muscles and glands.

synaptogenesis

An essential stage in the formation of the nervous system responsible for the specificity of neural circuits.

syntagm. *See* phrase

syntax

The set of rules determining the organization of words in a sentence and whether statements are well-formed according to the grammar of the language.

timbre

Particular quality of a sound independent of its pitch or its intensity, but specific to an instrument or to a voice.

tone language

A language in which variations of F0 contour on words or syllables have a linguistic function. In Chinese, for example, depending on the direction of the tone (high or low, rising or falling), *ma* may mean "mother," "horse," "hemp," or "to insult."

universal grammar

In Chomsky's theory, the grammatical principles that underlie all natural human languages and constrain the hypotheses that children can make in acquiring their native language.

velar

A consonant (such as /k/ and /g/) pronounced with the back of the tongue raised to touch the soft palate (or velum).

vocal cords. *See* larynx

vocal tract

The set of cavities through which air sent from the lungs passes on its way up to the glottis and the larynx—from the pharynx, through the oral and nasal cavities, separated by the hard and soft palates at the back of the mouth, and ending at the uvula in the upper pharynx. The vocal tract also contains articulators (the jaw, lips, and tongue) that modify the shape of the cavities through which the airstream passes.

voiced and unvoiced

A voiced sound is produced by a vibration of the vocal cords with the passage of air. A sound is said to be unvoiced when there is an interruption in the vibration of the vocal cords during the production of a consonant.

voicing lag

Delay that occurs between the constriction of the vocal tract for the production of a consonant and the resumption of voicing after closure is relaxed. The more or less rapid resumption of voicing constitutes an acoustic index that allows voiced consonants (such as /b/, /d/, and /g/) to be distinguished from unvoiced consonants (such as /p/, /t/, and /k/).

vowel

A phoneme pronounced without any constriction of the airstream (/a/, /e/, /i/, /o/, /u/ in English). A further distinction is made between compact vowels, whose spectral energy is concentrated in a zone of relatively limited frequency (such as /a/), and diffuse vowels, whose spectral energy is diffusely distributed over the range of frequencies (such as /i/).

vowel harmony

The assimilation of the vowel of a syllable in one word to the vowel of the syllable that comes before or after it. One observes such alterations in the evolution of adult language or in children's production of words (in French, for example, *assa* for *assis*).

vowel nucleus

The part of a syllable constituted by a vowel (or a diphthong) in which energy is largely concentrated.

vowel space

Space described on a diagram by relating the frequencies of the first two formants (or regions of high degrees of sound energy) of the vowels of a language.

Wernicke's area

Left rear and upper portion of the temporal lobe. Lesions in this area provoke deficits in comprehension of language.

Bibliography

Aldobrandino da Siena. (1911/13th c.) *Régime du corps*. Edited by L. Landouzy and R. Pépin. Paris: Champion.

Altmann, G. T. M. (ed.). (1990). *Cognitive Models of Speech Processing: Psycholinguistic and Computational Perspectives*. Cambridge, Mass.: MIT Press.

Altmann, G. T. M., and R. Shillcock (eds.). (1993). *Cognitive Models of Speech Processing: The Second Sperlonga Meeting*. Hillsdale, N.J.: Erlbaum.

Aslin, R. N. (1993). "Segmentation of Fluent Speech into Words: Learning Models and the Role of Maternal Input." In Boysson-Bardies et al., *Developmental Neurocognition*.

Augustine, Saint. (1960/circa 410). *The Confessions*. Translated with an introduction and notes by John K. Ryan. New York: Doubleday.

Bacri, N. (1984). "Pitch and Timing Cues in Speech Intelligibility: The Case of Child Language." In van den Broecke and Cohen, *Proceedings of the Tenth International Congress of Phonetic Sciences* (pp. 589–594).

Baillargeon, R. (1991). "Object Permanence in 3.5- and 4.5-Month-Old Infants." *Developmental Psychology* 23: 655–664.

Baillargeon, R., E. S. Spelke, and S. Wasserman. (1985). "Object Permanence in Five-Month-Old Infants." *Cognition* 20: 191–208.

Barthes, R. (1984). *Essais critiques IV: Le bruissement de la langue*. Paris: Seuil.

Bartholomaeus Anglicus (Bartholomew de Glanville). (1994/13th c.). *De proprietatibus rerum*. In Pierre Riché and Danièle Alexandre-Bidon (eds.), *L'Enfance au Moyen Âge*. Paris: Seuil and Bibliothèque de France.

Barton, D. (1978). *The Role of Perception in the Acquisition of Phonology*. Bloomington, Ind.: Indiana University Linguistics Club.

Bates, E., I. Bretherton, C. Shore, and S. McNew. (1983). "Names, Gestures, and Objects." In Nelson, *Children's Language* (vol. 4).

Bates, E., P. S. Dale, and D. Thal. (1995). "Individual Differences and Their Implications for Theories of Language Development." In Fletcher and Mac-Whinney, *The Handbook of Child Language* (pp. 96–151).

Bates, E., V. Marchman, D. Thal, L. Fenson, P. Dale, J. S. Reznick, J. Reilly, and J. Hartnung. (1994). "Developmental and Stylistic Variation in the Composition of Early Vocabulary." *Journal of Child Language* 21: 85–123.

Bell, A., and J. Hooper (eds.). (1978). *Syllables and Segments*. Amsterdam: North Holland.

Benedict, H. (1979). "Early Lexical Development: Comprehension and Production." *Journal of Child Language* 6: 183–200.

Bertoncini, J., R. Bijeljac-Babic, P. Jusczyk, L. Kennedy, and J. Mehler. (1988). "An Investigation of Young Infants' Perceptual Representations of Speech Sounds." *Journal of Experimental Psychology: General* 117: 21–33.

Bertoncini, J., and J. Mehler. (1981). "Syllables as Units in Infants' Speech Behavior." *Infant Behavior and Development* 4: 247–260.

Bertoncini, J., J. Morais, R. Bijeljac-Babic, S. MacAdams, I. Peretz, and J. Mehler. (1989). "Dichotic Perception and Laterality in Neonates." *Brain and Language* 37: 591–605.

Best, C. (1993). "Emergence of Language-Specific Constraints in Perception of Non-Native Speech: A Window on Early Phonological Development." In Boysson-Bardies et al., *Developmental Neurocognition* (pp. 289–304).

Best, C., H. Hoffman, and B. B. Glanville. (1982). "Development of Infant Ear Asymmetries for Speech and Music." *Perception and Psychophysics* 31, no. 1: 75–85.

Bickerton, D. (1990). *Language and Species*. Chicago: University of Chicago Press.

Bijeljac-Babic, R., J. Bertoncini, and J. Mehler. (1993). "How Do Four-Day-Old Infants Categorize Multisyllabic Utterances?" *Developmental Psychology* 29: 711–721.

Bishop, D., and K. Mogford, (eds.). (1993). *Language Development in Exceptional Circumstances*. Hillsdale, N.J.: Erlbaum.

Blake, J., and B. de Boysson-Bardies. (1992). "Patterns in Babbling: A Cross-Linguistic Study." *Journal of Child Language* 19, no. 1: 51–74.

Blake, J., and R. Fink. (1987). "Sound-Meaning Correspondences in Babbling." *Journal of Child Language* 14: 229–253.

Bloom, L. (1970). *Language Development: Form and Function in Emerging Grammars*. Cambridge, Mass.: MIT Press.

Bloom, L., L. Lightbown, and L. Hood. (1975). "Structure and Variation in Child Language." *Monographs of the Society for Research in Child Development* 40, no. 2.

Blount, B. (1970). "The Pre-Linguistic System of Luo Children." *Anthropological Linguistics* 12: 326–342.

Blount B. G., and E. Padgug. (1976). "Mother and Father Speech: Distribution of Parental Speech Features in English and Spanish." *Papers and Reports on Child Language Acquisition* 12: 47–59.

Bornstein, M. H., H. Azuma, C. S. Tamis-LeMonda, and M. Ogino. (1990). "Mother and Infant Activity and Interaction in Japan and the United States: A Comparative Microanalysis of Naturalistic Exchanges." *International Journal of Behavioral Development* 13: 267–287.

Bornstein, M., J. Tal, C. Rahn, C. Z. Galperin, M. Lamour, M. Ogino, M.-G. Pêcheux, S. Toda, H. Azuma, and C. S. Tamis-LeMonda. (1992). "Functional Analysis of the Contents of Maternal Speech to Infants of Five and Thirteen Months in Four Cultures: Argentina, France, Japan, and the United States." *Developmental Psychology* 28, no. 4: 1–10.

Bornstein, M. H., C. S. Tamis-LeMonda, M.-G. Pêcheux, and C. W. Rahn. (1991). "Mother and Infant Activity and Interaction in France and the United States: A Comparative Study." *International Journal of Behavioral Development* 14, no. 1: 21–43.

Boysson Bardies, B. de. (1976). *Négation et performance linguistique*. Paris and The Hague: Mouton.

Boysson-Bardies, B. de. (1993). "Ontogeny of Language-Specific Phonetic and Lexical Productions." In Boysson-Bardies et al., *Developmental Neurocognition*.

Boysson-Bardies, B. de, P. Hallé, L. Sagart, and C. Durand. (1989). "A Cross-Linguistic Investigation of Vowel Formants in Babbling." *Journal of Child Language* 16: 1–17.

Boysson-Bardies, B. de, L. Sagart, and C. Durand. (1984). "Discernable Differences in the Babbling of Infants According to Target Language." *Journal of Child Language* 11: 1–15.

Boysson-Bardies, B. de, S. de Schonen, P. Jusczyk, P. MacNeilage, and J. Morton (eds.). (1993). *Developmental Neurocognition: Speech and Face Processing in the First Year of Life*. Dordrecht: Kluwer.

Boysson-Bardies, B. de, and M. M. Vihman. (1991). "Adaptation to Language: Evidence from Babbling and First Words in Four Languages." *Language* 67, no. 2: 297–319.

Boysson-Bardies, B. de, M. M. Vihman, L. Roug-Hellichius, C. Durand, I. Landberg, and F. Arao. (1992). "Material Evidence of Infant Selection from the Target Language: A Cross-Linguistic Phonetic Study." In Ferguson, Menn, and Stoel-Gammon, *Phonological Development* (pp. 369–391).

Braine, M. D. S. (1963). "The Ontogeny of English Phrase Structure: The First Phase." *Language* 39: 1–14.

Bretherton, I. (1988). "How to Do Things with One Word: The Ontogenesis of Intentional Message-Making in Infancy." In Smith and Locke, *The Emergent Lexicon* (pp. 225–260).

Bril, B., and H. Lehalle. (1988). *Le Développement psychologique est-il universel?* Paris: Presses Universitaires de France.

Broca, P. (1969/1861). "Remarques sur le siège de la faculté du langage articulé, suivies d'une observation d'aphémie (perte de la parole)." *Bulletin de la Société d'Anthropologie* 6: 330–357, 398–407. Reprinted in Hécaen and Dubois, *La Naissance de la neuropsychologie du langage* (pp. 61–91).

Broca, P. (1969/1865). "Sur le siège de la faculté du langage articulé." *Bulletin de la Société d'Anthropologie* 6: 337–393. Reprinted in Hécaen and Dubois, *La Naissance de la neuropsychologie du langage* (pp. 108–121).

Broecke, M. P. R. van den, and A. Cohen (eds.). (1984). *Proceedings of the Tenth International Congress of Phonetic Sciences*. Dordrecht: Floris.

Brown, R. (1973). *A First Language: The Early Stages*. Cambridge, Mass.: Harvard University Press.

Bühler, C. (1927). "Die ersten sozialen Verhaltensweisen des Kindes." *Quellen und Studien zur Jugendkunde* 5: 1–102.

Butterworth, B. (ed.). (1983). *Language Production* (vol. 2). London: Academic Press.

Butterworth, B., B. Comrie, and Ö. Dahl (eds.). (1984). *Explanations of Linguistic Universals*. The Hague: Mouton.

Butterworth, G., and E. Cochran. (1980). "Towards a Mechanism of Joint Visual Attention in Human Infancy." *International Journal of Behavioral Development* 3: 253–270

Butterworth, G. E., and L. Grover. (1988). "The Origins of Referential Communication in Human Infancy." In Weiskrantz, *Thought Without Language* (pp. 5–24).

Caramazza, A., and A. E. Hillis. (1991). "Lexical Organization of Nouns and Verbs in the Brain." *Nature* 349: 788–790.

Carey, S., and R. Gelman (eds.). (1991). *The Epigenesis of Mind*. Hillsdale, N.J.: Erlbaum.

Castellan, N. J., D. B. Pisoni, and G. R. Potts (eds.). (1976). *Cognitive Theory* (vol. 2). Hillsdale, N.J.: Erlbaum.

Cendrars, B. (1983/1926). *Moravagine*. Paris: Grasset.

Changeux, J.-P. (1992). "Un modèle neuronal capable de raisonnement." *La Recherche* (vol. 3), no. 244: 711–713.

Changeux, J.-P. (1997/1983). *Neuronal Man: The Biology of Mind*. Translated by Laurence Garey with a new preface by Vernon B. Mountcastle. Princeton: Princeton University Press.

Changeux, J.-P., and A. Danchin. (1976). "Selective Stabilization of Developing Synapses as a Mechanism for the Specification of Neuronal Networks." *Nature* 264: 705–721.

Changeux, J.-P., and S. Dehaene. (1989). "Neuronal Models of Cognitive Functions." *Cognition* 33: 63–110.

Charles-Luce, J., and P. A. Luce. (1990). "Similarity Neighbourhoods of Words in Young Children's Lexicons." *Child Language* 17: 205–215.

Chomsky, N. (1957). *Syntactic Structures*. The Hague: Mouton.

Chomsky, N. (1959). "A Review of B. F. Skinner's *Verbal Behavior*." *Language* 35: 26–58.

Chomsky, N. (1965). *Aspects of the Theory of Syntax*. Cambridge, Mass.: MIT Press.

Chomsky, N. (1968). *Language and Mind*. New York: Harcourt Brace Jovanovich.

Chomsky, N., and M. Halle. (1968). *The Sound Pattern of English*. New York: Harper and Row.

Christophe, A., E. Dupoux, J. Bertoncini, and J. Mehler. (1995). "Do Infants Perceive Word Boundaries? An Empirical Study of the Bootstrapping of Lexical Acquisition," *Journal of the Acoustical Society of America* 3: 1570–1580.

Chukovsky, K. (1963/1971). *From Two to Five*. Translated and edited by Miriam Morton. Berkeley.

Cohen, N. J., and L. Beckwith. (1976). "Maternal Language in Infancy." *Developmental Psychology* 12: 371–372.

Cordemoy, G. de. (1970/1668). *Discours physique de la parole*. In *Les Oeuvres du feu M. de Cordemoy*, Paris, 1704. Reprint, Paris: Copedith, Bibliothèque du Graphe, 1970.

Curtiss, S. (1977). *Genie: A Psycholinguistic Study of a Modern-Day "Wild Child."* London: Academic Press.

Cutler, A. (1994). "Prosody and the Word Boundary Problem." In Morgan and Demuth, *Signal to Syntax*.

Cutler, A. (1994). "Segmentation Problems, Rhythmic Solutions." *Lingua* 92, no. 1: 81–104.

Cutler, A., and D. M. Carter. (1987). "The Predominance of Strong Initial Syllables in the English Vocabulary." *Computer Speech and Language* 2: 133–142.

Cutler, A., J. Mehler, D. Norris, and J. Segui. (1983). "A Language-Specific Comprehension Strategy." *Nature* 304: 159–160.

Cutler, A., and D. G. Norris. (1988). "The Role of Strong Syllables in Segmentation for Lexical Access." *Journal of Experimental Psychology: Human Perception and Performance* 14: 113–121.

Cyrulnik, B. (1993). *Les Nourritures affectives.* Paris: Odile Jacob.

Darwin, C. (1859). *The Origin of Species.* London: Murray.

Darwin, C. (1871). *The Descent of Man and Selection in Relation to Sex.* London: Murray.

Darwin, C. (1872). *The Expression of Emotions in Man and Animals.* London: Murray.

Dawson, G., and K. Fischer (eds.). (1993). *Human Behavior and the Developing Brain.* New York: Guilford.

DeCasper, A. J., and W. P. Fifer. (1980). "Of Human Bonding: Newborns Prefer Their Mothers' Voices." *Science* 208: 1174–1176.

DeCasper, A. J., J.-P. Lecanuet, M. C. Busnel, C. Granier-Deferre, and R. Maugeais. (1994). "Fetal Reactions to Recurrent Maternal Speech." *Infant Behavior and Development* 17, no. 2: 159–164.

DeCasper, A. J., and M. J. Spence. (1986). "Prenatal Maternal Speech Influences Newborn's Perception of Speech Sounds." *Infant Behavior and Development* 9: 133–150.

Dehaene-Lambertz, G. (1994). "Bases cérébrales de la discrimination syllabique chez le nourrison." *Annales de la Fondation Fyssen* 9: 43–49.

Dehaene-Lambertz, G., and S. Dehaene. (1994). "Speed and Cerebral Correlates of Syllable Discrimination in Infants." *Nature* 370: 292–295.

Demany, L., B. McKenzie, and E. Vurpillot. (1977). "Rhythm Perception in Early Infancy." *Nature* 266: 718–719.

De Schonen, S., M. Gil De Diaz, and E. Mathivet. (1986). "Hemispheric Asymmetry in Face Processing in Infancy." In Ellis, Jeeves, Newcombe, and Young, *Aspects of Face Processing* (pp. 199–208).

De Schonen, S., A. Van Hout, J. Mancini, and M. O. Livet. (1994). "Neuropsychologie et développement cognitif." In Seron and Jeannerod, *Neuropsychologie humaine* (pp. 487–527).

Deville, G. (1890). "Notes sur le développement du langage." *Revue de Linguistique et de Philologie Comparée* 23: 330–343 and 24: 10–42, 128–143, 242–257, 300–320.

Di Cristo, A. (1976). Contribution à l'étude de la structure prosodique de la phrase en français moderne. Doctoral thesis, Université de Provence.

D'Odorico, L., and F. Franco. (1985). "The Determinants of Baby Talk: Relationship to Content." *Journal of Child Language* 12: 567–586.

Dupoux, E., and J. Mehler. (1990). *Naître humain.* Paris: Odile Jacob.

Edelman, G. M. (1987). *Neural Darwinism*. New York: Basic Books.

Eibl-Eibesfeldt, I. (1970). *Ethology: The Biology of Behavior*. New York: Holt, Rinehart, and Winston.

Eimas, P. D., E. R. Siqueland, P. Jusczyk, and J. Vigorito. (1971). "Speech Perception in Infants." *Science* 171: 303–306.

Ellis, H. D., M. A. Jeeves, F. Newcombe, and A. Young (eds.). (1986). *Aspects of Face Processing*. Dordrecht: Nijhoff.

Entus, A. K. (1977). "Hemispheric Asymmetry in Processing of Dichotically Presented Speech and Nonspeech Stimuli by Infants." In Segalowitz and Gruber, *Language Development and Neurological Theory*.

Fenson, L., P. S. Dale, J. S. Reznick, E. Bates, D. J. Thal, and S. J. Pethick. (1994). "Variability in Early Communicative Development." *Monographs of the Society for Research in Child Development* 59, no. 5.

Ferguson, C. A. (1964). "Baby Talk in Six Languages." *American Anthropologist* 66, no. 6/2: 103–104.

Ferguson, C. A. (1977). "Baby Talk as a Simplified Register." In Snow and Ferguson, *Talking to Children*.

Ferguson, C. A., and C. B. Farwell. (1975). "Words and Sounds in Early Language Acquisition." *Language* 51: 419–439.

Ferguson, C. A., L. Menn, and C. Stoel-Gammon (eds.). (1992). *Phonological Development: Models, Research, Implications*. Timonium, Md.: York Press.

Fernald, A. (1985). "Four-Month-Old Infants Prefer to Listen to Motherese." *Infant Behavior and Development* 8: 181–195.

Fernald, A., and P. Kuhl. (1987) "Acoustic Determinants of Infant Reference or Motherese Speech." *Infant Behavior and Development* 10: 279–283.

Fernald, A., and H. Morikawa. (1993). "Common Themes and Cultural Variations in Japanese and American Mothers' Speech to Infants." *Child Development* 64: 637–656.

Fernald, A., and T. Simon. (1984). "Expanded Intonation Contours in Mothers' Speech to Newborns." *Developmental Psychology* 20: 104–113.

Fernald, A., T. Taeschner, J. Dunn, M. Papousek, B. de Boysson-Bardies, and I. Fukui. (1989). "A Cross-Language Study of Modifications in Mothers' and Fathers' Speech to Preverbal Infants." *Journal of Child Language* 16, no. 3: 477–501.

Fletcher, P., and M. German (eds.). (1979). *Language Acquisition: Studies in First Language Acquisition*. Cambridge: Cambridge University Press.

Fletcher, P., and B. MacWhinney (eds.). (1995). *The Handbook of Child Language*. Oxford: Blackwell.

Fodor, J. (1983). *The Modularity of Mind*. Cambridge, Mass.: MIT Press.

Fodor, J. A., and J. J. Katz (eds.). (1964). *The Structure of Language: Readings in the Philosophy of Language.* Englewood Cliffs, N.J.: Prentice-Hall.

Friederici, D. (1993). "Development of Language-Relevant Processing Systems: The Emergence of a Cognitive Module." In Boysson-Bardies et al., *Developmental Neurocognition.*

Furrow, D., K. Nelson, and H. Benedict. (1979). "Mother's Speech to Children and Synatctic Development: Some Simple Relationships." *Journal of Child Language* 6: 423–442.

Garnica, O. (1977). "Some Prosodic and Paralingual Features of Speech to Young Children." In Snow and Ferguson, *Talking to Children* (pp. 63–68).

Gerken, L. A., B. Landau, and R. E. Remez. (1990). "Function Morphemes in Young Children's Speech Perception and Production." *Developmental Psychology* 27: 204–216.

Geschwind, N., and A. M. Galaburda. (1987). "Cerebral Lateralization: Biological Mechanisms, Associations, and Pathology, I–III: A Hypothesis and a Program for Research." *Archives of Neurology* 42: 428–459, 521–552, 634–654.

Glanville, B. B., C. T. Best, and R. Levenson. (1977). "A Cardiac Measure of Cerebral Asymmetries in Infant Auditory Perception." *Developmental Psychology* 13: 54–59.

Gleitman, L. R. (1990). "The Structural Sources of Verb Meaning." *Language Acquisition* 1: 3–55.

Golinkoff, R. M. (ed.). (1983). *The Transition from Prelinguistic to Linguistic Communication.* Hillsdale, N.J.: Erlbaum.

Golinkoff, R. M., and K. Hirsh-Pasek. (1995). "Reinterpreting Children's Sentence Comprehension: Toward a New Framework." In Fletcher and Mac-Whinney, *The Handbook of Child Language.*

Golinkoff, R. M., K. Hirsh-Pasek, K. M. Cauley, and L. Gordon. (1987). "The Eyes Have It: Lexical and Syntactic Comprehension in a New Paradigm." *Journal of Child Language* 14: 23–45.

Greenberg, J. H. (ed.). (1978). *Universals of Human Language.* Stanford: Stanford University Press.

Grégoire, A. (1937). *L'Apprentissage du langage: Les deux premières années.* Paris: Félix Alcan.

Grieser, D. L., and P. K. Kuhl. (1988). "Maternal Speech to Infants in a Tonal Language: Support for Universal Prosodic Features in Motherese." *Developmental Psychology* 24: 14–20.

Hagège, C. (1985). *L'Homme de parole: Contribution linguistique aux sciences humaines.* Paris: Fayard.

Hallé, P. A., and B. de Boysson-Bardies. (1994). "Emergence of an Early Receptive Lexicon: Infants' Recognition of Words." *Infant Behavior and Development* 17: 119–129.

Hallé, P. A., and B. de Boysson-Bardies. (1996). "The Format of Representation of Recognized Words in Infants' Early Receptive Lexicon." *Infant Behavior and Development* 19: 463–481.

Hallé, P. A., B. de Boysson-Bardies, and M. Vihman. (1991). "Beginnings of Prosodic Organization: Intonation and Duration Patterns of Disyllables Produced by Japanese and French Infants." *Language and Speech* 34, no. 4: 299–318.

Hannequin, D., P. Goulet, and Y. Joanette. (1987). *Hémisphère droit et langage.* Paris: Masson.

Hécaen, H., and J. Dubois (eds.). (1969). *La Naissance de la neuropsychologie du langage, 1825–1865.* Paris: Flammarion.

Hirsh-Pasek, K., and R. M. Golinkoff. (1991). "Language Comprehension: A New Look at Some Old Themes." In Krasnegor et al., *Biological and Behavioral Determinants of Language Development* (pp. 301–320).

Hirsh-Pasek, K., D. G. Kemler-Nelson, P. W. Jusczyk, K. Wright-Cassidy, B. Druss, and L. Kennedy. (1987). "Clauses Are Perceptual Units for Young Infants." *Cognition* 26: 269–286.

Hirst, D. J., and A. Di Cristo. (1984). "French Intonation: A Parametric Approach." *Die Neuren Sprachen* 83, no. 5: 554–569.

Hohne, E. A., A. M. Jusczyk, and N. J. Redanz. (1994). "Do Infants Remember Words from Stories?" Paper presented at the meeting of the Acoustical Society of America, Cambridge, Mass., June 1994.

Hugo, V. (1985/1881) *L'Art d'être grand père.* Paris: Flammarion.

Itard, J. (1981/1801). "Mémoire et rapport sur Victor de l'Aveyron." Reprinted in Lucien Malson, *Les Enfants sauvages: mythe et réalité.* Paris: Éditions France Loisirs.

Izard, C. E., R. Huebner, D. Risser, G. McGinnes, and L. Dougherty. (1980). "The Young Infant's Ability to Produce Discrete Emotional Expressions." *Developmental Psychology* 16: 132–140.

Jakobson, R. (1972/1942). *Child Language Aphasia and Phonological Universals.* The Hague: Mouton.

Jakobson, R., and L. Waugh. (1979). *The Sound Shape of Language.* Bloomington: Indiana University Press.

Jeannerod, M., (ed.). (1991). *Attention and Performance, XII: Motor Representation and Control.* Hillsdale, N.J.: Erlbaum.

Johnson, H. M., and J. Morton. (1991). *Biology and Cognitive Development: The Case of Face Recognition.* Oxford: Blackwell.

Jusczyk, P. W. (1985). "On Characterizing the Development of Speech Perception." In Mehler and Fox, *Neonate Cognition*.

Jusczyk, P. W. (1993). "How Word Recognition May Evolve from Infant Speech Perception Capacities." In Altmann and Shillcock, *Cognitive Models of Speech Processing*.

Jusczyk, P. W., and R. N. Aslin. (1995). "Infants' Detection of the Sound Patterns of Words in Fluent Speech." *Cognitive Psychology* 29: 1–23.

Jusczyk, P. W., and J. Bertoncini. (1993). "Si 'd'instinct' nous apprenions à percevoir la parole?" In Pouthas and Jouen, *Les Comportements du bébé* (pp. 257–270).

Jusczyk, P. W., A. Cutler, and N. J. Redanz. (1993). "Infants' Preference for the Predominant Stress Patterns of English Words." *Child Development* 64: 675–687.

Jusczyk, P. W., and C. Derrah. (1987). "Representation of Speech Sounds by Young Infants." *Developmental Psychology* 23: 648–654.

Jusczyk, P. W., A. Friederici, J. Wessels, V. Svenkerud, and A. M. Jusczyk. (1993). "Infants' Sensitivity to the Sound Patterns of Native Language Words." *Journal of Memory and Language* 32: 402–420.

Jusczyk, P. W., K. Hirsh-Pasek, D. G. Kemler-Nelson, L. Kennedy, A. Woodward, and J. Piwoz. (1992). "Perception of Acoustic Correlates of Major Phrasal Units by Young Infants." *Cognitive Psychology* 24: 252–293.

Kelkar, A. (1964). "Marathi Baby Talk." *Word* 20: 40–54.

Kemler-Nelson, D. G., P. W. Jusczyk, D. R. Mandel, J. Myers, A. Turk, and L. A. Gerken. (1995). "The Headturn Preference Procedure for Testing Auditory Perception." *Infant Behavior and Development* 18: 111–116.

Kent, R. D. (1976). "Anatomical and Neuromuscular Maturation of the Speech Mechanism: Evidence from Acoustic Studies." *Journal of Speech and Hearing Research* 19: 421–445.

Kent, R. D. (1992). "The Biology of Phonological Development." In Ferguson, Menn, and Stoel-Gammon, *Phonological Development*.

Kent, R. D., and H. R. Bauer. (1985). "Vocalizations of One-Year-Olds." *Journal of Child Language* 12: 491–526.

Kent, R. D., and A. D. Murray. (1982). "Acoustic Features of Infant Vocalic Utterances at Three, Six, and Nine Months." *Journal of Acoustic Society of America* 72: 353–365.

Klatt, D. H. (1979). "Speech Perception: A Model of Acoustic-Phonetic Analysis and Lexical Access." *Journal of Phonetics* 7: 279–312.

Koopmans van Beinum, F. J., and J. M. Van der Stelt. (1979). "Early Stages in Infant Speech Development." *Proceedings of the Institute of Phonetic Sciences, University of Amsterdam* 5: 30–43.

Krasnegor, N., D. Rumbaugh, R. Schiefelbusch, and M. Studdert-Kennedy (eds.). (1979). *Biological and Behavioral Determinants of Language Development.* Hillsdale, N.J.: Erlbaum.

Kuhl, P. K. (1983). "Perception of Auditory Equivalence Classes for Speech in Early Infancy." *Infant Behavior and Development* 6: 263–285.

Kuhl, P. K. (1993). "Innate Predispositions and the Effects of Experience in Speech Perception: The Native Language Magnet Theory." In Boysson-Bardies et al., *Developmental Neurocognition* (pp. 259–274).

Kuhl, P. K., and A. N. Meltzoff. (1982). "The Bimodal Perception of Speech in Infancy." *Science* 218: 1138–1141.

Kuhl, P. K., and A. N. Meltzoff. (1984). "The Intermodal Representation of Speech in Infants." *Infant Behavior and Development* 7: 361–381.

Kuhl, P. K., K. A. Williams, F. Lacerda, K. N. Stevens, and B. Lindblom. (1992). "Linguistic Experience Alters Phonetic Perception in Infants by Six Months of Age." *Science* 255: 606–608.

Lecanuet, J.-P., and C. Granier-Deferre. (1993). "Speech Stimuli in the Fetal Environment." In Boysson-Bardies et al., *Developmental Neurocognition.*

Lecanuet, J.-P., C. Granier-Deferre, A. J. DeCasper, R. Maugeais, A. J. Andrieu, and M.-C. Busnel. (1987). "Perception et discrimination fœtale de stimuli langagiers, mise en évidence à partir de la réactivité cardiaque: Résultats préliminaires." *Comptes rendus de l'Académie des Sciences de Paris* 305 (Series III): 161–164.

Lecanuet, J.-P., C. Granier-Deferre, and B. Schaal. (1993). "Continuité sensorielle transnatale." In Pouthas and Jouen, *Les Comportements du bébé.*

Lenneberg, E. (1964). "The Capacity for Language Acquisition." In Fodor and Katz, *The Structure of Language.*

Lenneberg, E. (1967). *Biological Foundations of Language.* New York: Wiley.

Levelt, W. J. M. (1989). *Speaking: From Intention to Articulation.* Cambridge: MIT Press.

Levitt, A., and Q. Wang. (1991). "Evidence for Language-Specific Rhythmic Influences in the Reduplicative Babbling of French- and English-Learning Infants." *Language and Speech* 34: 235–249.

Lewis, M. M. (1936). *Infant Speech: A Study of the Beginnings of Language.* London: Routledge and Kegan Paul.

Liberman, A. M. (1957). "Some Results of Research on Speech Perception." *Journal of Acoustic Society of America* 29: 117–123.

Liberman, A. M., K. S. Harris, J. A. Kinney, and H. Lane. (1961). "The Discrimination of Relative-Onset Time of the Components of Certain Speech and Nonspeech Patterns." *Journal of Experimental Psychology* 61: 379–388.

Lieberman, P. (1980). "On the Development of Vowel Production in Young Children." In Yeni-Komshian, Kavanagh, and Ferguson, *Child Phonology 1.*

Lindblom, B. (1992). "Phonological Units as Adaptive Emergents of Lexical Development." In Ferguson, Menn, and Stoel-Gammon, *Phonological Development.*

Lindblom, B., P. MacNeilage, and M. Studdert-Kennedy. (1983). "Self-Organizing Processes and the Explanation of Phonological Universals." In Butterworth, Comrie, and Dahl, *Explanations of Linguistic Universals.*

Lindblom, B., and R. Zetterstrom (eds.). (1986). *Precursors of Early Speech.* New York: Stockton.

MacFarlane, J. A. (1975). "Olfaction and the Development of Social Preferences in the Human Neonate." In Porter and O'Connor, *Parent-Infant Interaction* (pp. 103–117).

MacKain, K., M. Studdert-Kennedy, S. Spieker, and D. Stern. (1983). "Infant Intermodal Speech Perception Is a Left-Hemisphere Function." *Science* 219: 1347–1349.

Macken, M. (1979). "Developmental Reorganization of Phonology." *Lingua* 49: 11–49.

Macken, M. A. (1980). "Aspects of the Acquisition of Stop Systems: A Cross-Linguistic Perspective." In Yeni-Komshian, Kavanagh, and Ferguson, *Child Phonology 1.*

Macken, M. A. (1993). "Developmental Changes in the Acquisition of Phonology." In Boysson-Bardies et al., *Developmental Neurocognition.*

MacNeilage, P. F. (1980). "The Control of Speech Production." In Yeni-Komshian, Kavanagh, and Ferguson, *Child Phonology 1* (pp. 9–21).

MacNeilage, P. F., and B. L. Davis. (1991). "Acquisition of Speech Production: Frames, Then Content." In Jeannerod, *Attention and Performance, XII.*

Mandel, D. R., P. W. Jusczyk, and D. G. Kemler-Nelson. (1994). "Does Sentential Prosody Help Infants Organize and Remember Speech Information?" *Cognition* 53: 155–180.

Mandel, D. R., P. W. Jusczyk, and D. B. Pisoni. (1995). "Infants' Recognition of the Sound Patterns of Their Own Names." *Psychological Science* 6: 315–318.

Markman, E. M., and J. E. Hutchinson. (1984). "Children's Sensitivity to Constraints on Word Meaning: Taxonomic versus Thematic Relations." *Cognitive Psychology* 16: 1–27.

Marler, P. (1984). "Song Learning: Innate Species Differences in the Learning Process." In Marler and Terrace, *The Biology of Learning.*

Marler, P., and H. S. Terrace (eds.). (1984). *The Biology of Learning: Report on the Dahlem Workshop on the Biology of Learning, Berlin, 1983, October 23–28.* Berlin: Springer Verlag.

Masataka, N. (1992). "Pitch Characteristics of Japanese Maternal Speech to Infants." *Journal of Child Language* 19: 213–223.

Mehler, J., J. Bertoncini, M. Barrière, and D. Jassik-Gershenfeld. (1978). "Infant Recognition of Mother's Voice." *Perception* 7: 491–497.

Mehler, J., E. Dupoux, and J. Segui. (1990). "Constraining Models of Lexical Access: The Onset of Word Recognition." In Altmann, *Cognitive Models of Speech Processing* (pp. 236–262).

Mehler, J. and R. Fox (eds.). (1985). *Neonate Cognition: Beyond the Blooming, Buzzing Confusion.* Hillsdale, N.J.: Erlbaum.

Mehler, J., P. W. Jusczyk, G. Lambertz, N. Halsted, J. Bertoncini, and C. Amiel-Tison. (1988). "A Precursor of Language Acquisition in Young Infants." *Cognition* 29: 143–178.

Mehler, J., J. Segui, and U. Frauenfelder. (1981). "The Role of the Syllable in Language Acquisition and Perception." In Myers, Laver, and Anderson, *The Cognitive Representation of Speech.*

Mehler, J., E. Walker, and M. Garrett (eds.). (1982). *Perspectives on Mental Representations.* Hillsdale, N.J.: Erlbaum.

Meisel, J. M. (1990a). "Grammatical Development in the Simultaneous Acquisition of Two First Languages." In Meisel, *Two First Languages* (pp. 5–22).

Meisel, J. M. (ed.). (1990b). *Two First Languages: Early Grammatical Development in Bilingual Children.* Dordrecht: Foris.

Meisel, J. M. (1995). "Parameters in Acquisition." In Fletcher and MacWhinney, *The Handbook of Child Language* (pp. 10–35).

Meltzoff, A. N., and M. K. Moore. (1977). "Imitation of Facial and Manual Gestures by Human Neonates." *Science* 1909. 75–78.

Menn, L. (1971)."Phonotactic Rules in Beginning Speech." *Lingua* 26: 225–241.

Menn, L. (1978). "Phonological Units in Beginning Speech." In Bell and Hooper, *Syllables and Segments.*

Menn, L. (1983). "Development of Articulatory, Phonetic, and Phonological Capacities." In Butterworth, *Language Production.*

Menyuk, P., and L. Menn. (1979). "Early Strategies for the Perception and Production of Words and Sounds?" In Fletcher and German, *Language Acquisition.*

Mills, D. C., S. A. Coffey, and H. J. Neville. (1993b). "Language Acquisition and Cerebral Specialization in Twenty-Month-Old Infants." *Journal of Cognitive Neuroscience* 5: 317–334.

Mills, D. C., S. A. Coffey, and H. J. Neville. (1993a). "Changes in Cerebral Organization in Infancy During Primary Language Acquisition." In Dawson and Fischer, *Human Behavior and the Developing Brain.*

Mogford, K., and D. Bishop. (1993). "Five Questions About Language Acquisition Considered in the Light of Exceptional Circumstances." In Bishop and Mogford, *Language Acquisition in Exceptional Circumstances.*

Molfese, D. L. (1990). "Auditory Evoked Responses Recorded from Sixteen-Month-Old Human Infants to Words They Did and Did Not Know." *Brain and Language* 38: 343–363.

Molfese, D. L., R. B. Freeman, and D. S. Palermo. (1975). "The Ontogeny of Brain Lateralization for Speech and Non-Speech Stimuli." *Brain and Language* 2: 356–368.

Molfese, D. L., and V. J. Molfese. (1979). "Hemisphere and Stimulus Differences as Effected in the Cortical Responses of Newborn Infants to Speech Stimuli." *Developmental Psychology* 15: 505–511.

Morgan, J. L., and K. Demuth (eds.). (1996). *Signal to Syntax: Boostrapping from Speech to Grammar: Early Acquisition.* Mahwah, N.J.: Erlbaum.

Morikawa, H., N. Shand, and Y. Kosawa. (1988). "Maternal Speech to Prelingual Infants in Japan and the United States: Relationships among Functions, Forms, and Referents." *Journal of Child Language* 15: 237–256.

Myers, J., P. W. Jusczyk, D. G. Kemler-Nelson, J. Charles-Luce, A. Woodward, and K. Hirsh-Pasek. (1996). "Infants' Sensitivity to Word Boundaries in Fluent Speech." *Journal of Child Language* 23: 1–30.

Myers, T., J. Laver, and J. Anderson (eds.). (1981). *The Cognitive Representation of Speech.* Amsterdam: North Holland.

Nelson, K. (1973). "Structure and Strategy in Learning to Talk." *Monographs of the Society for Research in Child Development* 38, no. 149.

Nelson, K. E. (ed.). (1983). *Children's Language* (vol. 4). Hillsdale, N.J.: Erlbaum.

Nelson, K., J. Hamson, and L. Kessler-Shaw. (1993). "Nouns in Early Lexicons: Evidence, Explanations, and Implications." *Journal of Child Language* 20: 61–84.

Newport, E. L. (1976). Motherese: The Speech of Mothers to Young Children." In Castellan, Pisoni, and Potts, *Cognitive Theory* (vol. 2).

Oller, D. K. (1980). "The Emergence of the Sounds of Speech in Infancy." In Yeni-Komshian, Kavanagh, and Ferguson, *Child Phonology* 1.

Oller, D. K. (1986). "Metaphonology and Infant Vocalizations." In Lindblom and Zetterstrom, *Precursors of Early Speech.*

Oller, D. K., R. E. Eilers, and M. L. Steffens, M. P. Lynch, and R. Urbano. (1994). "Speech-like Vocalization in Infancy: An Evaluation of Potential Risk Factors." *Journal of Child Language* 21: 33–58.

Oller, D. K., and M. P. Lynch. (1992). "Infant Vocalizations and Innovations in Infraphonology: Toward a Broader Theory of Development and Disorders." In Ferguson, Menn, and Stoel-Gammon, *Phonological Development.*

Oller, D. K., L. A. Wieman, W. Doyle, and C. Ross. (1975). "Infant Babbling and Speech." *Journal of Child Language* 3: 1–11.

Oviatt, S. L. (1980). "The Emerging Ability to Comprehend Language: An Experimental Approach." *Child Development* 51: 97–106.

Papousek, H., and M. Papousek. (1993). "Apprentissage chez le nourrisson: un point de vue synthétique." In Pouthas and Jouen, *Les Comportements du bébé* (p. 120).

Papousek, M., and H. Papousek. (1989). "Forms and Functions of Vocal Matching Interactions Between Mothers and Their Precanonical Infants." *First Language* 9: 137–158.

Papousek, M., H. Papousek, and M. Haekel. (1987). "Didactic Adjustments in Fathers' and Mothers' Speech to Their Three-Month-Old Infants." *Journal of Psycholinguistic Research* 16: 491–516.

Pegg, J. E., J. F. Werker, and P. J. McLeod. (1992). "Preference for Infant-Directed over Adult-Directed Speech: Evidence from 7-Week-Old Infants." *Infant Behavior and Development* 15: 325–345.

Peters, A. M. (1977). "Language-Learning Strategies: Does the Whole Equal the Sum of the Parts?" *Language* 53, no. 3: 561–573.

Petitto, L. A., and P. F. Marentette. (1991). "Babbling in the Manual Mode: Evidence for the Ontogeny of Language." *Science* 251: 1493–1496.

Pinker, Steven. (1994). *The Language Instinct: How the Mind Creates Language.* New York: Morrow.

Porter, R., and M. O'Connor (eds.). (1975). *Parent-Infant Interaction.* CIBA Foundation Symoposium 33. Amsterdam: Elsevier-North Holland.

Pouthas, V., and F. Jouen (eds.). (1993). *Les Comportements du bébé: expression de son savoir?* Liège: Mardaga.

Premack, D. (1977). *Intelligence in Ape and Man.* Hillsdale, N.J.: Erlbaum.

Prigogine, I. (1987). "La redécouverte du temps." Lecture delivered at the Sorbonne, Paris, 10 June.

Pye, C. (1983). "Mayan Telegraphese: Intonational Determinants of Inflectional Development in Quiché Mayan." *Language* 59: 583–604.

Querleu, D., X. Renard, and F. Versyp. (1981). "Les perceptions auditives du fœtus humain." *Médecine et Hygiène* 39: 2101–2110.

Quine, W. V. (1960). *Word and Object.* Cambridge, Mass.: MIT Press.

Quine, W. V. (1969). "Natural Kinds." In *Ontological Relativitity and Other Essays.* New York: Columbia University Press.

Rakic, P., J.-P. Bourgeois, M. F. Eckenoff, N. Zecevic, and P. S. Goldman-Rakic. (1986). "Concurrent Overproduction of Synapses in Diverse Regions of the Primate Cerebral Cortex." *Science* 232: 232–235.

Ratner, N. B., and C. Pye. (1984). "Higher Pitch Is Not Universal: Acoustic Evidence from Quiché Mayan." *Journal of Child Language* 11: 515–522.

Riché, P., and D. Alexandre-Bidon (eds.). (1994). *L'Enfance aux Moyen Âge.* Paris: Seuil and Bibliothèque de France.

Rousseau, J.-J. (1817). *Essai sur l'origine des langues: Où il est parlé de la mélodie et de l'imitation musicale.* Berlin.

Saussure, F. de. (1972/1916). *Cours de linguistique générale.* Paris: Payot.

Scaife, M., and J. Bruner. (1975). "The Capacity for Joint Visual Attention in Human Infancy." *Nature* 253: 265–266.

Schaal, B., H. Montagner, E. Hertling, D. Bolzoni, E. Moyse, and R. Quichon. (1980). "Les stimulations olfactives dans les relations entre l'enfant et la mère." *Reproduction, Nutrition, Développement* 20: 843–858.

Schaffer, H. R. (ed.). (1977). *Studies in Mother-Infant Interaction.* New York: Academic Press.

Schieffelin, B. B. (1986). "Teasing and Shaming in Kaluli Children's Inter-actions." In Schieffelin and Ochs, *Language Socialization across Cultures.*

Schieffelin, B. B., and E. Ochs. (1983). "A Cultural Perspective on the Transi-tion from Prelinguistic to Linguistic Communication." In Golinkoff, *The Tran-sition from Prelinguistic to Linguistic Communication.*

Schieffelin, B. B., and E. Ochs (eds.). (1986). *Language Socialization across Cul-tures.* New York: Cambridge University Press.

Segalowitz, S. J., and F. A. Gruber (eds.). (1977). *Language Development and Neurological Theory.* New York: Academic Press.

Seron, X., and M. Jeannerod (eds.). (1994). *Neuropsychologie humaine.* Liège: Mardaga.

Shibatani, M. (1990). *The Languages of Japan.* Cambridge: Cambridge University Press.

Shute, B. (1987). "Vocal Pitch in Motherese." *Educational Psychology* 7(3): 187–205.

Siqueland, E. R., and C. DeLucia. (1969). "Visual Reinforcement of Non-nutritive Sucking in Human Infants." *Science* 165: 1144–1146.

Skuse, D. H. (1993). "Extreme Deprivation in Early Childhood." In Bishop and Mogford, *Language Development in Exceptional Circumstances* (pp. 29–46).

Smith, M. D., and J. L. Locke (eds.). (1988). *The Emergent Lexicon: The Child's Development of a Linguistic Vocabulary.* New York: Academic Press.

Snow, C. E., and C. A. Ferguson (eds.). (1977). *Talking to Children: Language Input and Acquisition.* Cambridge: Cambridge University Press.

Spelke, E. S. (1982). "Perceptual Knowledge of Objects in Infancy." In Mehler, Walker, and Garrett, *Perspectives on Mental Representations.*

Spelke, E. S. (1985). "Perception of Unity, Persistence, and Identity." In Mehler and Fox, *Neonate Cognition*.

Spelke, E. S. (1991). "Physical Knowledge in Infancy: Reflections on Piaget's Theory." In Carey and Gelman, *The Epigenesis of Mind* (pp. 133–169).

Stager, C. L. (1995). *Phonetic Similarity Influences Learning Word-Object Associations in Fourteen-Month-Old Infants*. Ph.D. thesis, University of British Columbia.

Stern, D. N., S. Spieker, R. K. Barnett, and K. MacKain. (1983). "The Prosody of Maternal Speech: Infant Age and Context-Related Changes." *Journal of Child Language* 10: 1–15.

Stoel-Gammon, C., and J. Cooper. (1984). "Patterns of Early Lexical and Phonological Development." *Journal of Child Language* 11: 247–271.

Streri, A. (1987). "Tactile Discrimination of Shape and Intermodal Transfer in Two- to Three-Month Old Infants." *British Journal of Developmental Psychology* 5: 213–220.

Studdert-Kennedy, M. G. (1991). "Language Development from an Evolutionary Perspective." In Krasnegor et al., *Biological and Behavioral Determinants of Language Development*.

Tamis-LeMonda, C. S., M. Bornstein, L. Cyphers, S. Toda, and M. Ogino. (1992). "Language and Play at One Year: A Comparison of Toddlers and Mothers in the United States and Japan." *International Journal of Behavioral Development* 15, no. 1: 19–42.

Termine, N. T., and C. E. Izard. (1988). "Infants' Responses to their Mothers' Expressions of Joy and Sadness." *Developmental Psychology* 24: 223–229.

Thelen, E. (1991). "Motor Aspects of Emergent Speech: A Dynamic Approach." In Krasnegor et al., *Biological and Behavioral Determinants of Language Development* (pp. 339–362).

Thongkum, T. L., V. Panupong, P. Kullavanijaya, and M. R. Tingsabadh (eds.). (1979). *Studies in Thai and Mon-Kmer Phonetics and Phonology: In Honor of Eugenie J. A. Henderson*. Bangkok: Chulalongkorn University Press.

Toda, S., A. Fogel, and M. Kawai. (1990). "Maternal Speech to Three-Month-Old Infants in the United States and Japan." *Journal of Child Language* 17: 279–294.

Trehub, S. E. (1973). "Infants' Sensitivity to Vowel and Tonal Contrasts." *Developmental Psychology* 9: 91–96.

Trehub, S. E., D. Bull, and L. Thorpe. (1984). "Infants' Perception of Melodies: The Role of Melodic Contour." *Child Development* 55: 821–830.

Trevarthen, C. (1977). "Descriptive Analyses of Infant Communicative Behavior." In Schaffer, *Studies in Mother-Infant Interaction* (pp. 227–270).

Tuaycharoen, P. (1979). "An Account of Speech Development of a Thai Child: From Babbling to Speech." In Thongkum et al., *Studies in Thai and Mon-Kmer Phonetics and Phonology*.

Uzgiris, I. C. (1993). "L'imitation dans les interactions précoces." In Pouthas and Jouen, *Les Comportements du bébé*.

Valian, V. V. (1991). "Syntactic Subjects in the Early Speech of American and Italian Children." *Cognition* 40: 21–81.

Valian, V. V. (Forthcoming). Input and Innateness: Controversies in Language Acquisition. Working manuscript.

Valian, V. V. (Forthcoming). *Parental Replies: Linguistic Status and Didactic Role.* Cambridge, Mass.: MIT Press/Bradford Books.

Vihman, M. M. (1978). "Consonant Harmony: Its Scope and Function in Child Language." In Greenberg, *Universals of Human Language*.

Vihman, M. M. (1992). "Early Syllables and the Construction of Phonology." In Ferguson, Menn, and Stoel-Gammon, *Phonological Development* (pp. 393–422).

Vihman, M. M., and B. de Boysson-Bardies. (1994). "The Nature and Origins of Ambient Language Influence on Infant Vocal Production and Early Words." *Phonetica* 51: 159–169.

Vihman, M. M., C. A. Ferguson, and M. Elbert. (1986). "Phonological Development from Babbling to Speech: Common Tendencies and Individual Difference." *Applied Psycholinguistics* 7: 3–40.

Vihman, M. M., E. Kay, B. de Boysson-Bardies, C. Durand, and U. Sundberg. (1994). "External Sources of Individual Differences? A Cross-Linguistic Analysis of the Phonetics of Mothers' Speech to One-Year-Old Children." *Developmental Psychology* 30, no. 5: 651–662.

Vihman, M. M., and R. Miller. (1988). "Words and Babble at the Threshold of Lexical Acquisition." In Smith and Locke, *The Emergent Lexicon*.

Vygotsky, L. S. (1962). *Thought and Language.* Edited and translated by E. Hanfmann and G. Vakar. Cambridge, Mass.: MIT Press.

Wallon, H. (1942). *De l'acte à la pensée.* Paris: Flammarion.

Waterston, N. (1971). "Child Phonology: A Prosodic View." *Journal of Language* 6: 179–211.

Watson-Gegeo, K. A., and D. W. Gegeo. (1986). "Calling-Out and Repeating Routines in Kwara'ae Children's Language Socialization." In Schieffelin and Ochs, *Language Socialization across Cultures* (pp. 17–50).

Weiskrantz, L. E. (ed.). (1988). *Thought without Language.* Oxford: Clarendon Press.

Werker, J. F., J. H. Gilbert, K. Humphrey, and R. C. Tees. (1981). "Developmental Aspects of Cross-Language Speech Perception." *Child Development* 52: 349–353.

Werker, J. F., J. E. Pegg, and P. J. McLeod. (1994). "A Cross-Language Investigation of Infant Preference for Infant-Directed Communication." *Infant Behavior and Development* 17, no. 3: 323–333.

Werker, J. F., and R. C. Tees. (1984). "Cross-Language Speech Perception: Evidence for Perceptual Reorganization During the First Year of Life." *Infant Behavior and Development* 7: 49–63.

Wernicke, C. (1874). *Der aphasische symptomencomplex Cohn.* Breslau: Weigert.

Yeni-Komshian, G., C. Kavanagh, and C. Ferguson (eds.). (1980). *Child Phonology 1: Production.* New York: Academic Press.

Zack, M. (1987). Étude du comportement de refus de poursuivre la tétée. Doctoral thesis, École des Hautes Études en Sciences Sociales, Paris.

Zanzotto, A. (1986). "Élégie du pétel." *Arcanes* 17.

Index

Accent
  and babbling, 64, 69
Acoustic environment
  prenatal, 23
Acoustic segmentation, 18, 96
Adjectives
  in Asian languages, 178
  as early words, 186
  and first words, 146
Adult speech. *See also* Parents
  with children, 85
  lexical system of, 192
  psychoacoustic system of, 19
Adverbs
  and Japanese first words, 187
  and vocabulary structure, 148
Affection
  and name recognition, 28
Affective communication
  and motherese, 82–83
Affectivity, 94
Age
  and vocabulary growth, 139
Ambiguity
  and segmentation, 97
American children
  early words of, 184, 186
  vocabulary development of, 157
  vocabulary size of, 137

American mothers
  didactic technique of, 180
  expectations of, 158, 178
  and "vocabulary illusion," 179
Analytic style, 151–158, 175
Anglicus, Bartholomaeus, 84, 143
Animal names
  as first words, 147, 183
Animals
  communication among, 71
Aphasia, 30
Apraxia, 30
Arabic language
  baby talk in, 86
  vowels in, 58
Arcuate fasciculus, 30
Aristotle, 13
Art
  and language acquisition, 150
Articles
  at twenty months, use of, 207
  and vocabulary structure, 148
Articulation. *See also* Articulators
  cerebral control areas, 29
  components of, 15
  and construction of phonological
    system, 193
  control of, 17
  early consonant preferences, 61

Child language
  and creativity, 6, 213–214
  and linguistically impoverished
    environments, 90
Chinese language
  baby talk in, 86, 87
  vowels in, 58
Choice
  and early production, 174
  and language acquisition, 151, 213
Chomsky, N., 3, 6
Clauses
  infant recognition of, 103
Clitic subjects
  in French, 204
Closed syllables
  in early babbling, 46
Cognitive organization
  and early production, 174
  and turn-taking, 76
  and word learning, 129
Cognitive systems
  and innateness, 6
  and intermodal processing, 75
  modularity of, 7
Communication
  dependence on speech act, 4
  desire to engage in, 10, 147
  and expression, 71, 80
  and language acquisition, 9, 94
  and motherese, 83–90
  nonverbal, 120
Compactness
  of adult/infant vowels, 59
Comprehension
  after first year, 5
  lexicon, 145
  pathology of, 30
Concept formation
  and grammaticality, 201
  by infants, 213
Consonantal discrimination, 43, 104.
  by newborns, 26
  after three months, 34
Consonantal features
  infant manipulation of, 38

Consonantal harmonizations, 144
Consonants. *See also* Articulation;
    Articulators; Consonantal
    discrimination
  duration of, as segmentation cue, 98
  in early babbling, 46
  and early phonetic organization, 60
  early production of, 141
  omission of, 144
  as syllabic margins, 45
  vowels, associations with, 64
Context
  and emergence of stable vocabulary,
    111, 167
  and segmentation by adults, 97
  and word recognition, 123
  and word understanding, 109, 124
Conversation
  subjects of, among children, 182–183
Cooing, 38–39
Cordemoy, G. de, 5–6
Creativity
  and child language, 6, 213–214
Creoles
  and child language, 90
Critical periods, 91–94
Cross-linguistic differences
  in babbling, 56
  in baby talk, 85
  and children's styles, 157
  and diversity of styles, 175
  and early grammars, 201
  in early word recognition, 123
  and first words, 178
  and grammaticality, 209
  and production of first words, 151–
    152
  in two-word production, 200
Crying, 77
  universality of, 37
Cultural milieu
  and early words, 179–188
  and language, 177
  and language acquisition, 214
  and motherese, 85–90
Cypselus legend, 77

Darwin, C., 6–7, 78, 150
Deaf infants
  babbling in, 55
  and critical periods, 93
  and turn-taking, 76
Deictic sentences
  cultural differences in use of, 89
Demonstratives
  and early particle additions, 199
Dental babbling, 47. *See also* Babbling
Dichotic listening, 32
Discrimination. *See* Consonantal
    discrimination; Newborns;
    Prosody discrimination; Vowels
Diversity
  and child language, 213
  and early production, 174
  and early words, 183, 188
  and first sentences, 198
  and language acquisition, 149–176,
    214
Dominance, hemispheric, 33. *See also*
    Hemispheric development
Dutch language
  and phonotactic preferences, 107

Early words
  of American children, 184, 186
  and babbling, 141
  and cultural milieu, 179–181
  of French children, 184
  grammar, 189
  of Japanese children, 187
  and play, 183
  proper nouns, 185
  and representation of, 190–191
  of Swedish children, 184
  variation across cultures, 182–188
  verbs, 186
Echoes
  and turn-taking, 76
Embryogenesis, 13
Emotions
  expression of, 77
  infant interpretation of, 72, 77, 78
  sharing of, 78

Empathy, 78
Encoding. *See also* Representations
  of familiar words, 113
  and lexicon explosion, 192
  and word production, 141
English-speaking children
  vocabulary size of, 137
English language, 83
  baby talk in, 86
  and early words, 144, 186
  and expressive style, 167
  F0 contour in, 65
  infant vowel discrimination in, 41
  nouns in, 147
  and phonotactic preferences, 107
  stress in, 98, 106
  unit representation in, 116
  vowels in, 58
Environment
  and critical periods, 91
  and diversity of styles, 175
  first interactions with, 72
  and language acquisition, 150
  prenatal acoustic, 23
  and word learning, 129
Epiglottis
  early configuration of, 17
Error frequency
  and early word production, 144–
    145, 192
Event-related potentials
  auditory, 34
  as evidence of phonological
    encoding, 194
Evoked potentials. *See* Event-related
  potentials
Evolution
  and language, 4
Experience, role of, in language
    acquisition, 91, 107, 133, 149
Expression, 82, 86
  and communication, 71
Expressive style, 151–168
  and extroversion, 175
  and first sentences, 199
  and non-noun vocabulary, 148

Grammaticality
and early concepts, 201
and motherese, 89
Greetings. *See* Social communication
Grégoire, A., 37–38, 45, 51–52, 55, 56

Harmonic patterns
and word production, 144
HAS. *See* High-amplitude sucking
Haskins Laboratory, 18
Hearing-impaired children
earliest babbling in, 75
Hearing loss
and language acquisition, 93
and late speech, 171
Heart rate, prenatal
and mother's voice, 23
Hebrew language
and strong-weak preference, 106
Hemispheric development
and diversity of style, 175
functional equipotentiality, 31–32
intrauterine, 31
and late speakers, 174
and speech processing, 194
and word processing, 197
Hemispheric function, 30–32
High-amplitude sucking (HAS), 19
Hindi language
consonantal discrimination in, 43
Homo habilis, 4
Homo sapiens, 4
Hugo, V., 81
Humor
early understanding of, 78
and language acquisition, 214

Imagination
and language acquisition, 213, 214
Imitation, 39
and expression of emotions, 73
during first months, 37
and reciprocal behaviors, 74
role of, 6
Imperatives
in motherese, 89

Individuality
cerebral, 31
and language acquisition, 9
Infant cognition
and physical intuitions, 132
Infants. *See* Language acquisition, stages of; Newborns
Inflected languages, 3, 179
and diversity of styles, 176
Information sharing, 79
Instinct
and language, 6
and language acquisition, 150
Intellectual capacity
and diversity of styles, 175
Interaction
and language acquisition, 55, 213
Intermodal processing, 75
Interrogative sentences
in motherese, 89
Intonation. *See also* Prosody
adult, 84
and language of environment, 64, 65
and motherese, 82, 109
and segmentation, 97
variation of, across languages, 48
Intonation contour
and early productions, 151
and expressive style, 158, 162, 167, 175
and word production, 141
Intrauterine acoustics, and perception, 23
and right-hemisphere development, 30
Isolation
and critical periods, 92–93
Italian language
baby talk in, 86

Jakobson, R., 52
Japanese children
and critical periods, 91
early consonantal preferences of, 61
preference for aesthetic words, 186
and verb comprehension, 147
vocabulary size, 137

Memory
  and language acquisition, 6
  at nine months, 105
  and object names, 121
  and phonological lexicon, 190
  verbal, and vocabulary size, 140
  and word recognition, 110, 112
Mental representation of words, 115–
  119
  early words, 190
  after first year, 213
  global, 119
  and hemispheric development, 197
  and semantic awareness, 113
  and word learning, 129
  and word production, 141
  and word recognition, 112
Metrical feet
  as frame for words, 141
Middle Ages, 136
  theory of language learning in, 84,
  143
Middle-ear infection
  and language acquisition, 93
Modularity
  of cognitive systems, 7
Mora
  as unit of representation in Japanese,
  116
Morphology
  and phonological lexicon, 191
Motherese, 81–84
  and children's style, 157
  and diversity of styles, 175
  and expressive style, 168
  and first words, 178
  and prosodic grouping, 104
Mother's language. See also Motherese
Mother's voice, 72. See also Motherese
  effect on infant pitch, 39
  infant preference for, 21, 24–25
  prenatal recognition of, 23
Mother tongue, 80
Motor development, 15
  and first words, 63
  and sign-language babbling, 68

Mouth, muscles of. See also
    Articulators
  cerebral control area for, 29
  and speech production, 15
Music
  and right-hemisphere control, 30
Musical ability
  and expressive style, 168
Music/speech discrimination
  at two months, 33
Mutual gaze. See Looking behavior

Name recognition
  of infant's own name, 28–29
Names
  of animals, 147
  as early words, 185
  as first words, 147, 175
  of objects, 147
Nasal consonants
  in early babbling, 46
Native language
  and children's style, 157
Negation
  early expressions of, 208
Newborns, 15–21, 211. See also
    Language acquisition, stages of
  brain development, 14
  as non-talkers, 13
  preference for mother's voice, 72
  recognition of mother's smell, 72
  and speech–sound discrimination,
    20, 26
  talents, 26–28
Nominal subjects
  in speech of American children,
  202
Nonhuman primates
  sound production by, 15
  vocal tract of, 16
Nonlinguistic communication. See
    Nonverbal communication
Nonnutritive sucking, 19–22, 23–
  24
Nonspeaker
  linguistic designation of, 11

Phonological organization
and babbling, 57
Phonology, 191–194
and word acquisition, 127
Phrases
infant recognition of, 103
Phylogenetic evolution
and language, 4, 71, 212
and vocal tract, 16
Physical principles
and infant cognition, 129–133
Physiology
and language processing, 194–202
Pidgins
and child language, 90
Pitch
in adult speech, 84
in infant speech, 86
infant manipulation of, 38
infant sensitivity to, 101
modulation of, as segmentation cue, 98
and motherese, 82
Pitch languages. *See* Tone languages
Pivot words, 200
Place discrimination
by infants, 20
Place of articulation
early preference for, 61
Planum temporale, 31, 32
Play
and early words, 183
Pointing
emergence of, 79
Polish language
and phonetic perception, 107
Polysyllabic utterances
growth of early repertoire of, 49
Posterior temporal lobe, 29
Posture
and evolution of speech, 4
Preadaptation, 212
Prebabbling vocal play. *See* Cooing
Precocity
and vocabulary size, 139–140
Predicate forms
and first words, 146

Prenatal development, 22–26
and language acquisition, 8
Prigogine, I., 150
Primates
compared with humans, 4–5
synaptic development in, 14
Private language, 158
Production
and comprehension, 120
diversity in, 151
holistic style of, 151
lexicon, 146
and word representations, 116
Pronunciation
and construction of the phonological system, 191–194
and vocabulary assessment, 181
Proper nouns
as early words, 185
Prosody
in adult speech, 84
and clause recognition, 103
and discrimination of phonetic contrasts, 27
and discrimination of phonotactic contrasts, 107–108
and diversity of styles, 175
early memorization of, 40
and early representations of words, 116
and everyday speech, 28
and expressive style, 158
infant discrimination of, 21, 35, 37
infant language preference for, 22
infant sensitivity to, 101
and language of environment, 64
and motherese, 82–83
in motherese, 104
at one year, 88
prenatal perception of, 23
and recognition of mother's voice, 24
and recognition of organized forms, 102
and right-hemisphere control, 30
and segmentation, 96
Psantik I, 92

Psychoacoustic system
of adult speech, 19
Ptah, 2

Questions
and motherese, 89
Quiche Mayan language
baby talk in, 87
and segmentation, 106
Quine, W., 133

Reality
and word learning, 127, 128–129
Reason, gift of, 5
Reciprocal behaviors, 72, 73
and emergence of speech, 74
Recognitory comprehension, 121
Referential function
and reaction to names, 29
and word learning, 128
Referential style, 151–158
and differences among children, 175
and noun vocabulary, 148
Reformulation
of sentences, by mother, 88
Register. See Pitch
Repetition
cross-cultural role of, in language
learning, 87–88
Representation of words. See Mental
representation of words
Respiration, 15
early control of, 17
and evolution of speech, 4
Rhythm. See also Intonation; Prosody
and early production, 151
and expressive style, 161
infant sensitivity to, 101
Right hemisphere
and acoustic information, 30
function in adults, 197

Salish language
consonant discrimination in, 43
Saussure, F., 3
Second-language acquisition
limitations on, 40, 91

Segmentation. See also Categorization
acoustic, 18
by adults, 97
and language acquisition, 8, 95
and prosodic cues, 64, 65
and stress in English, 106
and word production, 141
Selection process
and vocal production, 55–56
Self-awareness
and language acquisition, 213
Semantic grammar, 201
Semantics. See also Meaning
acquisition of, 69, 95–125, 119, 128
and early expression, 79
early expression, 208
and early sentences, 200
and first words, 188
and language acquisition, 8
and name recognition, 29
and phonology, 192
and word recognition, 109–111
Sensory deprivation
and critical periods, 93
and language acquisition, 10
Sensory information, organization of
and language acquisition, 8
Sentences
and expressive style, 161
first, 198–209
and presentation of new words, 88
structure of, and infant sensitivity to,
84, 202
structure of, and verb comprehension, 147
two-word, 199–202
type, by age, 89
Siena, Aldobrandino da, 84, 143
Sign
character of, 3
Sign language
and babbling, 68
Smiling
as innate, 77
Social communication
emergence of, 39
in expressive style, 167

Social communication (cont.)
  and first words, 183, 186
  and Japanese first words, 187
Social identification
  through behaviors, 75
Socialization
  and language, 177
  and language acquisition, 214
Social relations
  and communication, 71
Social words
  as first words, 147
Soft palate, 15
  early configuration of, 17
  first sounds from, 38
Sound perception
  prenatal, 22
  and word learning, 129
Spanish language
  baby talk in, 86
Spatial intuition
  and infant cognition, 130–133
Species recognition, 72
Speech
  by adults to children, 81, 85
  analysis of, by infant, 18, 95
  as behavior, 10
  and communication, 9
  emergence of, 37–69
  as genetic program, 149
  infant perception of, 18
  intrauterine perception of, 24
  and language, 2
  normal rhythm of, 15
  pathologies of, 29–30, 31–32
  as peculiar to humans, 15
  "telegraphic" approach to, 200,
    208
  vocal apparatus for, 15
Speech/music discrimination
  at two months, 33
Speech processing
  dual system theory of, 194
  and hemispheric development, 194
  and left hemisphere, 30
  linguistic level, 110
  by newborns, 35

Speech signal
  infant preferences for, 25
Spoken language
  uniqueness to humans, 9
St. Augustine, 124
Staring behavior
  and emergence of speech, 73
Stress
  in English, 98, 106
  and word production, 157, 162
Strong-weak patterns. See Stress
Subjects of sentences
  in English and Italian, 202
Superior temporal lobe, 29
Swedish children
  preference for action words, 186
  early words of, 184
  and verb comprehension, 147
  vocabulary size of, 137
Swedish language
  early consonantal preferences in, 61
  infant vowel discrimination in, 41
Syllabic duration
  as segmentation cue, 98
Syllabic emphasis, 88
Syllabic omission, 144
Syllabic organization, 105. See also
    Syllables
Syllables, 39, 105
  and babbling stage, 45
  definition and description of, 45
  discrimination of
    at two months, 27
    at three months, 34
  in early babbling, 46
  and early motor limitations, 63
  and early phonetic organization, 60
  emphasis on, in teaching, 88
  as frame for words, 141
  and French word production, 144
  and production style, 151
  pseudo, 39
  terminal, 65
  as unit of representation in French,
    116
Sylvian sulcus, 29
Symbolic comprehension, 121

Symbolic function
and language acquisition, 213
Synaptic development
and redundancy, 14
Syntax
and early concepts, 201
motherese, emphasis on, 88, 104
and phonology, 192
and prosody, 104
and verb comprehension, 147
and vocabulary size, 140
and word acquisition, 127
and word comprehension, 124

Talk. *See* Speech
Taste
and facial expression, 73
Temporality
infant sensitivity to, 104
and recognition of organized forms,
103
Temporal lobe
as language control area, 29
Temporoparietal area
function of, in adults, 197
Terminal syllable
analysis of, 65
and expressive style, 162
Thai language
baby talk in, 87
Thoughts. *See also* Concept formation;
Mental representation of words
expression of, 3
and language, 4
Timbre, 57
Tone languages
baby talk in, 87
and diversity of styles, 176
and prosodic cues, 96
Tongue, 15
early configuration of, 17
early use of, 39
Transformations
of body image, 75
of word segments, 117
Trills
infant manipulation of, 38

Turkish language
motherese in, 88
Turn-taking, 76
and motherese, 83

Understanding
and late speech, 171
Universal grammar, 3, 6, 215
child-specific version of, 200

Velar babbling, 47. *See also* Babbling
Velar consonants
in early babbling, 46
Verbal memory
and vocabulary size, 140
Verbs
in Asian languages, 178
as early words, 186
and first words, 146
as French first words, 147
infant analysis of, 201
Vervet monkeys, 4
Visual attention, 76
and motherese, 82
Vocabulary
acquisition of, 127–148
comprehension, 123, 140
cross-linguistic assessment of, 182
emergence of, 110
expressive, 138
growth of, 130, 137, 138–140, 146–
148, 189–190
rapid development of, in American
children, 157–158
"Vocabulary illusion," 140, 179
Vocal apparatus, 15
early development of, 16, 37
Vocalization
and babbling by deaf infants, 68
and early babbling, 47
infant modulation of, 38–39, 48, 98
Vocal pitch. *See* Pitch
Vocal play. *See also* Cooing
increase in complexity of, 49–50
and turn-taking, 76
Vocal tract. *See also* Articulators
and evolution of speech, 4

Vocal tract (cont.)
  motivity of, in early babbling, 47
  and vowel production, 57
Voluntary behavior
  vocalization as first, 38
Vowel space
  mental representation of, 41, 60
Vowels
  association with consonants, 64
  cross-linguistic characteristics, 57
  discrimination of, 26, 40–41, 104
  duration of, as segmentation cue, 98
  in early babbling, 46
  first production of, 38
  as syllabic nucleus, 45

Weak-strong patterns. *See* Stress
Wernicke's area, 29, 198
Wolf children. *See* Feral children
Word form
  predictability of, in Western
    languages, 179
Word order
  infant analysis of, 201
Word production, 141
  phonological basis of, 191–194
Word recognition, 109–111, 113
  and consonantal discrimination, 43
  and language acquisition, 96
  and parental conversation, 84
Words
  boundary discrimination among,
    100, 101, 108
  early use of, 137
  and generalization, 135
  magic of, 2
  and objects, 133–136
  structure of, as segmentation cues, 99
  understanding of, 119–125
  uniqueness to human language, 9
  as units of meaning, 127
Words, first. *See* First words

Yoruba language
  consonant production in, 63

Zanzotto, A. 82